The
Adventure
of English

The Adventure of English

500AD to 2000
THE BIOGRAPHY OF A LANGUAGE

MELVYN BRAGG

SCEPTRE

Copyright © 2003 by Melvyn Bragg

First published in Great Britain in 2003 by Hodder & Stoughton
A division of Hodder Headline
This edition published in 2004

The right of Melvyn Bragg to be identified as the Author of
the Work has been asserted by him in accordance with the
Copyright, Designs and Patents Act 1988.

A Hodder & Stoughton book

1 3 5 7 9 10 8 6 4 2

A CIP catalogue record for this title is available from the British Library

ISBN 0 340 82993 1

Typeset in Adobe Garamond 3 by
Rowland Phototypesetting Ltd, Bury St Edmunds, Suffolk
Printed and bound in Great Britain by
Clays Ltd, St Ives plc

Hodder Headline's policy is to use papers that are natural, renewable and
recyclable products and made from wood grown in sustainable forests. The logging
and manufacturing processes are expected to conform to the environmental
regulations of the country of origin

Hodder and Stoughton
A division of Hodder Headline
338 Euston Road
London NW1 3BH

To
Greg and Sue
good friends

CONTENTS

Introduction   ix

1 The Common Tongue   1

2 The Great Escape   17

3 Conquest   33

4 Holding On   41

5 The Speech of Kings   54

6 Chaucer   69

7 God's English   80

8 English and the Language of the State   94

9 William Tyndale's Bible   105

10 A Renaissance of Words   116

11 Preparing the Ground   129

12 Shakespeare's English   141

13 'My America'   154

14 Wild West Words   172

15 Sold Down the River   187

16 Mastering the Language   199

Contents

17 The Proper Way to Talk   219

18 Steam, Streets and Slang   237

19 Indian Takeover   250

20 The West Indies   265

21 Advance Australia   276

22 Warts and All   287

23 All Over the World   297

24 And Now . . . ?   306

Acknowledgements   313

Picture Acknowledgements   317

Bibliography   319

Index   329

INTRODUCTION

The way in which a few tribal and local Germanic dialects spoken by a hundred and fifty thousand people grew into the English language spoken and understood by about one and a half billion people has all the characteristics of a tremendous adventure. That is the story of this book. English, like a living organism, was seeded in this country a little over fifteen hundred years ago. England became its first home. From the beginning it was exposed to rivalries, dangers and threats: there was an escape from extinction, the survival of an attempt at suffocation; there was looting, great boldness, chances taken and missed; there were and there are casualties. It has often been a fierce war over words – whose language rules? – but also there were and are treasures: literatures, unified governance, and today the possibility of a world conversation, in English.

This book is about where the English language came from and how it achieved the feat of transforming itself so successfully. It is about the words which describe the way we live, the words we think in, sing in, speak in; the words which nourish our imagination, words which tell us what we are. Although English only exists in the mouths, minds and pens of its many individual users, I came to feel that English had a character and presence of its own. This is not how professional linguists see it but just as some historians see 'England' with a life of its own at certain times, so the language itself, in my view, can be seen as a living organism.

It is not known with any certainty as yet when language evolved: one hundred thousand years ago? Later? It probably began as signs and calls, gestures and facial and bodily expressions, many of which we retain still. We speak of 'body language'. We can tell what someone is 'saying' by their expression. We 'talk' in our expressions still and our extreme calls of fear or ecstasy may not be much different from those of the first Homo sapiens a hundred thousand years ago. But then language began to build. We will never know who laid the foundations. Stephen Pinker and others think that Homo sapiens arrived with the gift of language innate – the language instinct. What remained to be done was to find the methods and opportunities to turn that instinct into words.

But who found the first words? Who finds new words today? We know that Shakespeare put into print at least two thousand new words but the majority of words come out of the crowd. An American frontiersman like Davy Crockett can be as good a word spinner as a Master of Trinity College, Cambridge. Early words came from those who worked the land, those whose centuries of nose to the earth made them acquainted with the minutiae of nature and most likely it was they who, often out of necessity, had to name what they saw: basic things, and creatures which might endanger or nourish them. The giving of names could be called the most democratic communal effort in our history. Language is the finest achievement of culture – and in my view, the English language is the most remarkable of the many contributions these islands have made to the world.

Some years ago I made twenty-five programmes for BBC Radio 4 called *The Routes of English*, whose general starting point was the way in which English had changed and developed on the tongue. My own starting point was a childhood in which I spoke a heavily accented dialect based on an Old Norse vocabulary unintelligible to all my teachers at the grammar school, for which I had to adopt Standard English or what was more commonly known as BBC English. Also in the dialect I spoke there was a seam of Romany, and the whole of the language was still based squarely in the world of agriculture, a world outside the city wall.

There was, though, I thought, another set of programmes I wanted to make, programmes which would describe the history of English, combining, I hoped, the history I had read at university with the English I had read before, during and since. ITV accepted this as a series. Although this book is far fuller than the programmes I wrote, it is based on their structure, which I decided early on would work best as an adventure story.

I am not a linguistic scholar, but I have been very greatly helped by scholars whose work is acknowledged in the book. But there is, in this country, a tradition, across many disciplines, of the permitted amateur – doctors who were biologists and ornithologists, landed gentlemen who were scientists, zoologists and historians, clergymen who were encyclopaedic – and I hope I will be admitted to the ranks of those amateurs.

One of the consequences of this is that the book, though as thoroughly researched as I could make it, is not an academic text. It is for the general reader. The spelling of words, for instance, which has changed so often and so radically, has been the subject of difficult decisions. Where the original spelling of the word is vital to the story, I have kept it. Where, in my opinion, the argument and the examples flow convincingly in a more modern version, I have opted for that.

Daniel Defoe famously wrote of 'Your Roman-Saxon-Danish-Norman English'. Were he to reformulate this today he would have to add several other sources: Indian, West Indian, your global-technical, but most of all your American. The American influence on English has been and continues to be crucially important and one of the lucky turns in the adventure is that it was English and not, as it just might have been, French or Spanish or German which adopted or was adopted by that new-found land – that engine of the new and the modern world. America has brought much treasure to the word-hoard but also, like the British Empire it succeeded, its

English has caused casualties, and in both empires they are part of this story.

This book travels across time and space from fifth-century Friesland to twenty-first-century Singapore, from the Wessex of King Alfred to the Wild West of Buffalo Bill, from the plains of India to the monasteries of Holy Island, from the Palace of Westminster to the black Gullah tongue in the Deep South of America. Along the way it reaches back to claw in Latin, Greek, Hebrew and Sanskrit: on its journey it takes from French, Italian, Arabic, Chinese and scores of other languages. English still uses the basic vocabulary of those first invaders but has added tower after tower of new words and new ideas. It has released feelings and thoughts all over the planet. It continues to reinvent new Englishes wherever it goes and shows no sign at all of slowing down.

I

The Common Tongue

S o where did it begin?
   How did the billion-tongued language of Modern English first find its voice? When and where did it stir itself, begin to assume the form we know, begin to sound like an English we can recognise? How did it set out from such a remote and unlikely small place on the map of the world to forge the way to its spectacular success?

As far as England is concerned, the language that became English arrived in the fifth century with Germanic warrior tribes from across the sea. They were first invited over as mercenaries to shore up the ruins of the departed Roman Empire, stayed to share the spoils and then, dug in. The natives, the Celts or Britons, were, the invaders asserted in their own triumphalist chronicles in an entry dated 449, 'worthless' and the 'richness of the land' was irresistible. This may have been written later but the point is clear enough: the place was ripe for plucking. The Anglo-Saxon historian Bede reports of 'the groans of the Britons' in a letter to the Roman Consul Aetius. The groans came from those Britons who had suffered at the hands of these Germanic tribes. 'The Barbarians', they called them, who 'drive us to the sea. The sea drives us back towards the barbarians – we are either slain or drowned.'

That is one powerful image – English arriving on the scene like a fury from hell, brought to the soft shores of an abandoned imperial outpost by fearless pagan fighting men, riding along the whale's way on their wave-steeds. It is an image of the spread of English which has been matched by reality many times, often savagely, across one and a half millennia. This dramatic colonisation became over time one of its chief characteristics.

There is another story. There were many who came as peaceful immigrants, farmers seeking profitable toil and finding a relatively peaceful home as they transported their way of life from bleak flat-lands to rich pastures. Through their occupation English was earthed. This ability to plant itself deep in foreign territory became another powerful characteristic of the language.

Moreover there were many tribes or small kingdoms – twelve at one stage – who came over at different times and in different strengths: principally the Saxons, the Angles and the Jutes, but splinter groups within and around, speaking different dialects. Though mutually intelligible, they were often at each other's throats. That variation too became part of the story not only in the regional dialects at home but in the sunburst of variation abroad.

Nor for all the 'groans of the Britons' did they give up that easily. The struggle with the British Celts went on for over a hundred years, and this largely rearguard action – which gave the British their greatest mythological hero, Arthur – achieved its aim. For the Celtic language so threatened by the hammering force of the German tribes was saved. In Wales, in Cornwall, in the north of Scotland, in Gaelic, it kept its integrity. That, too, is part of this adventure – there are both casualties and survivors as this hungry creature, English, demanded more and more subjects.

It would take it two to three hundred years for English to become more than first among equals. From the beginning English was battle-hardened in strategies of survival and takeover. After the first tribes arrived it was not certain which dialect if any would become dominant. Out of the confusion of a land the majority of whose speakers for most of that time spoke Celtic, garnished in some cases by leftover Latin, where tribal independence and regional control were ferociously guarded, English took time to emerge as the common tongue. There had been luck, but also cunning and the beginnings

of what was to become English's most subtle and ruthless characteristic of all: its capacity to absorb others.

If you go to Friesland, an industrious province by the North Sea in the
Netherlands, you can hear what experts believe sounds closest to what
became our ancestral language. This immediately shows one of the
limitations of print! On radio and television you can of course hear the
words and the ears can often understand what the eyes see only as a
fright of foreignness. When we hear Piet Paulusman, the local weather
forecaster, saying 'En as we dan Maart noch even besjoche, Maart hawwe
we toch in oantal dajan om de froast en friezen diet it toch sa'n njoggen
dagen dat foaral oan'e grun' or more accessibly 'trije' (three) or 'fjour'
(four), 'froast' (frost) or 'frieze' (freeze), 'mist' or 'blau' (blue) we may
pick something up, some echo, but we still flinch away. When you can
see the words on the screen at the same time as they are uttered, they
soon seem familiar. Careful listening does drop us back through time:
we were there once. Had the Normans not invaded England, we too
could be saying not 'Also there's a chance of mist, and then tomorrow
quite a bit of sun, blue in the sky' but 'En fierders, de kais op *mist*. En
dan *moarn*, en dan mei flink wat sinne, *blau* yn'e loft en dat betsjut dat.'

When you look around the island of Terschelling in Friesland,
you encounter words so close to English, again in the pronunciation
as much as in the spelling, that any doubts fade: Frisian was a strong
parent of English. 'Laam' (lamb), 'goes' (goose), 'bûter' (butter), 'brea'
(bread), 'tsiis' (cheese) are in the shops; outdoors we have 'see' (sea),
'stoarm' (storm), 'boat' (boat), 'rein' (rain) and 'snie' (snow). Indoors
there's 'miel' (meal) and 'sliepe' (sleep). Even entire sentences which
you overhear in the street, sentences which contain not one word that
you can translate, sound eerily familiar. For many English-speaking
non-Brits, I suspect, they are only a little less intelligible than one
of England's own current and proudly obstinate dialects, Geordie.
You feel you ought to know it; it is family.

But where did Frisian come from?

*

In 1786, Sir William Jones, a British judge and amateur linguist on service in India, after a close study of Sanskrit which had been in existence since at least 2000 BC in the Vedic hymns, wrote: 'Both the Gothik and the Celtick though blended with a very different idiom, have the same origin with Sanskrit.'

He was right. Proto Indo-European is the mother of us all and Sanskrit is certainly one of the older attested members of the family of languages out of which come all the languages of Europe (save Basque, Estonian, Finnish and Hungarian) and many in Asia. Sanskrit was an inflected language which relied on changes at the ends of words (inflections) to indicate grammatical functions in nouns (through case and number) and verbs (through person, tense and mood). Germanic formed a subgroup of the Western Indo-European family – as did Celtic and Hellenic. Germanic further divided itself into three smaller groups: East Germanic, now extinct; North Germanic – the Scandinavian languages, Old Norse in sum; and West Germanic – Dutch, German, Frisian and English, the last two of which were closely connected.

The similarities are remarkable. In Sanskrit the word for father is 'pitar'; in Greek and Latin it is 'pater'; in German, 'Vater'; in English, 'father'. 'Brother' is English, the Dutch is 'broeder', in German 'Bruder', in Sanskrit 'bhratar'. There can be few clearer examples of the spread and flow of language and the interconnection of peoples.

Somewhere, then, out on the plains of India more than four thousand years ago, began the movement of a language which was to become English. It was to drive west, to the edge of the mainland of Eurasia, west across to England, west again to America, and west across the Pacific where it met with Britain's eastern trade across Asia and into the Far East and so circled the globe.

According to Bede, writing at the beginning of the eighth century, Essex, Sussex and Wessex were planted by the Saxons; East Anglia, Mercia and Northumbria by the Angles; the Jutes took Kent and the Isle of Wight. They could be ruthless. Sometimes, as at Pevensey Castle, for instance, an ancient Roman fort in which the Celts took refuge, it is recorded that every man, woman and child was slaughtered by these invaders. Much the same happened in what became England, between AD 500 and, say, AD 750, to the native Celtic language.

Despite being spoken by an overwhelming majority of the population, despite preceding the Germanic invasion and creating an admired civilisation, the Celtic language left little mark on English. It has been calculated that no more than two dozen words were recruited to the conquering tongue. These are often words describing particular landscape features. In the mountainous Lake District where I live, for instance, there is still 'tor' and 'pen', meaning hill or hill-top, as in village and town names such as Torpenhow and Penrith; there's 'crag' as in Friar's Crag in Keswick, where the National Trust began, there's also 'luh' for 'lake' or 'lough'. And there are a few poignant others – several rivers – Thames, Don, Esk, Wye and Avon ('afon' is Welsh for 'river'). And two symbolic and significant English towns, Dover and London, bear Celtic names. How could it be that so few Celtic words infiltrated a language which was to grow by embracing infiltration?

One answer could be that the invaders despised those they overcame. They called the Celts 'Wealas' (which led to Welsh) but fifteen hundred years ago it meant slave or foreigner and the Celts became both of these in what had been their own country. Another answer is that the Celts and their language found countries of their own, most notably Wales but also Cornwall, Brittany and the Gaelic-speaking lands where they saved and nurtured the Celtic in a magisterial strategy of cultural continuity. More fancifully, I speculate that English, finding a new home, its powerful voice freed by water from old roots, groping towards the entity it would become, wanted all the space it could claim. For English to grow to its full power, others had to be felled or chopped back savagely. Until it grew confident enough to take on newcomers, it needed the air and the place to itself. The invaders were confident in their own word-hoard and in the beginning they stayed with it, building up its position in the new land.

Much the same happened with the Roman inheritance, though the invaders did borrow some Latin words spoken by the Celts. The Romans were in Britain from 43 BC to AD 410 and many Celtic Britons would have spoken or known some words from Latin. Yet the Roman influence on the first one hundred and fifty years of invaders' English is very slight – about two hundred words at most. 'Planta' (plant), 'win' (wine), 'catte' (cat), 'cetel' (kettle), 'candel' (candle), 'ancor' (anchor), 'cest' (chest), 'forca' (fork); a few for buildings, 'weall' (wall), 'ceaster' (camp), 'straet' (road), 'mortere' (mortar), 'epistula' (letter), 'rosa' (rose). The Roman influence was to be revived through the reintroduction of Christianity but, as with the Celts, we have the Angles, Saxons and Jutes taking on very little at first. It could be that they rejected the Romans because they did not want to kow-tow to a language, therefore a people, who had a historical claim to be their superior. The masses – the Celts – would be enslaved, their language rejected; and equally the relict of empire would be spurned, its great classical sentences also rejected. Less than three per cent of Old English, the bedrock vocabulary, are loan words from other languages. The invaders kept it tight, just as their heirs, the Puritans, a thousand years on, were to do when they went into America.

Though purists maintain that English did not fully exist until the late ninth century, the time of Alfred the Great, there is little doubt that as its many varieties increasingly consolidated, English in one of its dialects from much earlier on determined the common tongue.

We can see it most plainly in the places in which we live. The '-ing' ending in modern place names means 'the people of' and '-ing' is all about us – Ealing, Dorking, Worthing, Reading, Hastings; '-ton' means enclosure or village, as in my own home town of Wigton, and as in Wilton, Taunton, Bridlington, Ashton, Burton, Crediton,

Luton; '-ham' means farm – Birmingham, Chippenham, Grantham, Fulham, Tottenham, Nottingham. There are hundreds of examples. These were straightforward territorial claims. The language said: we are here to stay, we name and we own this.

Then came the great work, the laying of the foundations of the English language, and one which endures vigorously to this day.

Our everyday conversation is still founded on and funded by Old English. All of the following are Old English: is, you, man, son, daughter, friend, house, drink, here, there, the, in, on, into, by, from, come, go, sheep, shepherd, ox, earth, home, horse, ground, plough, swine, mouse, dog, wood, field, work, eyes, ears, mouth, nose – 'my dog has no nose' – broth, fish, fowl, herring, love, lust, like, sing, glee, mirth, laughter, night, day, sun, word – 'come hell or high water'. These words are our foundation. We can have intelligent conversations in Old English and only rarely need we swerve away from it. Almost all of the hundred most common words in our language worldwide, wherever it is spoken, come from Old English. There are three from Old Norse, 'they', 'their' and 'them', and the first French-derived word is 'number', in at seventy-six.

The hundred words are: 1. the; 2. of; 3. and; 4. a; 5. to; 6. in; 7. is; 8. you; 9. that; 10. it; 11. he; 12. was; 13. for; 14. on; 15. are; 16. as; 17. with; 18. his; 19. they; 20. I; 21. at; 22. be; 23. this; 24. have; 25. from; 26. or; 27. one; 28. had; 29. by; 30. word; 31. but; 32. not; 33. what; 34. all; 35. were; 36. we; 37. when; 38. your; 39. can; 40. said; 41. there; 42. use; 43. an; 44. each; 45. which; 46. she; 47. do; 48. how; 49. their; 50. if; 51. will; 52. up; 53. other; 54. about; 55. out; 56; many; 57. then; 58. them; 59. these; 60. so; 61. some; 62. her; 63. would; 64. make; 65. like; 66. him; 67. into; 68. time; 69. has; 70. look; 71. two; 72. more; 73. write; 74. go; 75. see; 76. number; 77. no; 78. way; 79. could; 80. people; 81. my; 82. than; 83. first; 84. water; 85. been; 86. call; 87. who; 88. oil; 89. its; 90. now; 91. find; 92. long; 93. down; 94. day; 95. did; 96. get; 97. come; 98. made; 99. may; 100. part.

English had also dug into family, friendship, land, loyalty, war, numbers, pleasure, celebration, animals, the bread of life, the salt of the earth. This deep, long-toughened tongue proved to be the basis for dizzying monuments of learning and literature, for surreal jokes and songs superb and slushy.

With the 20/20 vision of hindsight it seems as if English knew exactly what it was doing: building slowly but building to last, testing itself among competing tribes as in centuries to come it would be tested among competing nations, getting ready for as difficult a fight as was needed, branding the tongue. Even in its apparent simple directness and comparatively limited vocabulary — twenty-five thousand recorded words compared with the hundreds of thousands of today — it is always able to rise to greatness.

'We shall fight on the beaches,' said Churchill in 1940, 'we shall fight on the landing grounds, we shall fight in the fields and in the streets, we shall fight in the hills; we shall never surrender.' Only 'surrender' is not Old English. That, in itself, might be significant.

Rome came back, not with a sword but with a cross. In 597 Augustine arrived in Kent, sent from Holy Rome with all its authority by Pope Gregory, who had been impressed by the blond-haired Anglian boy-slaves ('non Angli,' said the apparently compulsively punning Pope, 'sed angeli'). In 635, Aidan independently arrived in the north of England with all the apostolic zeal and learned crusading ferocity of the Irish Celtic Church. In remote monasteries and enclosed orders, in arcane services and devoted godly scholarship, without threat and despite hindrance, these men and their successors fed the growing English with their Church Latin. Gradually English, partly I think because it could control these marginal praying clerics, took on Latin, the second classical tongue of the ancient world, and Latin smuggled in Greek. The English talent to absorb and its appetite for layerings had begun with what are called 'loan words'.

These words began by creeping in at the outer edges of the concerns of the pagan English. 'Angel', 'mass' and 'bishop' came in, as did 'altar', 'minster', 'abbess', 'monk', 'nun' and 'verse'. Greek slipped in via Latin with, for example, 'alms', 'psalm', 'apostle', 'pope' and 'school'. As importantly, existing Old English terms were given new powers, a new philosophy. Heaven and hell, for instance, or Halig Gast (Holy Ghost), Domesday (from Judgement Day). Eostre, a famous pagan goddess, gave her name to the most important of the Christian festivals. And through Christianity we have the first recorded entrance into our literature of the common man, Cædmon the swineherd who, untutored we are told and inspired wholly by faith, composed this hymn in English.

> Now we shall praise the Keeper of the Heavenly Kingdom
> The power of the Lord of Destiny, and his imagination . . .
>
> Nu scylun hergan hefaenricaes uard
> metudæs maecti end his modgidanc . . .

This Northumbrian version is from an eighth-century manuscript. But it is not his words alone which are of central importance here. What matters, I think, is that through the words comes a faith new to most of the Angles, Saxons and Jutes, the melders of English, and the ideas inside that faith. Ideas of resurrection, of a life after death, were in parts of the Germanic culture, but heaven and hell were of a different order. As was the idea of saints, the company of angels, of sin, and especially of a gentle Saviour, a non-warrior God. So were all the intellectual complexities of the Roman faith and its often tortuous and tormented way of looking at the material world. The word 'martyr', for instance, opened up astounding possibilities to non-Christians.

As the Church grew more pervasive in the land, not least through its recruitment of wealthy and learned aristocratic women like St Hilda, so its overall philosophy flourished and Latin slid under the carapace of English and would never be expelled or ignored again. This was the quietest but possibly in the long term the most success-ful grafting on to English for it brought to the barely literate lusty language book-tested ways of thinking and words which could and often did direct a whole view of life. The messages and words of Christianity would feed English for more than a thousand years. It was English's first encounter with an invading force of thought and slowly, over centuries, overcoming long-held practices and superstitions, English let it in. The tightly bonded local language began to open up.

Rich bishops went to Rome and brought back pictures, books, holy relics, craftsmen, but above all, as far as the adventure of English is concerned, they brought back writing and writing began to mould and advance the native language.

The Angles, Saxons and Jutes had not brought a script with them. They used runes. The runic alphabet (called the 'futhorc' named after the first letters of the runic alphabet, just as our 'alphabet' is from the first letters of the Greek alphabet) was made up of symbols formed mainly of straight lines, so that the letters could be carved into stone or wood or bone. This best equipped them for short practical messages. They are represented in the solutions to some of the Exeter Riddles. Runes were capable of poetry, as can be seen on the eighth-century Ruthwell Cross near Dumfries in Scotland, which shows events from the life of Christ. There are lines of runes as in the poem 'The Dream of the Rood' in which Christ's Passion is told from the point of view of the Cross on which he was crucified.

The Cross speaks:

ᛁᚻ ᚠᛖᚾ ᛗᛁᛈ ᛒᛚᚩᛞᚪ ᛒᛁᚾᛏᛗᛗᛁᛞ

Ic wæs miþ blodi bistemid [Old English translation]

I was with blood bedewed

Runes could not only be used for poetry, they were sufficiently developed to have coped with *War and Peace*. But these straight lines were designed to be cut, chiselled on hard surfaces: wood, metal, stone and bone. The Christians brought with them the manuscript book and a different script, a technology more suitable for the new medium of vellum and parchment. English was emerging from the tribal Babel as a resourceful tongue, but it had no great written language and without that it would be for ever condemned to the limbo of vernaculars all over the world whose attempt to live on by sound alone has often doomed them to insularity, then to irrelevance, finally to oblivion. Occasionally there is desperate resuscitation from a few survivors who know that to lose any language is to lose a unique way of knowing life. Only writing preserves a language. Writing gives posterity the keys it needs. It can cross all boundaries. A written language brings precision, forces ideas into steady shapes, secures against loss. Once the words are on the page they are there to be challenged and embellished by those who come across them later. Writing begins as the secondary arm but soon, for many, becomes the primary source, the guardian, the authority, the soul of language.

Written words stimulate the imagination as much as any other external reality – fire, storm, thunder – and yet they can express an internal reality – hope, philosophy, mood – in ways which also provoke the imagination, engage with that astounding faculty and set it off to make more words, adding to the visible map of the mind. Writing helps us fully to see what it is to be more completely human. 'The word was made flesh and dwelt among us' can apply to the alphabet as well as to Christ. The alphabet created and unleashed a new world.

The first manuscripts were in the Roman alphabet brought to Northumbria by Aidan and other Irish missionaries. That was the basis for the Old English alphabet, for in the monasteries the monks began to use the wonderfully flexible, clear and beautiful half-uncial majuscule script (which can be seen in the Lindisfarne Gospels). Monks recruited locally saw the signs and were converted. An alphabet most likely sown by anonymous clerics grew out of the Latin and remarkably early, by the seventh century, Old English had achieved its own alphabet. It was like discovering intellectual fire. A, æ, b, c, d, e, f, g, h, i, k, l, m, n, o, p, r, s, t, þ, ð, u, uu (to become w much later), y. Twenty-four letters to begin with but from those few letters has flowed an incalculable number of variations, fine distinctions and pyrotechnics, from Shakespeare to James Joyce, from David Hume to Noam Chomsky, from Francis Bacon to Crick and Watson's DNA, to tens of thousands of journals, novels, magazines and newspapers.

In the early years English knew its place and its place was literally in the margins: we see a small plain English hand crawling its shy translation above the towering, magnificently wrought Latin letters which brought the word of God to save the souls of the English. I have always been ridiculously pleased that the Lindisfarne Gospels, the first great English work of art, was a book. Though using crafts-men from other lands it was made in the Northumbrian part of what was to become England. The Lindisfarne Gospels were executed in brilliant colours, a mixture of Germanic, Irish and Byzantine motifs, elaborately designed letters, decorated with precious stones, works to awe the masses and to praise God.

A few miles away, in the monastery of St Paul in Jarrow – in the early eighth century – at about the same time as the Gospels were produced, a local boy who had gone into the monastery at the age of seven and become the great scholar Bede wrote *Ecclesiastical History of the English Nation* which gave status and lineage to the Angles, Saxons and Jutes. His transcendent skills and talents founded the history of the English speakers. He wrote more than thirty books in Latin but it is said that he believed that the language of the people should also be employed. Soon after Bede, English began to dare to compete. Mostly, written early English was used for practical matters – laws, charters, the daily stuff of definition – dull at the time but its information rusting to gold as centuries passed. Sometimes, though, and as early as the seventh century, the new language boldly enters into the heart of things.

> Our Father
> Who art in heaven
> Hallowed be thy name . . .

Fæder ure
Þu þe eart on heofonum
Si þin nama gehalgod . . .

It is so moving. Spoken aloud the similarity is all but a twinning. Even there on the page: ure/our; Fæder/Father; Þu/who; eart/art; heofonum/heaven. And later:

And forgyf us ure gyltas, swa we forgyfað urum gyltendum

And forgive us our trespasses, as we forgive those who trespass against us.

Forgyf/forgive; gyltas (guilts)/trespasses.

Across thirteen centuries the sounds come to us, the sound of our ancestral voices speaking across time and space, words holding ideas and ideals about the conduct of life with which we still engage today, words in the English common tongue.

As if that were not enough as the roots went down, English, with the self-confidence of the new player in the book, planted its claims to literature. When precisely works like *The Wanderer*, *The Seafarer* and *Beowulf* were composed is hard to establish but that they came out of the intellectual ambitions of this period – seventh, eighth century – seems possible. English, settled now, began to play. The Exeter Book with its riddles gives us insights into the word games so beloved of English crossword solvers and Scrabble addicts ever since. The seeds are already there in what were so long mis-called 'The Dark Ages'. This is from the sole remaining manuscript, in the library of Exeter Cathedral, which contains ninety-four riddles.

What is this?

I live alone, wounded by iron,
Struck by a sword, tired of battle-work,
Weary of blades. Often I see war,
Fight a fearsome foe. I crave no comfort,

That safety might come to me out of the war-strife
Before I among men perish completely.
But the forged brands strike me,
Hard-edged and fiercely sharp, the handwork of smiths,
They bite me in the strongholds. I must wait for
A more murderous meeting. Never a physician
In the battlefield could I find
One of those who with herbs healed wounds
But my sword slashes grow greater
Through death blows day and night.

The first four lines in Old English read:

Ic eom anhaga   iserne wund
bille gebennad,   beadoweorca sæd,
ecgum werig.   Oft ic wig seo,
frecne feohtan.   Frofre ne wene,

Answer: The Shield

The greatest of the Old English poems is *Beowulf*, a Scandinavian hero who goes to the aid of Hrothgar, the Danish king, to defend him against the monster Grendel. It has been called the first great epic poem in the English language. It begins:

Hwaet,   we Gar-Dena   in geardagum

So,   the Spear-Danes   in days gone by

We are, yet again, hearing our own language, but this time through the art of the poet or poets using techniques which are the property of poetic literature. The language has been alchemised into literature.

Seamus Heaney's recent translation interprets the work for our own age while providing an echo of the original, which reads, speaking of Grendel the monster:

Mynte se manscaða   manna cynnes
summa besyrwan   in sele þam hean.

Heaney writes of Grendel:

> The bane of the race of men
> roamed forth, hunting for prey in the high hall.
>
> Onbræd þa bealohydig,   þa he gebolgen waes,
> recedes muþan . . .
>
> ac he gefeng hraðe   forman siðe
> slæpendne rinc   slat unwearnum,
> bat banlocan,   blod edrum dranc,
> synsnædum swealh;   sona haefde
> unlyfigendes   eal gefeormod,
> fet ond folma.
>
> When his rage boiled over
> He ripped open the mouth of the building
> Maddening for blood . . .
>
> He grabbed and mauled a man on his bench
> Bit into his bone lappings, bolted down his blood
> And gorged on him in lumps
> Leaving the body utterly lifeless
> Eaten up, hand and foot.

Heaney has called this a 'fully developed poetic language capable of great elaboration'. Its alliterative powers and percussive effects tend to overlay the subtleties. He finds it 'terrific for action, terrific for description'. One point he made which seemed almost the clincher in Early English's claim on poetic greatness is its capacity to make up extra words: 'ban-hus' – bone-house, for 'body'; 'gleo-beam' – glee-wood, for 'harp'; 'wig-bord' – war-board, for 'shield'; 'whale's-way' for 'sea'; 'wave-steed' for 'boat'.

Between the Lord's Prayer, laws of the land, and *Beowulf*, English had already sunk deep shafts into written language. Latin and Greek had created great bodies of literature in the classical past. In the East at about this time, Arabic and Chinese were being used as the languages of poetry. But at that time, no other language in the Christian world could match the achievements of the *Beowulf* poet and his anonymous contemporaries inside and outside the Church.

Old English had found its home. It had fought its way to preeminence in a new, rich and diverse country. The adventure was under way.

But just as the springs of English had come from the shores of Friesland in the fifth century so, in the late eighth century, a potential destroyer of the language was ordering his battle fleets in another tongue, five hundred miles to the north.

2

The Great Escape

One of the manuscripts of the *Anglo-Saxon Chronicle* for 793 reads: 'In this year dire portents appeared over Northumbria and sorely frightened the people. There were exceptional flashes of lightning, and fiery dragons were seen flying in the air. A great famine immediately followed these signs, and a little after that in the same year, on the eighth of June, the ravages of heathen men miserably destroyed God's church on Lindisfarne.'

The Vikings were unloosed and for almost three centuries raids and settlements by these Scandinavian warriors devastated huge tracts of these islands and threatened to supplant the language which had begun to show such astonishing promise. The Norwegians raided the northern and western rim of Scotland and flooded into Cumbria in the north-west of England. It was the Danes, though, who came with greatest force, their armies looting and then occupying substantial territories in the Midlands and in the east of the country. They were, as the *Anglo-Saxon Chronicle* pointed out, heathen, very effective on the battlefield and with no reason to abandon their own tongue, which came from the same root as English but had evolved into a different language. English was in danger of being overrun or exiled as the Celtic languages had been.

It is important to emphasise that when we use the word English we have to be careful. It is likely that some Celtic was still spoken and the mutually intelligible but differing dialects of the Germanic tribes were by no means unified. Yet we have, for example, our great and founding historian, Bede, calling his book *The Ecclesiastical History of the English Nation* and that in itself, together with its early translation into Old English, is a strong indication that the fabric of a cohering language was in place. The Danes tore through that.

They ripped the jewels from the costly bindings of manuscripts like the Lindisfarne Gospels and wore them as ornaments. The Gospels themselves escaped, some would say miraculously. The year after they plundered Lindisfarne they returned and sacked Jarrow and burned down the great library which had nourished Bede. Despite some survivals it was as if their raids were designed to stamp out that which had given the tongue its greatest opportunity for survival – the books. By the middle of the ninth century the Danes were the dominating force. In 865 they landed a powerful army in East Anglia and moved south for the final kill. In 878 they won what appeared to be a decisive victory at Chippenham. Wessex, the last of the old kingdoms, was set to disappear. Alfred, the leader of that English army, fled into the baffling marshes of Somerset, known as the Levels. He and his small group of survivors moved, according to a contemporary record, 'under difficulties, through woods and into inaccessible places'. The Danes ruled. What they said went.

Alfred is the only English monarch to be known as 'The Great'. He has been hailed as the Saviour of England. That may be debatable in the strict sense – there was not as yet one 'England', more a federation waiting to be moulded into one. Alfred can, though, lay claim to saving the English language. It is in one of his own translations – in the preface to Gregory's *Pastoral Care* – that one of the first appearances of the word 'Englisc', describing the language, is recorded. But Alfred not only saved the language, he dug it even more deeply into the minds of his people by using English as a rallying force and even more importantly as the conduit for an intense programme of education.

That, though, must have seemed impossible as the young king, disguised we assume, sat in the legendary cottage of the poor woman and dreamed away, only to be scolded for burning the wheaten cakes he had been set to mind. He had in defeat proved to be enterprising in irregular warfare and mounted guerrilla attacks against the occupying forces of Guthrum, the Danish invader.

He realised that guerrilla warfare would never be enough. To defeat the Danes he had to bring them to open battle. His army had been scattered and many had been slaughtered. But they were not wiped out. In the spring of 878, Alfred sent out a loyalty call to the men of the shire fyrds – the county armies, the basis of the great county regiments. About four thousand men joined him, mainly from Wiltshire and Somerset. We are told they were armed only with shields, battle-axes and throwing spears.

They mustered at Egbert's Stone, where trackways and ridgeways met. Two days later they advanced against the Danish army of about five thousand men, who had positioned themselves brilliantly on high ground at Ethandune (Edington, in Wiltshire) on the western edge of Salisbury Plain. Drumming their shields and led from the front by the young king, they stormed the heights. Contemporary accounts tell us that what followed was a rout, a slaughter of the Danes. Modern historians question that, but there is no doubt that Alfred and his men prevailed. His crown and his kingdom were repossessed. The Danes surrendered. Their leader Guthrum was baptised as a Christian with Alfred in conciliatory attendance. A great white horse was carved into a Wiltshire hillside to commemorate the victory – undoubtedly a key victory for an emerging England and a crucial victory for English. Alfred had saved the language.

It is worth spending a few sentences on what might have been. The Danes were fierce and conquering tribes and had they occupied the whole of the land it is very likely that the final tongue would have come out of their dialects and not the 'English' dialects. Would that have mattered? Very likely, yes, I think. Their written records were meagre compared with the traditions already well established in the rich lands they had all but overrun. Their basic attitude to written language was to burn it or, more helpfully for the future, toss it aside. And though their version of a Germanic dialect might over time have dug in, it would have taken centuries and who knows whether it would have held English's vital combination of deep obstinacy and, when faced with real extinction, astonishing flexibility and that vital survival technique, the power to absorb.

What happened to English after the Battle of Ethandune was that it not only endured, it thrived, it grew. Having held steady under fire, it moved forward. The two principal reasons for this were Alfred himself and what seems to me to be the profoundly self-preserving nature of the language which had so slowly and doggedly alchemised into English.

Sometimes I think that it is a pity that the Victorians dubbed Alfred 'The Great'. It makes rather a nursery hero of him. He was much better than that. This is not the place to describe the full range of his achievements but with regard to English his contribution was unique.

The Danes had been defeated but they were a persistent enemy. They would and they did come back again and again. Alfred had won a victory but the war was not over. He knew that the kingdom and tribes he now commanded were still wounded from the defeats they had suffered. They needed to feel safe, they needed to feel protected, they needed to feel part of a winning side. Alfred's use of the English language united them. He was the first but by no means the last to see that loyalty and strength could come through an appeal to a shared language. He saw that inside the language itself, in the words of the day, there lay a community of history and continuity which could be invoked. He set out to teach the English English and make them proud of it, gather around it, be prepared to fight for it.

He recognised that the Danes would not accept subjugation, and nor had he the manpower to enforce it. So he drew a line diagonally across the country from the Thames to the old Roman road of Watling

Street. The land to the north and east would be known as the Danelaw and would be under Danish rule. The land to the south and west would be under West Saxon, becoming the core of the new England. This was no cosmetic exercise. No one was allowed to cross the line, save for one purpose – trade. This act of commercial realism would more radically change the structure of the English language than anything before or since. Trade refined the language and made it more flexible.

The Vikings had brought their own languages, particularly that of the Danes, but also the language based on the kindred Norwegians. Up to about AD 1000, these were pretty much undifferentiated and known as Old Norse. Deep inside the Danelaw they were attempting to impose this speech as much as they imposed their martial sovereignty. The interesting result was that, apart from the crucial matter of grammar, their success was rather limited. In its later phases, English became a language with an immense capacity to absorb others, to convert others, certainly to take on board other languages without yielding the ground on its own basic vocabulary and meanings. Yet here at this earlier stage – four hundred years on since the Frisian tribes and others had transported the roots of English into the people who would bear that name – it was still surprisingly obstinate. Only about a score of Celtic words had been admitted; only about two hundred Roman words and even now, from these overwhelming Danish invaders, no more than about one hundred and fifty words were added to a national word-hoard of about twenty-five thousand. This was partly because the power was at Winchester and texts from all around the country were copied into the West Saxon dialect there. But also it is as if at this stage English had dug in so very deeply that it would not be moved. And the result of this obstinacy, in my opinion, made it so powerfully earthed that later, when the Normans came with far more devastating consequences, it could still feed off its deep taproots.

Nevertheless the Vikings – Danes and Norwegians – brought

words which enriched the language greatly. In northern parts of England the new invaders' words predominate much more than in the south, exposing the north—south divide; and the accents too, from what linguists tell us – the Yorkshire, the Northumbrian, the Geordie, the Cumbrian – reach back to the sounds of the men in those longships whose peerless shipbuilding crafts enabled them to launch themselves as far as America and into the Mediterranean.

The Vikings live on most strikingly in the place names which spread like a rash over what was the land of the Danelaw. Locally it struck hard and has stayed fast. There are said to be at least one thousand five hundred of these names, more than six hundred of which, for example, end in '-by', the Scandinavian word for farm or town.

I was brought up in the far north-west of England, a few miles outside the Lake District, a place of more than four hundred mountains and thirty-three lakes deeply settled by Norwegian Vikings, most of whom came across from their stronghold in Dublin. The words they brought were bedded into the local dialect for more than a thousand largely undisturbed years. To use '-by' as an example: within a few miles of the town in which I grew up, Wigton, there are Ireby, Thursby, Wiggonby, Corby, Lazenby, Thornby, Dovenby and Gamblesby; more widely known examples would be Derby, Naseby and Rugby. The '-thorpe' ending, which denotes a village, is seen in Scunthorpe, Althorp, Linthorpe. The '-thwaite' ending, which denotes a portion of land, is again all over the north, and in the Lake District alone you have Bassenthwaite, Ruthwaite, Mickle-thwaite and Rosthwaite; '-toft', which means a homestead (the site of a house and its outbuildings), can be seen in Lowestoft, Eastoft, Sandtoft. And there are less popular but still extant Viking names: the word valley was 'dale' in Old Norse and the Lake District is furrowed with them – Borrowdale (a valley with a fort), Wasdale (a valley with a lake), Langdale, Eskdale, Patterdale. Sometimes there is a blend as in the Cumbrian village of Blennerhasset, 'blaen' being Celtic top of hill, and the Old Norse 'heysætr' – hay pasture. And Keswick, one of the prime towns in the Lakes, is a hardened form of the Old English name 'cesewic' meaning cheese farm. But without the Viking influence it would most likely be called Cheswick or Cheswich. In short, the Danes pitched camps and named them as their own and with such emphasis that they still stand today.

As do the Viking family names, again much more emphatically in the north. The Danish way of making a name was to add '-son' to the name of the father. If you look in the local papers inside the old Danelaw you find these sons everywhere. At my own school there were Johnsons, Pattisons, Robsons, Harrisons, Rawlinsons, Watsons, Nicholsons, Gibsons, Dickinsons, Hudsons, Hewitsons, Stevensons. And it is still true today that despite the centuries of people moving around these comparatively small islands, there are still markedly more shop names, 'Harrison', 'Johnson', 'Wilkinson', more sons, than in any other part of the country.

So they marked their places of arrival and they brought their names. The number of their words which entered into general use was not as many as the strength of the invasion might have promised. But as it were to compensate for that, many of them have become key words. For instance, 'they', 'their' and 'them' slowly replaced earlier forms (though they did not enter the language of London until the fifteenth century). Early loan words include 'score', and 'steersman' is modelled on an Old Norse word, but they could also spread into the common tongue with 'get' and 'both' and 'same', 'gap', 'take', 'want', 'weak' and 'dirt'. What is impressive is its ordinariness. Other Norse loan words include 'birth', 'cake', 'call', 'dregs', 'egg', 'freckle', 'guess', 'happy', 'law', 'leg', 'ransack', 'scare', 'sister', 'skill', 'smile', 'thrift' and 'trust'. The 'sk' sound is a characteristic of Old Norse and English borrowed words like 'score', 'skin' and 'sky'. Other words from Old Norse include 'knife', 'hit', 'husband', 'root' and 'wrong'.

So it could be argued that although they were not numerous these words became part of the soil of the language. Perhaps English was at a stage where it would only admit words which could help it describe its own world, words which could bed in without disturbing the existing word-hoard. This can best be seen by the early pairings. (In all cases the Old Norse is given first.) 'Hale' was used as well as 'whole'. In Norse you were 'ill', in Old English you were 'sick'. Old Norse 'skill' settled down alongside 'craft', 'skin' joined 'hide'. (Some of these words appear widely only after the Conquest.) Although they most likely began their life in the common language pointing to the same thing or the same condition, they held a slightly different meaning which was used, as time went on, to make finer distinctions. This twinning, which later split and went rather different ways, became one of the most fertile and inventive characteristics of English. We can see it clearly at work in a modest but enduring number of word-pairings, here in pre-Norman times.

And along the line of the Danelaw, in the trading outposts, the great grammar shift began to take place. This is the only case in our history in which the whole structure of the language changes.

In Old English, sense is carried by inflection – it worked in the same way that Latin did. The essential thing about it was that word order was much freer than it is today. On the whole, Old English tended already to use the order that we do now: subject, verb, object is the most common. But that wasn't a hard and fast rule. So if an Angle wanted to say 'the dogs killed the cat', he'd have to have the accusative form of cat, and the verb in the right form, to make his meaning clear, i.e. so that the message pointed to the death of the cat and not the dogs. Their sentences came not through word order but by tacking on endings to words, like articles and pronouns and nouns. When English came into contact with the not wholly dissimilar Danish language, a lot of the inflected endings began to lose their distinctive nature. The new grammatical meld tended to happen in the borderland market towns; words followed the trade. Clarity for commerce may have been the chief driving force.

Word endings fell away. Prepositions came in which took the language away from the Germanic and made it more English. Instead of adding a lump on the end of words, you could use 'to' or 'with'. 'I gave the dog *to* my daughter.' 'I cut the meat *with* my knife.' The order of words became important and prepositions became more common as signposts around sentences.

It is not necessarily simpler than an inflected language but it did give English a shove towards modernity. It is also easier for second-language users to make themselves understood, easier to get the words wrong and still make sense when the word order has so much meaning hard-wired into it. The grammar change made it capable of greater flexibility.

This had in some degree already begun to happen before the Vikings arrived. It was a gradual, even a hesitant, process not fully settled for centuries. But it was accelerated along the line of the Danelaw and it became another strength.

Perhaps my interest in English began when I was speaking at least two versions of it in my childhood. And within these two were, I suspect, something like the jumbled, shifting sound and sense of much earlier centuries of English.

I spoke a heavily accented dialect in Cumbria until I was about sixteen. There was also a considerable purely local vocabulary. Then the influence of school and BBC English began to erode that accent. The local dialect words were discarded once I began to travel out of the county, simply because no one understood them. But for years I could revert to that accent and remembered those words. Friends back home still employ some of them. They, like me, could switch into the more mainstream English when necessary. The vocabularies intermeshed, sometimes a new word rubbed out an old, it was a jumble, not at all difficult to manage, subject to teasing, snubbing, and as the old yielded more to the new, some regret.

I thought that my experience on a local and much smaller scale might bear some resemblance to the spoken English in the ninth century. To test that, I went through a Cumbrian dialect glossary to look at some of the words I used most commonly.

First, though, the accent. In the 1940s and 1950s, Wigtonians, like so many others everywhere else in small towns and villages, were still largely immobilised in one small area save when wars took off the men or emigration lured away desperate or daring families. It was still heavily influenced by agriculture and agricultural terms which had been just as common more than a hundred, even two or three hundred years before. Its accent was broad. To refined speakers it could appear coarse. Class climbers could even pretend it was unintelligible and subhuman. Yet it carried the deep history of our language and perhaps it had carried it intact for centuries in sound as well as in vocabulary.

The word 'I' would always be pronounced 'Aah'. The definite article 'the' would often be clipped to 't' – 'the bike' to 't bike', 'the horse' to 't horse'. 'R' would be given justice, as in 'rrreet', for right and even the last 'r' on 'remember' would be hit.

People were acutely aware of differences so nuanced that to an outsider the shadings would be as impenetrable as those between Darwin's first gradations of finches. Wigton's dialect would be different from that of Aspatria eight miles away and that of Carlisle eleven miles away and hugely different from that of Newcastle sixty miles away. It could still be called more a tribal collection of mutually intelligible dialects rather than a canopy of English under which were several divisions. In short it flourished from the ground up, much, I think, as it did in the ninth century and in many cases for another thousand years.

We thee'd and thou'd each other as if we had just got off the *Mayflower*. The King James Bible gave us not only cadences and rhythms but metaphors and references. There were a lot of Romany words around because of the gypsy encampments long established in the Wigton area and horse dealing brought in new words. The Romany word for horse was 'grey' and a 'good grey' was a good horse. Or it could have been a 'baary grey', 'baary' also meaning good. 'Togs' for 'clothes', 'cady' for 'hat', 'chaver' for 'boy', 'mort' for 'girl', 'paggered' for 'winded', were all words from the gypsies whose women used to make swill baskets from reeds and sell them along with clothes pegs door to door for 'lure', money, to us 'gadjis' men.

'Cower' was a thing, any thing, and 'mang nix' was say nothing. There were also hundreds of local pronunciations of non-dialect words – a book was a 'byeuk', water was 'watter' (as in Wordsworth) and up was 'oop', down was 'doon', words like play and say would sound like 'plaay' and 'saay', us would be 'uz', face would be 'feace', finger would be 'fing-er'. 'Siste' came from seest thou – nowadays we would say 'do you see'. No doubt we also mixed in words from Latin, French, Italian and Spanish and Indian, but the burr of it and the look of it when put on a page is nearer to Old English than Modern English. It was a Tower of Babel underpinned by English.

'Deke's you gadji ower yonder wid't dukal an't baarry mort gaan t'beck.' (Look at that man over there with the dog and the sexy girl going down to the river.) All us under-twelves in the 1940s spoke like that. We loved to sound just 'uz'.

When we said 'blud' for 'blood' and 'grun' for 'ground', we were way nearer Old than BBC English. No one told us that in the 1940s and 1950s. Had they done so we might have been proud that our way of speaking was in direct descent from the great warrior founding tribes of our language one and a half millennia ago. It might have done us good. Instead, whenever we strayed from our Cumbrian patch, especially when we left the boundaries of the ancient Northumbrian kingdom and heaved up in what we felt were more polished locations, we felt like rude mechanicals. We were encouraged to wipe that dialect off our lips.

The passage of history had reduced the once fierce language of power and rule into local speech, if not of the oppressed then certainly of those outside the pale of a tongue which calculated its civilisation partly by its distance from what had become a dialect. The transformed tongue was still built on the rock of Old English, the common words, the keys to the language, the grammar, the forceful expression of feelings. That, it seems, will survive any attempt to change. But the accent and context which had bred and nurtured it was lost to the new powers and it was pushed to the margins, as Celtic had been.

But in my youth it flourished still. In the 1940s, for instance, a young soldier called Harold Manning went to Iceland when the Allies occupied that country. He came from South Cumbria and his vocabulary was freckled with Norse words from the dialect. In Iceland, perhaps the most formaldehyde-protected of the Old Norse tongue, he used words from his home dialect and made himself understood. Within a week or two he was conversant with the Icelanders. Old Norse was that deeply bitten into the Old North.

And it is that Nordic element, always building on Old English but in the north clawing deeply into the language, which lies at the core of the fundamental separation – so often noted – between north and south. It is a divide which even today, with the levelling out of the language, distinguishes the north from the rest of Britain and will perhaps provide a platform for a return to a form of regional government for Northumbria as England finally loosens its hold on its first colonies. But that is another story. In the ninth century such a prospect would have been a luxury. English had a surprisingly slender chance and but for a visionary strategy it could well have slid away.

So I would say 'Aah's gaan yem.' 'Gaan', or 'gan' or 'gangan', meaning to go, was an Anglo-Saxon word also known to the Vikings. 'Yem' means home in Scandinavian. In Old Norse it is 'heim'. I would 'laik in t beck'. 'Leika' is an Old Norse word for 'play'; 'bekkr' a word for 'stream'. I would 'axe for breed'. 'Axe' is from the Anglo-Saxon 'acsian', 'breed' is northern but Anglo-Saxon in origin, meaning bread. I would say 'nowt' (nothing) and 'owt' (anything) from the Anglian words 'nawiht' and 'awiht'. I would climb a 'yek' (oak) tree to get a 'yebby' (stick). 'Claggy' was sticky, and like 'clarty' (muddy), it most likely comes from Scandinavian. I wore 'claes' (clothes), Anglo-Saxon, and as a 'lad' (Anglo-Saxon) I would 'loup' (Old Norse) 'ower a yat or yet' (a gate – northern pronunciation) or 'gawp' (stare) at a 'brock' (Celtic, badger). And 'yen' will always be one.

Hybrid county dialects like these, which used to be spoken by the majority in a Britain of proud geographical minorities, are now disappearing as we move to cities and as the way of life which informed the way of speech falls away. It is impressive to see the efforts being made by dialect societies and local publishers to keep the tongue alive, to keep in touch, through the history in speech, with that period when we were stitching together languages old and new. But until very recently we still sounded not unlike those who had brought them from the western European shorelands more than a millennium ago.

English not only survived the Danish invasion, eventually it benefited. When Alfred looked around at the state of the written culture, he found it to be in ruins. He used English to help weld together a demoralised and fragile people. It is also true that his stern sense of Christian duty – another of the factors which so endeared him to discerning Victorians – drove him to reinstitute the scholarship and learning which a century of Danish raids, often on the soft targets of monasteries, had so badly depleted. The high days of Bede and the tradition he exemplified had gone.

In the whole of Wessex, Alfred could barely find a handful of priests would could read and understand Latin. If they could not understand Latin they could not pass on the teachings of the religious books that told people how to lead virtuous lives. They could not save souls. Alfred found a chronic spiritual sickness in his kingdom and, as in war, he led from the front. At the age of forty, he learned Latin to help with the translations. For he had come up with a radical solution that hinged not on Latin but on English through translations. And in doing this, he took English to new heights of achievement.

In the preface to his own translation of Pope Gregory's *Pastoral Care*, Alfred wrote: 'I remember how, before it was all ravaged and burned, I'd seen how the churches throughout all England stood filled with treasures and books. And there was also a multitude of God's servants who had very little benefit from those books because they could not understand anything of them since they were not written in their own language.'

Their own language was, of course, English. Alfred decided to come to the study of Latin through English. The best scholars could then go on to learn Latin and join holy orders. The rest would still have access to spiritual guidance but it would be written in English. Centred on his capital town of Winchester, he drew up an extraordinarily imaginative plan – unmatched anywhere else in Europe – to empower the written vernacular which would not only bring the word of God to many denied it but also promote literacy, encourage scholarship and help unite the realm.

'We should,' he wrote, 'translate certain books which are most necessary for men to know into the language that we can all understand and also arrange it as, with God's help, we very easily can if we have peace, so that all the youth of free men now among the English people, who have the means to be able to devote themselves, may be set to study, for as long as they are of no other use, until the time that they are able to read English writing well.'

And English, the word 'Englisc', was here used as confidently as the word 'Latin'. Alfred's power and intelligence put it on the map of languages.

He had five books of religious instruction, philosophy and history translated from Latin into English. This was a laborious and costly undertaking but consistent in its thoroughness and vision with the man who drew a line across England to keep the peace, founded a navy and built up Winchester into a royal capital city. Copies of these books were then sent out to the twelve bishops in his kingdom. Further to emphasise the importance he attached to these books, Alfred also sent the bishops a costly pointer used to underline the text.

The head of one of those pointers was discovered in 1693 in Somerset. It is crafted in crystal, enamel and gold and is now on show at the Ashmolean Museum in Oxford. It is inscribed 'Ælfred had me made' – in English. Alfred the Great had made the English language the jewel in his crown. His Wessex dialect would become the first Standard English.

In Winchester he established what was effectively a publishing house. His sense of being English ran through everything he published. For instance, the *Anglo-Saxon Chronicle* had existed for centuries in different versions. Alfred brought these together in an act of compilation which seems as much an act of patriotism as of scholarship.

A hundred years on from Alfred, the Danes would again be on the rampage. At the Battle of Maldon in 991, the Danes defeated the English once more; the Danegeld was levied and in 1013 King Æthelred was exiled into Normandy. The Danish King Sweyn succeeded him. Authority in the land was once again decided on battlefields. But thanks to Alfred, authority in the language had been settled. The poem describing the Battle of Maldon is in Old English, full of the fury of alliteration, worked with words wisely woven. And still used today. Words like 'heard' (hard), 'swurd' (sword), 'wealdan' (wield), 'feoll' (fell), 'god' (good) and, best of all, I think, 'word' (word). Usually it is the victors who write the history. Here the defeated English did that service, proving that although the Danes had the land again, they could not possess the language.

For even in the worst period of the renewed Danish invasions, the monk Ælfric was working in Winchester and then in Cerne Abbas, teaching Latin in the language of English to the same peoples, 'the youth of free men', whom Alfred had originally targeted. Ælfric was prolific in English; his books on the lives of saints, for example, were dramatic and popular. His colloquies, in Latin, were a series of dialogues between a master and his pupils, and Ælfric did it through drama. He would assign his pupils a role – a ploughman, a fisherman, a baker, a shepherd, a monk – and Ælfric would ask them questions about what they did. This gave the pupils a chance to answer in their own words, be spontaneous, individual, inventive. And when, some years later, Old English was written above the Latin, these teaching aids brought that free discipline to English itself.

It is just as fascinating to look at the work of Archbishop Wulfstan, who wrote a sermon to the English when the Danes persecuted them most severely, in 1014. Called 'Sermo Lupi', it begins:

Beloved men, recognise what the truth is: this world is in haste and it is drawing near the end – there fore the longer it is the worse it will get in the world. And it needs must thus become very much worse as a result of the people's sins prior to the Advent of Antichrist, and then indeed it will be terrible and cruel throughout the world. Understand properly also that for many years now the Devil has led this nation too far astray and that there has been little loyalty among men although they spoke fair, and too many wrongs have prevailed in the land.

A few of the same words in the Old English in which it was originally written will indicate similarities and differences. It begins: 'Leofen men, gecnawað þaet soð is: ðeos worold is on ofste and hit nealæcð þam ende.'

At that time it was widely believed that the world was about to end – a thousand years after either Christ's birth or death. Apocalyptic signs would announce that. It seems to me at least possible that Wulfstan was aligning the Danes with the Apocalypse, even the Antichrist, while not missing out on this opportunity to lecture his countrymen on their sins and terrible shortcomings. In that sense he is on both sides, serving two territorial masters, excusing the invaders by giving them Apocalyptic trappings and urging his own to repent. On a more practical level, Archbishop Wulfstan served the English king Æthelred and was equally active in designing and preparing legislation for the Danish king's court. The nationality of the rulers changed. The language and those who commanded the language remained, entrenched now in a power through words given them by Alfred.

The Danes would be overthrown and once more an Englishman would be sworn in as sovereign. As he took his oath, in English, in the middle of the eleventh century, he inherited Alfred's legacy, whose range of written vernacular history, philosophy, law and poetry had no peers anywhere in mainland Europe. Not only England but English seemed secure when Harold became king. But he would face other invaders and with them the greatest threat the English language has ever encountered.

3

Conquest

A victory in battle by Alfred saved the English language. Less than two hundred years later a defeat in battle by Harold threatened to destroy it. It was an event which had a greater effect on the English language than any other in the course of its history. Eighty-five per cent of Old English vocabulary would eventually be lost as a result of that defeat and though some historians now regard the survival of English as inevitable, it seemed very unlikely at the time. Chroniclers three centuries on from the Conquest still feared for the language. England, and English, were overwhelmed, suppressed and beaten out of the controlling conversations of the time. The savagery and completeness of the defeat at Hastings, we are told, amazed all Europe.

The year 1066 is such a smiling date in our history that we find it rather difficult today to load it with doom; *1066 and All That*, the jolly title of the most entertaining version of our history, only emphasises its status as a harmless old granddad of a date. 'We have never been conquered,' Elizabeth I is reported, perhaps apocryphally, to have said. 'Save by the Normans,' replied a bold courtier. 'But they could not have done it unless they had been us,' said the Virgin Queen, and in its way it is true: English eventually absorbed the conqueror.

This is a translation of one of the versions of the *Anglo-Saxon Chronicle* for 1066. The chronicle had earlier been rescued and rearranged by Alfred but not with this record in mind:

Then Count William came from Normandy to Pevensey on Michaelmas eve, and as soon as they were able to move on they built a castle at Hastings. King Harold was informed of this and he assembled a large army and came against him at the hoary apple tree. And William came against him by surprise before his army was drawn up in battle array. But the king nevertheless fought hard against him, with the men who were willing to support him, and there were heavy casualties on both sides. There King Harold was killed and Earl Leofwine his brother, and Earl Gyrth his brother, and many good men, and the French remained masters of the field, even as God granted it to them because of the sins of the people.

The first thing to say about this *Anglo-Saxon Chronicle* is how clear and authoritative it is. It gives us an excellent historical account in what had become a language capable of exact record, rare anywhere and at any time, all but unique in the world of the eleventh century.

This passage does not refer to the background of the invasion – a background depicted in the Bayeux Tapestry: the illuminated window to the *Anglo-Saxon Chronicle*. There we see Edward the Confessor, a lover of Normandy, who named William, Duke of Normandy as his successor. There we see the richest and most powerful of the English earls, his wife's brother, Harold Godwineson, Earl of East Anglia, pledging loyalty to William, in Normandy, on two caskets of holy relics. Was what happened next treachery? The tapestry shows Harold being crowned in Westminster Abbey on the very day that Edward was laid to rest there.

But William thought he had God on his side. The *Chronicle* concurs by writing of 'the sins of the nation' – the English defeat was a just punishment. Harold's risky strategy, hurling all his best men into the front line in a make-or-break battle following a hurried march from the Battle of Stamford Bridge, deprived the land of English earls and chieftains, the very leaders and organisers who could have regrouped to fight another day against an opponent whose lines of communication were unreliable. But God had given William the fair wind to be denied both Philip II's colossal Armada and Napoleon Bonaparte's brooding mass of becalmed flotillas. Thanks to Harold's comprehensive defeat, there was no one left to oppose William post-1066 save the northern earls who believed they could deal independently with the Conqueror. They tried. They failed. The north was wasted. As the chronicler goes on to say in that same passage: 'Bishop Odo and Earl William stayed behind and built castles far and wide throughout this country, and distressed the wretched folk, and always after that it grew much worse. May the end be good when God wills!'

The chronicler seems to have readjusted his perspective here: 'evil has increased very much' he writes, and earlier, 'he ravaged all the country that he overran'. He was careful to give due to his new masters and put God on their side: he was scrupulous, too, in revealing something of the power of what became the Norman juggernaut: 'England' was taken over. It had become, and would for a long time remain, the offshore appendage of a Normandy-based power who saw it as a treasure-house of land and loot. Much as the Frisians had done.

English was also in danger. The Anglo-Saxons had all but eliminated the existing Celtic language from what was to become English. The Viking Danes had come within a whisker of doing the same to English. In the first case, Old English had shown its ruthless determination to take on no other tongue. In the second, it had been assisted by a most extraordinary warrior-scholar king. It had also begun to treat with that threatening language, the Danish, to draw it in, take what it needed. But now? Leaderless, oppressed, under the Norman heel?

There is an immediate clue in the name itself. The word 'Hastings' came from -ing (Old English), 'the people or district of' Hæsta, a warrior, whose name comes from 'hæst', an Old English word for violence. So into the unconscious went a place marking a defeat but by some necessity of survival, its name was subversively inspirational: not entirely unlike that other great inspirational defeat, Dunkirk. It was English which held the naming day. And yet the actual site of the engagement was named not with an English word like 'fight' but with a word from the language of the Norman victors, battle. This was the new reality.

The Normans who conquered England were Norsemen by blood and there could be reasonable expectation that the languages would mesh. But by the time their ships landed at the old Saxon shore of Pevensey – the precise spot where Frisians had landed in 491 – the language they spoke was a variety of French. The Darwinian properties had worked their evolutionary ways on the human tongue and French had swallowed up their Old Norse. Its roots now were not in the Germanic languages which had come to England, but in Latin. It is fascinating that the Norsemen's language was all but completely wiped out in France whereas its close kin in England, in the north, put up a real fight and forced its way into Old English, even into the roots of its grammar.

But the Normans came with an alien tongue and they imposed it. On Christmas Day 1066, William was crowned in Westminster Abbey. The service was conducted in English and Latin. William spoke French throughout. It is said that he attempted to learn English but gave up. French ruled. And the French language of rule, of power, of authority, of superiority, buried the English language.

William held his new realm by building a string of stone castles which at that time and for long afterwards must have seemed impregnable. He had no hesitation – in York for instance – in razing whole areas of a large town to plant his castle prominently and surrounded by open land to give it most advantage. When we see a castle such as the one at Rochester, even now, broken though it is, we see power manifest. Those walls guarded those in charge and protected them. Cathedrals too would be built to confirm and emphasise the stone power of the Norman conquerors. God is on our side, those great cathedrals – Durham, York – said. Look at the mighty works that we conquerors can make and despair of ever rising up against us. The size, structure and massiveness of those buildings in a single-storeyed or, more unusually, double-storeyed society of lowly architecture must have created an awesome effect. A new world had landed.

As with stone, so with words. Over the next two centuries, French rained heavily on the English. Words of war: 'army' (from armée), 'archer' (from archer), 'soldier' (from soudier), and 'guard' (from garde) all come from the victors. French was the language which spelled out the new language of the social order. 'Crown' (from corune), 'throne' (from trone), 'court' (from curt), 'duke' (from duc), 'baron' (baron), 'nobility' (from nobilité), 'peasant' (from paisant), 'vassal' (from vassal), servant (servant). The word to 'govern' comes from French (governer), as do 'authority' (from autorité), 'obedience' (obedience) and 'traitor' (from traitre).

From that short sample a new world emerges. We know who is in charge: those who have the language. We see a system being put in place – to reinforce the invaders; the language tells us that. It renames the rules and the ruled, it manacles English to the command words of French. And it spread everywhere.

In the law, for instance, 'felony' comes from felonie, 'arrest' from areter, 'warrant' from warant, 'justice' from justice, 'judge' from juge, 'jury' from juree. On it goes: to 'accuse' from acuser, to 'acquit' from aquiter, 'sentence' from sentence, to 'condemn' from condemner, 'prison' from prisun, 'gaol' from gaiole.

It has been estimated that in the three centuries following the Conquest perhaps as many as ten thousand French words colonised English. They did not all come at once – though the words of authority and law and rule were imposed immediately – but 1066 opened up a stream for French vocabulary which raced through until the fourteenth century and has continued to course into English, on and off, ever since. 'Battle', conquest', 'castle'; 'arms', 'siege', 'lance' and 'armour' came first and came to stay. Today they sound as English as 'ground' or 'blood' or 'sword' or 'son'. The new court motto: 'Honi soit qui mal y pense' (Evil be to him that thinks evil). The Normans seized the centre of power and it was their language which described the new order they brought to bear.

Over the next three hundred years French words, loan words which have since become 'our own', were imposed in control positions in art, architecture and building, Church and religion, entertainment, fashion, food and drink, government and administration, home life, law and legal affairs, scholarship and learning, literature, medicine, military matters, riding and hunting and social ranking.

How was English to survive this invasion and one led by those to whom obedience was unyieldingly demanded? The only way for even moderately ambitious English men and women to breathe any air of power or culture was to learn French and leave English in the kitchen.

But even in the kitchen it was not safe. Nearly five hundred words dealing with food, eating and cooking entered English from French. In any 'city' (from cité), there would be 'porters' (portiers) trading in, say, fish. In 'salmon' (from saumoun), in 'mackerel' (from mackerel), 'oysters' (from oistres), 'sole' (sole); or in meat, 'pork' (from porc), 'sausages' (from saussiches), 'bacon' (from bacon); or in fruit (from fruit), 'oranges' (orenges), and 'lemons' (limons), even 'grapes' (grappes). Or for a 'tart' (tarte), a 'biscuit' (bescoit), some 'sugar' (çucre) or 'cream' (cresme).

If you go into a restaurant and ask for a menu (French words that came in during the nineteenth century – the invasion of terms describing and contextualising food has never stopped) you will certainly also encounter words that came in during the Middle Ages. (We will of course sit at a table, on a chair, eating from a plate with a fork – all from French or widened into a modern meaning by French influence.) 'Fry' (from frire), 'vinegar' (from vyn egre), 'herb' (from herbe), 'olive' (olive), 'mustard' (from moustarde) and, key to it all, 'appetite' (from apetit).

This density of occupation affected all of the fifteen categories I listed above: and always appeared to take over the key positions. French was as ruthless and strategically shrewd as the Norman French army: the former found the means to dominate the language just as the latter found the way to dominate the land.

Domesday was a good word for it. Twenty years after the Battle of Hastings, William sent out his officers to take stock of his kingdom. The monks of Peterborough were still recording the events of history in the *Anglo-Saxon Chronicle* and they noted, disapprovingly, that not one piece of land escaped the survey, 'not even an ox or a cow or a pig'. William claimed all.

There are two volumes of the Domesday Book (one called Little Domesday, the return from East Anglia) and they show how complete the Norman takeover of English land was and how widespread their influence and their language. Half the country was in the hands of just one hundred and ninety men. Half of that was held by just eleven men. Here are a few of them:

Odo of Bayeux and Robert of Mortain (both half-brothers of
    William)
William de Warenne
Roger of Mowbray
Richard fitzGilbert
Geoffrey de Mandeville
William de Briouze

Not one of these great landowners spoke English.

The Domesday Book was written in Latin. This was to emphasise its legal authority in a way English was now thought incapable of doing.

If you believe that words carry history and meaning often deeper than their daily purpose, then we see with the coming of the Normans an almighty shift of power. The words that regulated society and enforced the hierarchy, the words that made the laws, the words in which society engaged and enjoyed itself were, at the top, and pressing down relentlessly, Norman French. Latin stood firm for sacred and high secular purposes. English was a poor third in its own country.

It is easy with hindsight to say that 'obviously' English has survived. But hindsight is the bane of history. It is corrupting and distorting and pays no respect to the way life is really lived – forwards, generally blindly, full of accidents, fortunes and misfortunes, patternless and often adrift. Easy with hindsight to say we would beat Napoleon at Waterloo: only by a whisker, according to the honest general who did it. Easy to say we would win the Second World War: ask those who watched the dogfights of the Battle of Britain in Kent in 1940. Easy to say the Berlin Wall was bound to fall. Which influential commentator or body of opinion said so in the 1980s? Hindsight is the easy way to mop up the mess which we call history; it is too often the refuge of the tidy-minded, making neat patterns when the dust has settled. As often as not, when the dust was flying, no one at the time knew what the outcome might be.

In that spirit, I would suggest that for many English people, certainly the educated, it must have seemed the end of their authority in the land and the end of their language as any sort of authority. Just as some Celts had become Romanised, so some English became Normanised. It was the only way up, the only way out. The effects on English were severe for at least a hundred and fifty years and for another hundred and fifty the language had to continue to struggle, not so much for survival this time, as with the Danes, but somehow to swallow, digest and absorb this monstrous regiment of foreign words. They were pile-driven into the vocabulary and needed to be denied, defeated or somehow to become 'our' 'English' words, other-wise French would certainly depress, effectively eliminate English and overrule any claim it had to primacy.

When, three hundred years later, English did finally emerge, it had changed dramatically. But first it had to take on its conqueror and somehow reconquer it. The language had to do what Harold Godwineson's army had failed to do in 1066.

Harold, King Harold, would be the last English-speaking king, the last king to take his oath in English, for three hundred years.

4

Holding On

Under William the state of England became an estate of Normandy. When the new king ordered the construction of the White Tower by the Thames in London in 1077, he declared his hand. It was to be part palace, part treasury, part prison and part fortress. Even today it stands splendid and formidable, the sleek and fierce ravens which appear to guard it seeming to contain still the savage powers of the last invader of England who brought with him such a cargo of Norman French that not only the territory but the tongue of the land was threatened.

William's successors continued his simple policy of brutal appropriation. Across the land William's men took over every position of power in the state and in the Church. Within sixty years of the Battle of Hastings, the monk and historian William of Malmesbury wrote: 'No Englishman today is an Earl or Bishop or Abbot. The newcomers gnaw at the wealth and guts of England, nor is there any hope of ending the misery.' Those who, armed with much later evidence, speak of the inevitability of the survival of English might do well to imagine a conversation in the early twelfth century with that level-headed historian. His view, a view from the battlefront, would have been far less confident. He wrote in Latin. Written English which had established itself so magnificently before the Conquest was being rapidly sidelined.

One of its proudest functions had been as a language of record in the

Anglo-Saxon Chronicles, which had recorded the great events of the past six hundred years. In Peterborough Abbey, in the mid twelfth century, that prime function of English, that unique tradition, breathed its last. These *Chronicles* had been written in the language of the people; there was nothing like them anywhere in mainland Europe. England was already a place with a long history written in its own language.

The *Chronicles* were kept at several monastic institutions. After the Conquest, one by one they were abandoned. The Peterborough Chronicle was the last survivor. In 1154 a monk at Peterborough Abbey recorded that the abbey had a new abbot with the French name of William de Waterville.

'He has made a good beginning,' the monk writes. 'Christ grant that he may end as well.' With this last entry in English, more than six centuries of written history came to an end. Old English ceased to be the recognised and respected language of record in its own land. History was no longer with the Anglo-Saxons: and their language was of no consequence to those who saw the past in their own image. One way to destroy a personality is to cut out memory: one way to destroy a state is to cut out its history. Especially when that history comes out of the native language. Status is gone; continuity is disconnected; all that went into the making of the people the *Anglo-Saxon Chronicles* had recorded so carefully was of no account. The written language which bound it together guttered out.

Yet just as Celtic in the fifth and sixth centuries was certainly the language spoken by the overwhelming majority of those who lived in 'England' (then a loose aggregation of often warring kingdoms), so now English after 1066 was still the language of the people. It has been estimated that in the beginning the Norman French accounted for no more than three or five per cent of the population. The Romans had proved that an even smaller percentage could subdue great tracts of land and the force of arms in many empires has been minute in number, disproportionate it would seem: the British in India for example, the French in Central Africa, Islam around the

Mediterranean and the East. A conquering military elite can build up an astonishing momentum and the Norman French are among those who proved that. It helped that the English were virtually leaderless, their finest warriors slaughtered or captured or fled, their final northern power base no match alone for the invaders. And the invaders gave no quarter: misery, waste, pillaging, ravaging, these are the words that describe their Genghis Khan-like progress through a fatally weakened land.

The language of the occupied no longer counted. But, as if language itself were a resistance movement, it continued not only to be spoken but to evolve, despite the heavy hand of Norman French which pressed it down, pushed it under the controlling conversations of society, its laws, its court talk, its churchmen. It may seem curious to bring grammar to bear on evidence here but grammar – rarely a word that strikes a welcoming note – is useful evidence. For if the grammar is changing, setting itself and meeting new challenges, if the internal engine of the language is still geared for change and adaptability in its own terms regardless of the new dominating tongue, that is good proof that a language is alive even if it is under siege.

Dr Katie Lowe has pointed out that when the Danes and the Wessex-led English began to trade across the Danelaw in the tenth century, the rub between the two not dissimilar languages led to changes which profoundly affected the way they talked then and we talk now. She took the sentence 'The King gave horses to his men,' and used that as an example. In English that would be 'Se cyning geaf blancan his gumum.'

There is no preposition, no 'to' in that sentence: it's all done by the endings of the words. The 'um' at the end of 'gumum' tells you that the noun ('guma' – man) is plural and that it's the indirect object of the sentence: as such in this sentence 'um' equals 'to'. Now the plural for horse is formed by putting an 'an' on it, so 'blancan' means horses. The problem was that the 'ums' and 'ans' became less distinct as these languages attempted to meld together. So instead of 'gumum' (to his men), we could get 'guman' (men, identical with the simple plural). Instead of 'his blancan' (horses) we could get 'his blancum' (to his horses). Even this straightforward sentence, therefore, could end up as 'The King gave men [guman] to his horses [blancum].' And of course the more complicated the sense, the more scope for misunderstanding. The word 'to' solved that and many more prepositions came into play around that time.

It is significant that this is still going on in the twelfth century. Especially in the north, this seeking for clarification had not ceased. In Old English, plurals could be signalled in a variety of ways. About this time it is noticeable that more plurals were being formed by adding an 's' – as many Old English nouns did. 'Naman', for example, the Old English plural of 'names', became 'nam-es', which became 'names'. Prepositions like 'to', 'by' and 'from' were performing more of the functions of the old word endings and word order itself was becoming more fixed. 'The' becomes used instead of the Old English bewildering range of different words used for the definite article.

So despite being the officially ignored language, despite being driven out of much of its written inheritance, English continued to change, to endure, both resisting and absorbing the invader's language, selecting, nursing itself like an exiled and wounded animal, hoping for the opportunity to re-emerge.

In 1154, it did not seem remotely possible. That fateful Peterborough Chronicle of 1154 also recorded that in that year the people of England acquired a new king, Count Henry of Anjou, grandson of William the Conqueror and the first of the Plantagenets. He was a lover of learning who spoke fluent Latin as well as French: but no English. His queen was Eleanor of Aquitaine, the daughter of William X of Aquitaine.

Henry II was crowned in Westminster in a lavish ceremony which announced and displayed a new force of Frenchness on the English scene. The clergy wore silk vestments more costly than anything ever seen before in England. The king and queen and the greater barons wore silk and brocade robes – such luxury was fitting, it was thought, for an occasion that solemnised the bringing together of so much land and wealth. So much, indeed, that in its own way, it threatened English every bit as much as the heavy horsemen who had benefited so greedily from the victory in 1066.

Henry II brought his inheritance of William the Conqueror's land in England and northern France. Eleanor, the greatest heiress in the western world, brought with her a great swathe of what is now France, from the Loire to the Pyrenees, from the Rhône to the Atlantic. This was a huge kingdom, the greater part of it made up of French-speaking lands across the Channel. As it grew, the English lands and the English language became an ever less significant part of it. French and Latin were even more firmly entrenched as the language of government, of the court, of the new culture.

Yet even on this great occasion, when England seemed to be reduced even further, there was still life and even hope in the language. As Henry and Eleanor processed up the Strand in London, it is reported that the people shouted 'Wes hal!' and 'Vivat Rex' – wishing them long life in Old English and in Latin. The language was alive on the streets.

Henry and Eleanor brought yet more new words. In the first century after the Conquest, most imported words came from Normandy and Picardy. But in Henry II's reign (1154–89), other dialects, especially Central French or Francien, contributed to the speech of the country. So 'catch', 'real', 'reward', 'wage', 'warden' and 'warrant' from Norman French sat alongside 'chase', 'royal', 'regard', 'gauge', 'guardian' and 'guarantee' from Francien (all given Modern English spelling).

Perhaps more important than the vocabulary were the ideas which winged in beside them. This is a clear example of what happened time and again: new words seeded new ideas. In the palace, new ideas from across the Channel were now in the air. The new words that expressed them included 'courtesy' (cortesie), 'honour' (honor), 'damsels' (damesieles), 'tournament' (torneiement). The vocabulary of 'romance' and 'chivalry' brought the biggest culture shock to England since Alfred set out to re-educate the people: but where

Alfred did this for God and for unity, the court of Henry and Eleanor did it for culture and pleasure. Eleanor was considered the most cultured woman in Europe. She attempted to change the sensibility of this doom-struck, crushed, occupied outpost of an island and it was she more than anyone else who patronised poets and troubadours whose verses and songs created the Romantic image of the Middle Ages as the Age of Chivalry — a glorious vision, little, if at all, realised outside the beautifully illustrated and ornamented pages of medieval literature.

But the new ideas came in and they bedded themselves in England and worked their way through the culture for at least seven centuries to come, as the gentle knight became the gentleman. Before Eleanor arrived in England the word 'chevalerie', formed around the word for horse, had simply meant cavalry. It was the fierceness of the mounted warriors that had carried the day at Hastings and since then many of the English knew the Norman chevalerie as little more than mounted thugs and bullies.

Now, under the influence of Eleanor, mounted horsemen began their transformation into knights. The word 'chivalry' came to mean a raft of ideas and behaviour, infused with honour and altruism. Words that prescribed how to act towards one's liege-lord, friends, enemies and, most of all, towards fair, cruel ladies. This, the preserve of the court, took the preoccupations of the state even further away from English, which had no place in the throne room. The way the society regarded itself had been pointed in a dramatically different direction, and initially it was nothing to do with Old England or Old English. Neither was needed.

It was in Eleanor's reign that poets brought the stories of Arthur and his Knights out of history or legend into poetry and a strengthening of the legend. There was a growing poetic tradition in this newly enriched language. The twelfth century saw the flourishing of the great Arthurian Romance poet Chrétien de Troyes and the poetess of magical fables Marie de France. Both were writing courtly verse in French; Marie by her own account was writing it in England.

Interestingly there is some evidence that both these writers plundered the riches of the locals as all colonisers do. Chrétien derived his material from England – possibly through Wace's French translation of Geoffrey of Monmouth's *Historia Regum Brittaniae*. Marie de France tells us that she translated some of her stories from English into French ('de l'engleis en romang').

The language was cultivated for itself and became far richer than that of the first Norman settlers. The poets rhapsodised about Eleanor, celebrating her as the most beautiful woman in the world, pouring out the impossible longing for the perfect woman that was at the heart of courtly love. That too had and still has a tremendous influence on poetry and songs of affairs of the heart, of the joy and pain of love. It propelled forward a line in literature that ran through Shakespeare's sonnets to Romantic love poetry, to the popular song lyrics of today. It is impossible to weigh, to quantify the effects of such ideas at the time. It is indisputable, though, that those imported, French, courtly ideas sank deep wells into our ways of thinking how we ought to and could behave and be in and out of love.

Eleanor's favourite troubadour was Bertrand de Born and his most famous work is 'Rassa tan cries e monte e poia'. The poet sings about the physical attractions of his noble lady (body as white as hawthorn flower, breasts firm, back like a young rabbit's – admittedly the last may have lost some of its erotic power in the last seven hundred and fifty years) and ends by singing:

> pois m'a pres per chastiador
> prec li que tela car s'amor
> et am mais un pro vavassor
> qu'un comte o duc galiador,
> que la tengues a dezonor.

since she has taken me for her counsellor, I pray that she holds her love dear and shows more favour to a worthy vassal than to a count or duke who would hold her in dishonour.

It is a long way from *Beowulf*. That sinewy alliterative epic of high poetry which showed the dreams and nightmares of Old English society was replaced by a subject and a way of thinking about life which the author(s) of *Beowulf* would have found totally foreign.

The first medieval biography of an English layman was of the Knight William Marshall, Earl of Pembroke, a professional soldier, royal adviser, champion of tournaments and Regent of England. It is a poem of more than nineteen thousand lines, written in the early thirteenth century. It is written in French. English, well fit for the task, was not considered adequate even for the biography of an Englishman.

Yet the English written word did not entirely disappear. In the first hundred and fifty years it lived on in the margins, much as the English dialects did after the triumph of eighteenth-century Enlightenment drove them outside the pale of 'literature' to the lower reaches of society.

In the late twelfth century, for instance, there was a book called *Ormulum* written by the monk Orm (a Danish man) who lived in North Lincolnshire. He wanted to teach the faith in English and his verses were to be read aloud. Here is Orm's description of his book:

> This book is called Ormulum
> Because Orm it wrought [made] . . .
> I have turned into English
> [the] gospel's holy lore,
> after that little wit that me
> my Lord has leant [granted]

> þiss boc iss nemmned Orrmulum
> forrþi þat Orrm itt wrohhte . . .
> Icc hafe wennd inntill Ennglissh
> Goddspelles hallghe lare
> Affterr þatt little witt þat me
> Min Drihhtin hafeþþ lenedd

This is local, it is near the Fen lands of Hereward the Wake, one of the last Saxons to stand up to the Normans; it is in that long tradition of devoted clerics who have used local freedoms to good effect. It is touching and important but there is the feeling that it is in a bywater, not part of a countrywide push to make the gospels accessible to ordinary men, more an isolated endeavour, even the end of a line.

A poem, 'The Owl and the Nightingale', was written at almost exactly the same time, largely in a south-eastern dialect. It is attributed to Master Nicholas of Guildford:

I was in a summery valley, in a very secluded corner. I heard an owl and a nightingale holding a great debate. The argument was stubborn and violent and strong, sometimes quiet and sometimes loud.

> Ich was in one sumere dale
> In one suþe digele hale
> Iherde Ich holde grete tale
> An hule and one nihtingale
> Þat plait was stif an starc an strong
> Sumwile softe an lud among

The rhyming scheme is French or French-inspired, four beat lines in rhyming couplets. This does not of course make it any less of a poem and, according to many scholars, a remarkable poem. It is written in English which stands as proof of a continuing readership for written English. Yet even here, even in the heartland of written English, poetry, the French influence would not be denied. It has been suggested it is written in the style of Marie de France.

There is a song which most refreshingly indicates that English was alive in the fields if not in the court. It was found in Reading Abbey complete with musical notation and is one of the first pieces of English that is still comparatively easy to recognise today. Even the few words which can seem a bit strange – 'med' (meadow), 'lhouþ' (lows), 'verteth' (farts) and 'swik' (cease) – fall into place.

This is the first verse:

> Sumer is icumen in
> Lhude sing, cuccu.
> Groweþ sed and bloweþ med
> And springþ the wude nu.
> Sing cuccu.
> Awe bleteþ after lomb
> Lhouþ after calve cu
> Bulluc sterteþ, bucke verteþ,
> Murie sing cuccu!
> Cuccu, cuccu
> Wel singe þu cuccu
> Ne swikþu naver nu.

The remarkable thing about this song is that there is not a word of French in it. Words like 'summer', 'come' and 'seed' go directly back to the Germanic. 'Spring' and 'wood' can be found in *Beowulf*. 'Loud' and 'sing' are in works authorised by Alfred the Great. There's a pure line of Old English vocabulary and a taste for English song that comes from the land as far from the chivalric songs of Bertrand de Born as can be imagined. The French culture of Henry and Eleanor has not eliminated the common tongue.

It was always bound to be a race against time. The longer Norman French dominated all the heights of communication the weaker English would become.

In the first hundred and fifty years or so, the system of feudalism, introduced by William, defined all economic and social relations, expressed in French words like 'villein' and 'vassal', 'labourer' and 'bailiff'. In the countryside, where ninety-five per cent of the population lived in the Middle Ages, still speaking in a language oppressed or ignored, the English were essentially 'serfs', another French word, not technically slaves but tied for life to their lord's estate, which they worked for him and, at subsistence level, for themselves.

While the English-speaking peasants lived in small, often one-roomed mud and wattle cottages, or huts, their French-speaking masters lived in high stone castles. Many aspects of our modern vocabulary reflect the distinctions between them.

English speakers tended the living cattle, for instance, which we still call by the Old English words 'ox' or, more usually today, 'cow'. French speakers ate prepared meat which came to the table, which we call by the French word 'beef'. In the same way the English 'sheep' became the French 'mutton', 'calf' became 'veal', 'deer' became 'venison', 'pig' 'pork', English animal, French meat in every case.

The English laboured, the French feasted.

This cut-off, though, may well have worked to English's advantage. A more extreme – though not too dissimilar – case would be that of slaves taken from their country of origin and holding on to their own language for identity, for secret communication, out of love and certainly out of stubbornness. The feudal system had cut-offs at several points, spaces between functions, between classes, gaps which were very rarely bridged. Conquered English could hunker down, brood on the iniquity of the French and the injustices of the world, cosset the English language as the one true mark of identity and dignity, bide its time, stealthily steal from the rich foreigners.

Sport unsurprisingly provides proof of that. French seemed unstoppable everywhere. Falconry, a pursuit of the aristocracy which made many demands on the underlings, provides one example over these early centuries. The word 'falcon' itself comes from French, as does 'leash', which referred to the strip of material used to secure the bird, and 'block', on which the bird stood. All early and easily assimilated. Our word 'codger' may come from the often elderly man who assisted the falconer by carrying the hawks on a 'cadge' or cage. 'Bate' described the bird beating its wings and trying to fly away; 'check' meant at first refusing to come to the fist. The word 'lure' comes from the leather device still used in training the hawk. 'Quarry' was the reward given to the falcon for making a kill. When a bird moulted it was said to 'mew' and from that comes the name of the buildings in which the hawks were kept, the 'mews'.

Nine French words came into English from that one activity. French influence on English in terms of vocabulary was unmatched by any other language. Yet they soon became 'English' in pronunciation, in their eventual common use.

The French also replaced English words – 'fruit' for instance replaces Old English 'wæstm'. But often enough English words stand side by side with them – Old English 'æppel' used to mean any kind of fruit. It retreats to the apple itself as 'fruit' takes over: it does not disappear.

Looking at these words today, words that came in during the three hundred or so years after the Conquest, we are struck by how very English they now seem. In the home: 'blanket', 'bucket', 'chimney', 'couch', 'curtain', 'kennel', 'lamp', 'pantry', 'parlour', 'porch', 'scullery'; there's an English domestic novel inside that selection. In the arts: 'art' itself, 'chess', 'dance', 'melody', 'music', 'noun', 'paper', 'poet', 'rhyme', 'story', 'volume' – an arts magazine could use each word for a section of 'prose' (another). In law: 'arrest', 'bail', 'blame', 'crime', 'fine', 'fraud', 'pardon', 'verdict'; in clothing and fashion: 'boot', 'buckle', 'button', 'frock', 'fur', 'garment', 'robe', 'veil', 'wardrobe'. In science and scholarship: 'calendar', 'grammar', 'noun', 'ointment', 'pain', 'plague', 'poison'. General nouns such as 'adventure', 'age', 'air', 'country', 'debt', 'dozen', 'hour', 'joy', 'marriage', 'people', 'person', 'rage', 'reason', 'river', 'sound', 'spirit', 'unity', 'vision'. General adjectives: 'active', 'calm', 'cruel', 'honest', 'humble', 'natural', 'poor', 'precious', 'single', 'solid', 'strange' . . . and on they go, in administration, in religion, in the army, in turns of phrase: 'by heart', 'do justice', 'on the point of' and 'take leave'. These are terms from Middle English, but how, we now think, could they ever have been anything *but* English? The influence of French words in the Middle Ages could fill more than fifty of these pages. We now see that they have been successfully anglicised.

Yet English was deluged with French words. It was the great flood and there seemed no ark in sight. How did English survive and re-emerge?

It took wars, it took patriotic resilience and it took one of the greatest natural disasters anyone had ever seen.

5

The Speech of Kings

Trade loosened the bonds between the Norman French and the natives. In the middle of the thirteenth century, the wool trade made parts of England rich. Great churches were built even in modest villages. Towns grew in size, sometimes French boroughs and English settlements together, as at Norwich and Nottingham. London's population was to double in the course of the century, drawing in English speakers from the countryside. It seemed all but impossible for English to storm the castles: the cities might provide a better opportunity. There were French-speaking court officials, administrators, lawyers and great merchants, but surely English could get a foot on the language ladder further down.

Even here it seems it was difficult. The French also brought over craftsmen who gave us the French names for the tools of the trade: 'measure' for example, 'mallet', 'chisel', 'pulley', 'bucket', 'trowel'. Again the deal seemed one way only. The name of Petty France in London is evidence that it originally housed a community of French immigrants which then became a business-trading centre (there were areas like this in many English towns). English and French speakers mingled but it was French which controlled the market. 'Merchant' (marchant), 'money' (monai), 'price' (pris), 'bargain' (bargaine), 'contract' (contract), 'partner' (parcener), 'embezzle' (enbesilier) – all French.

It still appeared that wherever it turned English met yet another phalanx of French. They even took its names away. The Old English names began to die out: out went Ethelbert, Aelfric, Athelstan, Dunstan, Wulfstan, Wulfric; in came Richard, Robert, Simon, Stephen, John, and most popular and sycophantic (or was it politic?) of all, William.

Despite the great numerical superiority of its followers, English was a mass without leaders or a strategy, its words sung in the fields and flickering into manuscripts but no match at all for the French. It was helpless, it seemed, before an inevitable pressing down, a percolation which would eventually eat away at it and so reduce its powers that more and more of its speakers would feel compelled to put it aside. It was not a language of advancement, a language of power, a language of hard commerce or even of educated conversation.

A defeat on the field of battle and in France itself in 1204 was the first truly encouraging sign that all might not be lost. John, King of Normandy, Aquitaine and England, lost his Norman lands in a war with the much smaller kingdom of France. The Norman dukedoms, ancestral lands of William the Conqueror, his cultural and linguistic homelands, were part of another empire now. The Norman barons of England had to choose where their allegiance lay: Philip II of France would tolerate no split loyalties. Choices were made. Simon de Montfort, for example, took over all his brother's English holdings and gave him his own land in Normandy in return.

Most importantly of all, the French began to be thought of as foreigners. That can scarcely be overestimated. When, later in the thirteenth century, Henry III did the natural French-speaking Norman thing and considerably strengthened the French representation at his court, there was strong anti-French feeling and complaints that London was full of foreigners. One defeat had threatened English; one hundred and twenty-eight years later, another defeat gave it hope. The Normans in England had to begin to consider themselves as anti-Norman.

This was the first step on a very long journey. England was now home because many had little choice, but the adoption of English did not follow. When the barons rebelled against King John and presented their demands in the most famous document in our history, Magna Carta, they had it drawn up in Latin. Latin was the language of God, the language of deep tradition, the common language of the western civilised world, a sacred language. Even when there was another rebellion, this time against Henry III in 1258, the barons again wrote to the king in Latin. But they also sent a letter around the shires to tell the people what they wanted and that was written in English. Royalty however was not to be addressed in the basic language of the land over which it ruled, and indeed it was the fight to seduce and force the kings of England publicly to acknowledge English which was to be the first of many major and necessary victories before the language regained the position it had held under Alfred the Great and Harold Godwineson.

There was, however, a fifth column: English women. The evidence for intermarriage is early and strong and although the English women would marry into households dominated by French and may well have learned and been obliged to learn French, they could scarcely have left their English outside the back door. It penetrated those unassailable castles in ways no English band of insurgents could hope to do. And they would bring their own servants, their own wet nurses. It has been said many times that the hand that rocks the cradle rules the world and in some households children may have grown up bilingual, as easily able to switch languages or codes as many children can today from their dialects, their patois, their inherited home-talk, to the standard speech demanded by the school or the state.

We have some lyrics of the period. This one may have been sung as a lullaby to many an infant Norman lordling:

> Merry it is while summer lasts
> Amid the song of the birds
> But now the wind's blast approaches
> And hard weather.

> Alas, how long the night is
> And I, most unjustly used,
> Sorrow and mourn and fast.

It would have been sung in Old English:

> Mirie it is, while sumer ilast
> Wið fugheles song
> Oc nu necheð windes blast
> And weder strong.
> Ei, ei! What þis nicht is long!
> And Ich wið wel michel wrong
> Soregh and murne and fast.

And yet, even after the middle of the thirteenth century, the record shows that French words continue to stream into English. The worrying thing, when you do the sums, is that far more words came in after 1250 than before. Even though England was setting itself up against France, French words, having found a breach, poured across the Channel unstoppably in their thousands. Here are a few of them: 'abbey' (abbaïe), 'attire' (atirer), 'censer' (censier), 'defend' (defendre), 'leper' (lepre), 'malady' (maladie), 'music' (musik), 'parson' (persone), 'plead' (plaidier), 'sacrifice' (sacrifice), 'scarlet' (escarlate), 'spy' (espier), 'stable' (stable), 'virtue' (vertue), 'park' (parc), 'reign' (regne), 'beauty' (bealte), 'clergy' (clergie), 'cloak' (cloke), 'country' (cuntrée), 'fool' (fol).

Each one of those words could nourish two or three paragraphs on what was brought to England through the word. A word like 'virtue', for instance, part of the theme of chivalry now woven into the thinking, brought a secular sense of moral attainment into a land where the Church had provided all the words and thoughts for any elevated morality. The word then took off and metamorphosed into several other meanings: it allied itself with honour and with courage, for example, embellishing both; it became a boast, it became a weakness to be satirised; from rare and aristocratic it became common and earnest. It came to mean reason or merit or worth. 'By virtue of the power vested in me' it began to dip below the horizon of well-used words. Soon it may be obsolete. Yet in its life, for eight hundred years, virtue alone, that one word, has illuminated and explained something of what we think we are, it has enriched our description of ourselves, uncovered yet more of the human condition which seems to crave infinite description. It is not just a word but a little history of our thought and actions. Virtue might or might not be its own reward. It was certainly ours.

Because French was at that time the international language of trade, it acted as a conduit, sometimes via Latin, for words from the markets of the East. Arabic words that it then gave to English include: 'saffron' (safran), 'mattress' (materas), 'hazard' (hasard), 'camphor' (camphre), 'alchemy' (alquimie), 'lute' (lut), 'amber' (ambre), 'syrup' (sirop). The word 'checkmate' comes through the French 'eschec mat' from the Arabic 'Sh h m t', meaning the king is dead. Again, as with virtue and as with hundreds of the words already mentioned, a word, at its simplest, is a window. In that case, English was perhaps as much threatened by light as by darkness, as much in danger of being blinded by these new revelations as buried under their weight.

Yet the best of English somehow managed to avoid both these fates. It retained its grammar, it held on to its basic words, it kept its nerve, but what it did most remarkably was to accept and absorb French as a layering, not as a replacement but as an enricher. It had begun to do that when Old English met Old Norse: hide/skin; craft/skill. Now it exercised all its powers before a far mightier opponent. The acceptance of the Norse had been limited in terms of vocabulary. Here English was Tom Thumb. But it worked in the same way.

So, a young English hare came to be named by the French word 'leveret', but 'hare' was not displaced. Similarly with English 'swan', French 'cygnet'. A small English 'axe' is a French 'hatchet'. 'Axe' remained. There are hundreds of examples of this, of English as it were taking a punch but not giving ground.

More subtle distinctions were set in train. 'Ask' – English – and 'demand' – from French – were initially used for the same purpose but even in the Middle Ages their finer meanings might have differed and now, though close, we use them for markedly different purposes. 'I ask you for ten pounds'; 'I demand ten pounds': two wholly different stories. But both words remained. So do 'bit' and 'morsel', 'wish' and 'desire', 'room' and 'chamber'. At the time the French might have expected to displace the English. It did not and perhaps the chief reason for that is that people saw the possibilities of increasing clarity of thought, accuracy of expression by refining meaning between two words supposed to be the same. On the surface some of these appear to be interchangeable and sometimes they are. But much more interesting are these fine differences, whose subtleties increase as time carries them first a hair's breadth apart and then widens the gap, multiplies the distinctions: just as 'ask' has evolved far away from 'demand'.

Not only did they drift apart but something else happened which demonstrates how deeply not only history but class is buried in language. You can take an (English) 'bit' of cheese and most people do. If you want to use a more elegant word you take a (French) 'morsel' of cheese. It is undoubtedly thought to be a better class of word and yet 'bit', I think, might prove to have more stamina. You can 'start' a meeting or you can 'commence' a meeting. Again, 'commence' carries a touch more cultural clout though 'start' has the better sound and meaning to it for my ear. But it was the embrace which was the triumph, the coupling which was never quite one.

That's the beauty of it. That was the sweet revenge which English took on French: it not only anglicised it, it used the invasion to increase its own strength; it looted the looters, plundered those who had plundered, out of weakness brought forth strength. For 'answer' is not quite 'respond'; now they have almost independent lives. 'Liberty' isn't always 'freedom'. Shades of meaning, representing shades of thought, were massively absorbed into our language and our imagination at that time. It was new lamps and old; both.

The extensive range of what I would call 'almost synonyms' became one of the glories of the English language, giving it astonishing precision and flexibility, allowing its speakers and writers over the centuries to discover what seemed to be exactly the right word. Rather than replace English, French was being brought into service to help enrich and equip it for the role it was on its way to reassuming.

Even that great redoubt of French, the royal family, unbelievably slow in appreciating their good fortune in ruling the country they did with the language it was relentlessly replenishing, began to take notice.

In Westminster Abbey on the tomb of Edward I there are the words 'The Hammer Of The Scots' – in Latin. More important for English was Edward's relationship with his new great enemy, France. When the French King Philip IV threatened to invade England in 1295, Edward used the English language as a symbol of nationhood to galvanise support.

'If Philip is able to do all the evil he means to,' he said, 'from which God protect us, he plans to wipe out our English language entirely from the earth.' Coming from a king whose first language was French, whose immediate ancestors had put England and English under the heel, he may have meant it, but it was richly ironic. But he saw it as the rallying cry for this new mongrel people. The invasion never came and Edward put aside his opportunistic loyalty to English: in all official matters Latin and French were still the controlling languages of the Church and state.

Yet Edward's desperate and inspired flash of English had been well calculated. As the thirteenth century gave way to the fourteenth, English was becoming the one language out of the three that everyone in the country could be counted on to know. In 1325, the chronicler William of Nassington could write:

> Latyn, as I trowe, can nane
> But þo þat haueth it in scolè tane
> And somme can Frensche and no Latyn
> Þat vsed han cowrt and dwellen þerein . . .

A prose translation would read: 'I believe that no one can speak Latin except those who have taken it at school, and some who are accustomed to the court and live there know French and no Latin.' It goes on: 'And some whose grasp of French is shaky know a bit of Latin. And some understand English well who know neither Latin nor French. But educated and uneducated, old and young, they all understand the English tongue.'

That last sentence signals a thaw. English, for so long frozen, underground, so many of its words withered by the icy blast from Normandy, had begun to come through, above ground once more, still far from its old commanding position but ready to move upward. Songs in the French troubadour style now had English words. In some places, the Old English religious homilies had continued to be copied and circulated and this began to affect other aspects of Christian teaching.

The Bestiary, in which birds and animals were portrayed and their behaviour made the basis of lessons in Christian morality, was a particular medieval form. It was believed that the animal and plant worlds were symbolic of religious truths and that 'the creatures of this sensible world signify the invisible things of God'. They were usually written in Latin, but a late-thirteenth-century example gave the text not in Latin but in English. In Modern English it reads: 'The deer has two properties. He draws out the adder from the stone with his nose and swallows it. The venom causes the deer to burn. Then he rushes to the water and drinks . . . The whale is the largest of all fish. He looks like an island when he is afloat. When he is hungry he gapes and out comes a sweet scent.'

The description of the lion can be used to show more clearly how the Bestiary worked. By penetrating this homely but intellectually imaginative Latin form, English demonstrated its hunger for growth, its willingness to tackle subjects which in the post-Conquest world would have been thought above its station.

A few lines of Middle English:

e leun stant on hille & he man hunten here
Oðer ðurg his nese smel smake ðat he negge,
Bi wilc weie so he wile to dele niðer wenden . . .

A literal translation of the lion's nature and qualities reads: 'The lion stands on a hill, and when he hears a man hunting or through his sense of smell scents that he is approaching, by whatever way he will go down to the valley.'

And the symbolic meaning in terms of Christ, the devil, good and evil, reads:

> Very high on the hill that is the Kingdom of Heaven
> Our Lord is the lion that lives there, above.
> Oh! When it pleased Him to come down to earth,
> Might never the devil know though he hunts secretly,
> How he came down nor how he lodged himself
> In that gentle maiden called Mary
> Who bore him for the benefit of mankind.

It would be a lengthy, bloody, martyr-strewn and bitter fight that English would have to claim its proper place in the Church. This infiltration was an omen. It came in quietly and stealthily through the beasts.

As did the greatest of all recorded plagues. In 1348 Rattus rattus, the Latin-named black rodent, was the devil in the Bestiary. These black rats deserted a ship from the Continent which had docked near Weymouth. They carried a deadly cargo, a term that modern science calls Pasteurella pestis, that the fourteenth century named the Great Pestilence and that we know as the Black Death.

The worst plague arrived in these islands and much, including the language, would be changed radically.

The infected rats scaled out east and then north. They sought out human habitations, building nests in the floors, climbing the wattle and daub walls, shedding the infected fleas that fed on their blood and transmitted bubonic plague. It has been estimated that up to one-third of England's population of four million died. Many others were debilitated for life. In some places entire communities were wiped out. In Ashwell in Hertfordshire, for instance, in the bell tower of the church, some despairing soul, perhaps the parish priest, scratched a short poignant chronicle on the wall in poor Latin. 'The first pestilence was in 1350 minus one ... 1350 was pitiless, wild, violent, only the dregs of the people live to tell the tale.'

The dregs are where our story of English moves on. These dregs were the English peasantry who had survived. Though the Black Death was a catastrophe, it set in train a series of social upheavals which would speed the English language along the road to full restoration as the recognised language of the natives. The dregs carried English through the openings made by the Black Death.

The Black Death killed a disproportionate number of the clergy, thus reducing the grip of Latin all over the land. Where people lived communally as the clergy did in monasteries and other religious orders, the incidence of infection and death could be devastatingly high. At a local level, a number of parish priests caught the plague from tending their parishioners; a number ran away. As a result the Latin-speaking clergy was much reduced, in some parts of the country by almost a half. Many of their replacements were laymen, sometimes barely literate, whose only language was English.

More importantly, the Black Death changed society at its roots – the very place where English was most tenacious, where it was still evolving, where it roosted.

In many parts of the country there was hardly anyone left to work the land or tend the livestock. The acute shortage of labour meant that for the first time those who did the basic work had a lever, had some power to break from their feudal past and demand better conditions and higher wages. The administration put out lengthy and severe notices forbidding labourers to try for wage increases, attempting to force them to keep to pre-plague wages and demands, determined to stifle these uneasy, unruly rumblings. They failed. Wages rose. The price of property fell. Many peasants, artisans, or what might be called working-class people discovered plague-emptied farms and superior houses which they occupied.

The English and English were breaking through. Wat Tyler led the Peasants' Revolt which in its mere five days of life threatened to do for England in 1381 most of what the French revolutionaries did for France in 1790. If it can be said to have failed by one act and one man, then that man was the boy king – thirteen years old – Richard II. He stopped it by having the guile and the guts to meet Wat Tyler and his conquering army (they had taken the hitherto impregnable White Tower of London) at Smithfield, addressing him in English. At Smithfield, using English under duress, he pulled Wat Tyler into a trap in which he was murdered and immediately and daringly rode across to the rebels and addressed them, also in English. He gave promises which placated them and turned them home, promises which he soon broke, homes in which they were hunted down. But English was at the heart of it. As far as we know, Richard II is the first recorded example of a monarch using only English since the Conquest. And he reached for it when he was within a few minutes of seeing his kingdom transformed utterly.

Just as importantly, though, the revolt was fired by the preacher John Ball, whose words were already notorious and whose sermon at Greenwich the day before the rebels marched on London began: 'When Adam delved and Eve span, who was then the gentleman?' The heft of what he said, all in English, with his gift for rhyme, was far nearer the Old English epics than the graces of the imported French troubadours.

John Ball, priest of Saint Mary, greeteth well all manner of men and bids 'em in the name of the Trinity, Father and Son and Holy Ghost, stand manly together in truth, and helpeth truth, and truth shall help you. Now reigneith pride in price, and covetousness is held wise, and lechery without shame, and gluttony without blame. Envy reigneth with treason, and sloth is taken in great season. God make the reckoning, for now is time. Amen.

English was the language of protest and protesting its right to be heard and taken account of before the highest in the land. And the highest of the land used it in 1381, to chop down the revolt of thousands of English speakers.

It was about this time that English replaced French in the school-rooms and for that we have the authority of the Cornishman John of Trevisa (d. 1402). In 1387, at Oxford, he translated Ranulf Higden's Latin *Polychronicon*, the chronicle of many ages from the Creation to 1352. Higden reviews the language situation before the first plague and comes to conclusions which must cause us to challenge assumptions based on the benign (for English) effects of Anglo-Norman mixed marriage and hence the bilingualism among Anglo-Norman children. In his view, English was in great peril from 1066 onwards. Higden saw a decline in English pre- the plague and accounted for it in this way: John Trevisa's translation tells us: 'On ys for chyldern in scole agenes þe vsage and manere of al oþer nacions, buþ compelled for to leue here oune longage . . .'

In Modern English:

One [reason] is that children in school, contrary to the usage and custom of all other nations, are compelled to abandon their own language and carry on their lessons and their affairs in French, and have done so since the Normans first came to England. Also the children of gentlemen are taught to speak French from the time that they are rocked in their cradle and learn to speak and play with a child's trinket, and rustic men will make themselves like gentlemen and seek with great industry to speak French to be more highly thought of.

Higden's view is tougher than the more easy-going view of inter-marriage, that it bred English-speaking children who would carry native language with them inside the fortresses of the foreigner. No doubt there is truth in both accounts, but I like Higden's stern note, its reminder of what occupation meant and how it affected not only the progeny but the generality, not only the children in the cradle but the rustics learning French, seeking to join the ruling club.

However, Trevisa's own footnote to this part of his translation, written about fifty years after the original, says: 'Þis manere was moche y-vsed tofore þe furst moreyn . . .'

This practice was much used before the first plague and has since been somewhat changed. For John Cornwall, a teacher of grammar, changed the teaching in grammar school and the construing of French into English; and Richard Penkridge learned that method of teaching from him, and other men from Penkridge, so that now, AD 1385, the ninth year of the reign of the second King Richard after the Conquest, in all the grammar schools of England, children abandon French and compose and learn in English . . .

This was a sea change.

As education and literacy spread, so did the demand for books in English. The language was recommencing its long march.

In 1362, for the first time in almost three centuries, English was acknowledged as a language of official business. Since the Conquest, court cases had been heard in French. Now the law recognised that too few people understood that language, perhaps because many of the educated lawyers, like the clergy, had died in the plague. From now on, it was declared, cases could be pleaded, defended, debated and judged in English. In that same year, Parliament was opened in the hammer-beamed Great Hall in the Palace of Westminster. For the first time ever, the Chancellor addressed the assembly not in French but in English. Surprisingly, there is no record of the words spoken: what follows is a reasonable guess, based on forms of words used in other contemporary documents. 'For the worship and honour of God, King Edward has summoned his Prelates, Dukes, Earls,

Barons and other Lords of his realm to his Parliament, held the year of the King . . .'

But that was not the crown. It took thirty-seven more years for Norman-French royalty to bend the kingly knee to the English language. Stoked no doubt by an interminable war with France which had already lasted on and off for sixty-one years, those who sat on the throne of England felt forced to use their people's tongue.

The country had not had a monarch take the crown in English since Harold Godwineson in 1066. It is debatable whether it had a first-language English-speaking king since then. But English was about to capture the crown.

In 1399, King Richard II was deposed by Henry, Duke of Lancaster. The document deposing him and his speech of abdication are in English. Parliament was summoned to the Great Hall at Westminster. The dukes and lords, spiritual and temporal, were assembled. The royal throne, draped in cloth of gold, stood empty. Then Henry stepped forward, crowned himself, and claimed the crown. In a great symbolic moment he made his speech not in the Latin language of state business, not in the French language of the royal household, but in what the official history, tellingly, calls 'His Mother Tongue'. English.

In the name of Fadir, Son, and Holy Gost, I, Henry of Lancaster chalenge this rewme of Yngland and the corone with all the members and the appurtenances, als I that am disendit be right lyne of the blode comying fro the gude lorde Kyng Henry Therde, and thorghe that ryght that God of his grace hath sent me, with the helpe of my kyn and of my frendes, to recover it – the whiche rewme was in poynt to be undone for défaut of governance and undoing of the gode lawes.

In the name of the Father, Son and Holy Ghost, I, Henry of Lancaster, claim this realm of England and the crown with all its property and privileges – because I am legitimately descended from the blood of the good lord King Henry the Third – and by that right that God's grace has granted me, with the help of both my family and my friends, to recover it; the which realm was in danger of being ruined by lack of government and the undoing of good laws.

Henry, Duke of Lancaster became King Henry IV and English was once again a royal language. It had been touch-and-go many times. And Latin and French had not lost their grip as the languages of official business and of the Church. But English had made its boldest public gain for three centuries and it sat once more on the throne. At last the tide seemed to be turning in its favour, although there would be much blood spilled before it gained status as the first language in all matters to do with English life.

Now, though, as if in celebration of this victory, it would welcome its first truly great literary champion, a writer who could harness its new capabilities to produce great stories, and poetry, a literature fit for the language that had come through.

6

Chaucer

Chaucer was the first writer of the newly emerged England. He told us what we were. In *The Canterbury Tales* in particular he describes characters we can still see around us today and he writes of them in the new English, Middle English, English that had somehow withstood the battering given by French and come back to begin its fight to regain control of the country in which it had been nourished.

David Crystal in his *Encyclopaedia of the English Language* writes: 'In no other author . . . is there better support for the view that there is an underlying correspondence between the natural rhythm of English poetry and that of English everyday conversation.'

Here, at the end of the fourteenth century, English speakers talk directly to us, through skilful stories told by a group of pilgrims to ease the time as they ride from Southwark in London to Canterbury Cathedral. There are several reasons to pause and look around the world of English with Chaucer but most importantly for me, he brings on to the stage the range of individually realised characters, high and low, broad and refined, and of words apt for each, coarse and delicate, satirical and mock-heroic, which signpost not only much of future English literature but much of English life. Most importantly of all, he decided to write not in Latin – which he knew well – not in the French from which he translated and which might have given him greater prestige, but in English, his own English, London-based English. Power had moved out of Wessex away from

Winchester and it was now London, together with the twin universities of Oxford and Cambridge, which increasingly would set the
often much resented and resisted Standard English.

Chaucer was not alone. There is Langland's *Piers Plowman*, there
is *Sir Gawain and the Green Knight*, there are homilies, sermons,
rhymes and verses bursting out all over, a springtime of English not
just released from bondage but energised and fortified by it. Chaucer
was supreme at that time and by concentrating on him, telling his
story along the way of our journey as his pilgrims did on their
journey we will, I hope, get some understanding of what English
had achieved in these three hundred Normanised years. There is
plenty to work on: he wrote forty-three thousand lines of poetry,
two substantial prose works and curiosities such as *A Treatise on the
Astrolabe* for the education of his son, Lewis.

The man's life is well enough known, probably more certain in its
details than the life of Shakespeare two centuries later. He was a
Londoner, born in the mid 1340s, son of a London vintner, John
Chaucer. In his adolescence, he became a page in the service of the
Duke of Clarence and later served in the household of Edward III. It is
important to emphasise that London was tiny by modern-day comparisons – a population of about forty thousand. Grandeur and the gutter
were twinned in confined, crowded, sometimes dangerously infected
places in which you did not risk drinking the water. A page at court
would most likely be sent on messages and little missions all over the
city and be able to savour all the variety of life on offer, life then being
much lived on the streets. Dickens, the great fictional cartographer of
London, is prefigured in Chaucer and both were steeped in the place.

Chaucer served in one of the campaigns in the Hundred Years
War, was taken prisoner, and ransomed. There was material here
well used and his rather grand marriage, to the daughter of Sir Payne
Roet, whose sister later linked him by marriage to John of Gaunt,
gave him high gossip at least, and access very likely to the centre of
power. The idea of a writer making a living solely through writing
was not entertained at that time. Chaucer had an income to find. He

discovered ways to do this which in retrospect seem brilliantly planned to develop his art as a writer while satisfying his need for a purchase on the worlds of money, intellectual engagement, diplomacy and status. In the 1370s he began to travel abroad on diplomatic missions for the king. There was a trade agreement he negotiated at Genoa; on a mission to Milan he encountered the dazzling achievements of Italian poetry. Petrarch and Boccaccio were alive and Dante was cherished and much discussed. There is evidence of their influence in much of his work.

After about ten years in the saddle abroad, during which time he composed *The Parliament of Fowls*, *Troilus and Criseyde* and translated Boethius' *The Consolation of Philosophy*, he settled in London to become Controller of the Petty Customs. In 1386 he was elected as a Knight, or MP, for the shire of Kent. He began work on *The Canterbury Tales* and it is in this period that his fortunes fluctuate as the youth of Richard II helped provoke court intrigue: Chaucer gets into debt; he recovers to become Clerk of the King's Works; he soon quits that for the unprepossessing post of Deputy Forester at Petherton in Somerset; he takes a lease on a house in the garden of Westminster Abbey in 1399 and dies the following year. It is a life which covered much of the important waterfront of the time and that knowingness, that lived experience is one of the factors which gives *The Canterbury Tales* its historical strength. Of course the characters and the stories are inventions but nevertheless, we feel, grounded in close observation of and some participation in the world as it was then. Chaucer's England is a believable place.

These are the opening lines of *The Canterbury Tales* in a Modern English translation; they begin in spring in the rain:

> When April with his sweet showers
> Has pierced the drought of March to the root
> And bathed every vein in such moisture
> Which has the power to bring forth the flower,
> When also Zephyrus with his sweet breath

Has breathed spirit into tender new shoots
In every wood and meadow . . .
Then people love to go on pilgrimage.

So in his own language, a language written to be read aloud to a
public more than read alone in private, Chaucer calmly, leisurely,
gathers his listeners and readers together:

Whan that Aprill with his shoures soote
The droghte of March hath perced to the roote
And bathed every veyne in swich lycour
Of which vertu engendred is the flour;
When Zephirus eek with his sweete breeth
Inspired hath in every holt and heeth
The tendre croppes . . .
Thanne longen folk to goon on pilgrimages.

About twenty to twenty-five per cent of the vocabulary used by
Chaucer is from the French. In that short extract there's an average
of at least one French word per line: 'April', 'March', 'perced', 'veyne',
'lycour', 'vertu', 'engendred', 'flour', 'inspired'. Often they have meanings now lost: 'lycour' = moisture; 'vertu' = power. Later, 'corage' =
heart; 'straunge' = foreign, distant. 'Zephirus' is from Latin, 'root' is
from Old Norse. But there is no sense that English had been taken
over. This language is English. All the words called by linguists
'function words' – pronouns and prepositions – are from Old English;
the nuts and bolts and the basic structure held.

And specially from every shires ende
Of Engelond to Caunterbury they wende,
The hooly blisful martir for to seke,
That hem hath holpen [helped] whan that they were seeke.

The martyr was the murdered Archbishop, Thomas à Becket.
And that is the basic structure of the tales. Within that, as within
the language, the variations through the stories themselves are numer-

ous and exhilarating. They meet at the Tabard Inn in Southwark, five minutes' walk from where the Globe would be built. In Chaucer's as in Shakespeare's time and until quite recently, it was a 'mixed' area of London, a place of pickpockets, prostitutes, markets, pubs, traffic and foreign seamen crowding the twisting streets from the Thames, 'real London' in Chaucer's day and still now.

The characters ride in:

> A knyght ther was, and that a worthy man,
> That fro the tyme that he first bigan
> To riden out, he loved chivalrie,
> Trouthe and honour, fredom and curteisie.

Here Chaucer has inherited and appropriated the language and the ideas brought over by Eleanor of Aquitaine and in doing so he has created a figure who would feature in English history and in English literature deep into the twentieth century. He may be lurking yet: the man of quality and privilege who was also a man of integrity, modest and courteous especially to women, a man prepared to fight for a cause that was good but not brutalised by war, a gentle man. The element of irony is there: this roll-call of battle honours can also be described as a catalogue of massacres. Yet, idealised, satirised, caricatured, lovingly rediscovered century after century, Chaucer's Knight is the first of many characters who defined what we thought or wanted to believe one aspect of being English was.

This brief paragraph could be repeated for almost all the pilgrims. Through his English, Chaucer gave England its first National Portrait Gallery.

> Ther was also a Nonne, a Prioresse,
> That of hir smylyng was ful symple and coy;
> Hire gretteste ooth was but by Seinte Loy;
> And she was cleped [called] madame Eglentyne.

> A Monk ther was, a fair for the maistrie [fit to wield authority],
> An outridere, that lovede venerie [hunting]

A Marchant was ther with a forked berd,
In mottelee, and hye on horse he sat;

The Millere was a stout carl [fellow] for the nones;
Ful byg he was of brawn . . .

Perhaps part of the appeal is what we might call the canny cross-class cluster. Not only from different parts of England but from different strata of society they come, joined in a common purpose, and whipped into line by the landlord, Harry Bailey. They take their turn to tell their stories. This gallery rises above feudalism, it presents a society of people happy to deal on equal terms before God and in story-telling. It has the deep attraction of a Golden Age and gives off the warm feeling that these were people who had come through a long tunnel and wanted to go together towards a new light, riding on the pleasure of their language and its new subtle abilities to etch them into history.

What Chaucer did most brilliantly was to choose and tailor his language to suit every story and its teller. The creation of mood and tone and the realisation of characters through the language they use is something we expect of writers today, so it is difficult to realise how extraordinary it was when Chaucer did it. He proved that the re-formed English was fit for great literature.

The range and variety of the language can clearly be seen by looking at just two of the stories. In the Nun's Priest's Tale, the language of high Romance — used with open sincerity and admiration in the Knight's Tale — is used satirically to tell the mock-Romantic comic story of a vain cockerel and his favourite chicken:

This courtly cock had at his command
Seven hens to do his pleasure
They were his sisters and his paramours
And marvellously like him in colouring
Of them the one with the most beautifully coloured throat
Was named the fair damsel Pertelote.

> This gentil cok hadde in his governaunce
> Sevene hennes for to doon al his plesaunce,
> Whiche were his sustres and his paramours,
> And wonder lyk to hym, as of colours;
> Of whiche the faireste hewed on hir throte
> Was cleped faire damoysele Pertelote.

French words dominate here – 'governaunce', 'plesaunce', 'paramours'. 'Governaunce' and 'plesaunce' are quite new, first recorded around the middle of the fourteenth century. Chaucer liked French borrowings and enjoyed introducing his own synonyms. English had the noun 'hard': Chaucer introduced the French (from Latin) 'difficulté'. He gave us 'disadventure' for 'unhap', 'dishonesté' for 'shendship', 'edifice' for 'building', 'ignoraunt' for 'uncunning'. Chaucer's reputation in France was high in his own lifetime and looting the old conqueror's language was fair game. He was unselfconscious about this new English: there was no rigid fundamentalism about it, eclecticism and elasticity were all.

The greatest contrast to the Nun's Priest's Tale is the Miller's Tale, where Absolon, the parish clerk, makes a midnight assignation with a neighbour's wife which, as it were, backfires:

> Then Absolon wiped his mouth very dry
> The night was dark as pitch or coal
> And out of the window she stuck her hole
> And Absolon fared neither better nor worse
> But with his mouth he kissed her naked arse.

> This Absolon gan wype his mouth ful drie,
> Derk was the nyght as pich, or as the cole,
> And at the wyndow out she putte hir hole,
> And Absolon, hym fil no bet ne wers,
> But with his mouth he kiste hir naked ers.

The style is direct, colloquial, with few French words. For earthy words he goes to Old English – or to the streets for 'ers'.

Sir Geoffrey Chaucer, courtier and scholar, had no problem with what we might call rude or saucy words. When Harry Bailey tells the Chaucer character to shut up (Chaucer has sent himself up with a tale of Sir Thopas in dreadful doggerel), he says:

> 'By God,' quod he, 'for pleynly, at a word,
> Thy drasty rymyng is nat worth a toord!'

There are plenty of other examples, the bluntest of which is probably that uttered by the sexually demanding Wife of Bath:

> What eyleth yow to grucche thus and grone?
> Is it for ye wolde have my queynte alone?

What really offended people then was swearing by God or by parts of God. When Harry Bailey asks them to tell a tale 'For Goddes bones', the Parson protests at this sinful swearing.

'Swerian' is an Anglo-Saxon word and probably began as the description of someone taking a solemn oath. Surprisingly few of our popular swear words are Anglo-Saxon in origin. The terrible oaths in Chaucer were profanities. In the Pardoner's Tale, Chaucer writes:

> And many a grisly ooth thanne han they sworn,
> And Cristes blessed body they torente [torn apart]

There's 'Goddes precious herte' and 'Goddes armes' and 'Jhesu shorte thy lyf'. To avoid the wrath of the Church, shorthand became a fashion. God's Blood became ''Sblood!', Christ's wounds became ''Swounds!', then ''Zounds!' This could deflect censure. It is a reminder of how very powerful the Church was, how pervasive its authority. These minced oaths came into full play much later, in Shakespeare's time.

As you would expect of a writer whose purpose, conscious or unconscious, seems to have been to round up as many Englishes as he could and drive them along the same road to Canterbury, Chaucer was well aware of the dialects. It was still the case that words in southern English would have to be translated in some measure certainly for northern and possibly for Midland English. John Trevisa complained that Yorkshire English was so 'scharp, slyttyng, and frotyng, and vnschape' (shrill, cutting, grating and ill-formed) that southerners like him could not understand it.

Chaucer in the Reeve's Tale gives us our first 'funny northerner', a character who has been with us ever since. He says 'ham' for 'home', 'knaw' for 'know', 'gang' for 'gone', 'nan' for 'none', 'na' for 'no', 'banes' for 'bones'. He would be comfortably at home in 2003 in the north-east and Newcastle, in Cumbria around Wigton and in Yorkshire around Leeds. Why it was thought to be funny in itself is the beginning of an independent study to do with the south's suspicion of the north, its fear of it to which it responded savagely in earlier times and later tried to tame through nervously superior laughter, and much later a felt superiority in wealth, privilege, culture and accent. There was class, of course, although as some of the greatest old English and old Norse families hailed from the north that was not always an easy one. But as language became one of the markers of class, all non-London dialects began to feel they were condescended to.

Chaucer planted English deeply in the country which bore its name, with a brilliance and a confidence that meant that there was no looking back: Confidence in England and English was growing. The increasing use of the surname may perhaps be an oblique confirmation of this. They were needed, to differentiate between people with the same Christian names, as the pool of Christian names in common use was very small at this period. 'Geoffrey' is Germanic but came to England through the Normans. 'Chaucer' is French, from the Old French 'Chausier', shoemaker, perhaps from the place in which his grandfather had lived in Cordwainer (Leatherworker) Street. We saw that in the north the suffix -son became prevalent: Johnson, Rawlinson, Arnison, Pearson, Matheson, Dickson, Wilson. More generally, in this Chaucerian period, other surnames came in, often based on where people lived – Hill, Dale, Bush, Fell, Brook, Field, or words ending in -land and -ton. Maybe this was a belated catching up with the Norman-French nobility, all of whom were 'de' somewhere or other, de Montfort, for instance. Then there were the occupational surnames: Butcher, Baker, Carver, Carter, Carpenter, Gardiner, Glover, Hunter, Miller, Cooper, Mason, Salter, Thatcher, Weaver. Place, occupation, inheritance, all these had to be stamped through man and woman, fastening them to their place, giving them full identities in a language and a country that was beginning to feel like theirs.

Yet Chaucer, anxious that he be read everywhere by those who could read English or understand it when it was read aloud to them, was still worried by the variety and confusion of languages in the land. He bids one of his poems, *Troilus and Criseyde*, a rather poignant and even a troubled farewell:

> Go, litel bok . . .
> And for ther is so gret diversite
> In Englissh and in writyng of oure tonge,
> So prey I God that non miswryte the [thee].
>   . . .
> That thow be understonde, God I bseche!

I find it touching that Chaucer could have such fears but how could he have known that with later modifications his language, fed by the Central and West Midlands, nourished in wealthy London, aided by the development of printing in London, would become the basis for a Standard English which would go in 'litel boks' not only all over England but all over the world?

We still have over fifty handwritten copies of *The Canterbury Tales* from the fifteenth century and we know that he reached an audience which included London merchants and Richard of Gloucester, the future King Richard III. Before the fifteenth century was out, William Caxton had printed two editions of *The Canterbury Tales* and they have never been out of print since. They have been enjoyed, imitated, copied, re-translated, put on stage, screen and radio, and generations have rightly regarded Chaucer as the father and founding genius of English literature.

A century and a half after his death, a monumental tomb was erected in his honour in Westminster Abbey. It is in what has become Poets' Corner, just a stone's throw from the house in which he died in 1400.

I think the best way to end this chapter is to quote from another great writer, Dryden, in the seventeenth century, writing of Chaucer:

He must have been a man of a most wonderful comprehensive Nature, because, as it has been truly observed of him, he has taken into the Compass of his Canterbury Tales the various Manners and Humours (as we now call them) of the whole English Nation, in his Age . . . the Matter and Manner of their Tales and of their Telling, are so suited to their different Educations, Humours and Callings, that each of them would be improper in any other Mouth . . .'Tis sufficient to say, according to the Proverb, that 'here is God's Plenty'.

7

God's English

Where English took poets, others wanted to follow. In the fourteenth and fifteenth centuries the movement was under way to force English into a central and commanding place in the society whose first and expanded tongue it was. The state had to be challenged, and the Church. It was with the Church that English had its most violent struggle. The brutalities involved beggar belief.

Later medieval Britain was a religious society. The Roman Catholic Church controlled and pervaded all aspects of earthly life including the intimately sexual. It also held the keys to a heaven and hell which were very real in the minds of most who were fed ceaselessly and cleverly with priestly persuasions, stories of miracles, promises of eternal happiness and threats of eternal torture and damnation. You challenged the might of the Church only if you were extremely powerful and even the powerful would quail and crack when the full range of the Church's instruments of power and conviction were brought to bear. But there were those in England, men of faith, totally committed to the idea that English should become the language of God and in a series of heroic efforts they set out to make that happen even though it would invoke the fearsome wrath of the Holy Roman Catholic Church.

The central power of words in fourteenth-century England lay in the Bible. There was no Bible in English. There had been some piecemeal translations of the Gospels and parts of the Old Testament in Old English and there were Middle English versions of the Psalms. In formal terms, God spoke to the people in Latin. Latin though not the monopoly of the clergy was certainly fortressed by it. The proper relationship between the believer and the Bible was one mediated by the priest in Latin. He would interpret scripture for the common people. It was not unlike a single party state with a single party line on everything. The Bible was in Latin – a language wholly inaccessible to the vast majority, and Bibles were few. The justification was that this was the word of God and to know God was a blessing and a richness beyond all understanding. The priest, it was argued, being ordained a true man of God, would avoid sinful misinterpretation and heresy. He would make sure the devil was shut out. This meant that it was impossible for most English people to know the Bible for themselves.

If you wanted to communicate with God in English, you might be lucky with an idealistic local priest who would preach a sermon on a biblical text – but his starting point and his finishing point would be in Latin: 'In nomine Patris et Filii et Spiritus Sancti. Amen.' There were other ways. Most notably there were the Mystery Plays such as those which began to be performed in York outside the cathedral, the minster, a building every bit as big and daunting as its twin, the Norman castle on the other side of the city.

These Mystery Plays tell the Christian story from the creation of God to the birth, death and resurrection of Christ. They are religious plays but they are not, nor were they allowed to be, the scriptures. They could be called a biblical soap opera. Every year, even today, one of the dozen plays, each originally put on by an often appropriate guild (the carpenters took care of the Crucifixion), is given in the English of the fourteenth century.

In 2002, it was the turn of the Shepherds' Play. In these few lines, the shepherds wonder what gift they can offer to Christ; first, here's a literal translation:

> Now look on me, my lord so dear
> Although I put me not in press.
> Ye are a prince without a peer,
> I have no present that may you please.
> Lo: a horn spoon that I have here,
> And it will hold good forty peas.
> This will I give you with good cheer.

In Middle English, a little later than Chaucer:

> Nowe loke on me, my lorde dere,
> Þof all I putte me noght in pres.
> Ye are a prince withouten pere,
> I haue no presentte that you may plees.
> But lo! An horne spoone that haue I here –
> And it will herbar fourty pese.
> Þis will I giffe you with gud chere.

There can be little doubt of the fear and love most of the population had for their religion and for their Church, and their reliance on it for comfort, for hope and for everyday pleasures, feast days, saints' days, grand processionals. But the common people were on the outside, as can still graphically be seen in York every year as the Mystery Players circle the town and perform in the shadow of the minster, but are not allowed through its doors.

When they went into the minster to stand or kneel respectfully at the back – and everyone had to go, church attendance was compulsory – the service was a remote affair. The whole emphasis was on the mystery of it, the priests like a secret society, the Latin words so awesome in their ancient verity that, although some phrases would have stuck over the years, the whole intention was to impress and to subdue and not to enlighten. There was of course no English Hymnal, and no Book of Common Prayer. You were at the mercy of the priests. Only they were allowed to read the word of God and they did even that silently. A bell was rung to let the congregation know when the priest had reached the important bits. The priest stood not as a guide to the Bible but as its guardian and as a guardian against common believers. They would not be allowed to enter into the Book.

It would be a formidable struggle to wrench that power from the priests, to replace that Latin with English. It is an inspiring passage in the adventure of English, a time of martyrdom and high risk, of daring, scholarship and above all a generous and inclusive belief that the word of God should be in the language of the people. The battle would eventually tear the Church in two, an inconceivable outcome when the first rumblings began in the second half of the fourteenth century. It would claim many lives. But many were ready to die for it, to make English the language of their faith.

The prime mover in the fourteenth century was a scholar, John Wycliffe, probably born near Richmond in Yorkshire, admitted to Merton College, Oxford, when he was seventeen, charismatic, we are told, and a fluent Latinist. He was a major philosopher and theologian who believed passionately that his knowledge should be shared by everyone. From within the sanctioned, clerical, deeply traditionalist honeyed walls of Oxford, Wycliffe the scholar launched a furious attack on the power and wealth of the Church, an attack which prefigured that of Martin Luther more than a hundred years later.

His main argument was to distinguish the eternal, ideal Church of God from the material one of Rome. In short, he maintained that if something is not in the Bible there is no truth in it whatever the Pope says – and, incidentally, the Bible says nothing at all about having a Pope. When men speak of the Church, he said, they usually mean priests, monks, canons and friars. But it should not be so. 'Were there a hundred popes,' he wrote, 'and all the friars turned to cardinals, their opinions on faith should not be accepted except in so far as they are founded on scripture itself.'

This was inflammatory and cut away the roots of all established authority, especially as he and his followers like John Ball coupled this with a demand that the Church give away all its worldly wealth to the poor. The Church saw no option but to crush him. For Wycliffe went even further. He and his followers attacked transubstantiation, the belief that, administered by the clergy, the wine and bread turn miraculously into the blood and body of Christ; he attacked clerical celibacy, which he thought of as an institutional control system over the army of the clergy; he attacked enforced confession, the method, Wycliffe argued, by which the clergy could trap dissidents and check errors in thought; and indulgences, the purchase of which were said to bring relief from purgatory but also brought wealth to the Church; pilgrimages, as a form of idolatry; and mystery plays, because they were not the word of God. Wycliffe took no prisoners.

His prime and revolutionary argument, one which, if accepted in any shape or form would have toppled the Church entirely, was that the Bible was the sole authority for religious faith and practice and that everyone had the right to read and interpret scripture for himself. This would have changed the world and those who ruled the world knew it. He was to become their prime enemy. It is ironic that his main arguments had to be written in Latin – the international language of scholarship and theology – though there are English sermons by him and his followers.

It is remarkable enough that a young man in a quiet clerical college in a country long thought by Rome as on the 'outermost edges of the known world' should raise up his fist against the greatest authority on the earth. He must have been fully aware of the risk he was taking. It is even more remarkable that he went on and did something, did so much, to put his ideas into practice and to enlist so much help from other scholars who also must have seen their whole life and life's work imperilled by this breathtaking venture.

What sustained them, I think, was the state of the Church as they saw it every day. It was intolerable to these Christian scholars. It was often lazy and corrupt. Bible reading even among the clergy appears to have been surprisingly rare, for often they did not have the Latin. When, for example, the Bishop of Gloucester surveyed three hundred and eleven deacons, archdeacons and priests in his diocese, he discovered that a hundred and sixty-eight were unable to repeat the Ten Commandments, thirty-one did not know where to find those Commandments in the Bible and forty could not repeat the Lord's Prayer. To men of true conscience, integrity and faith, men like Wycliffe and his followers, this state of decay and lack of care in what mattered most, this debilitated belief and betrayal of vocation had to be got rid of and defeated. The chief weapon, the natural weapon for a scholar, was a book: the Bible, in English.

A full Bible in English was unauthorised by the Church and potentially heretical, even seditious, with all the savage penalties including death which such crimes against the one true Church exacted. Any translation was very high risk and had to be done in secrecy.

Wycliffe inspired two biblical translations and rightly they bear his name. Both versions are made from the Latin Vulgate version and follow it so closely that it can be incomprehensible. Wycliffe prepared the first translation but the burden of it was undertaken by Nicholas Hereford of Queen's College, Oxford. He would have needed the help of many friends as well as recourse to a great number of books. It was not only the translation itself, a mammoth task, which faced them: the Bible had to be disseminated too. Rooms in quiet Oxford colleges were turned into revolutionary cells, scriptoria, production lines were established turning out these holy manuscripts and from the number that remain we can tell that a great many were made. One hundred and seventy survive, a huge number for a six-hundred-year-old manuscript, which tells us that there must have been effective groups of people secretly translating it, copying it, passing it on. Later, hundreds would be martyred, dying the most horrible deaths, for their part in creating and distributing to the people the first English Bible.

It is difficult to appreciate the extent and the audacity of this enterprise. Wycliffe was leading them into the cannon's mouth. All of them knew it and yet behind the obedient honey-coloured Latinate walls of Oxford colleges, the medieval equivalent of the subversive samizdat press which bypassed Stalin's controls in Russia was organised, and effectively. The operation is a long way from the image of medieval Oxford as a cloistered community of rather quaint time-serving scholarly clerks. Oxford was then the most dangerous place in England, leading the fight in an underground movement which challenged the biggest single force in the land and called into the public court the authority of the revealed language of God. Yet Wycliffe and his men believed they were to change the world and for a brief moment, it seemed, they had. The Wycliffe English Bible was completed. It was scaled out. It was read.

Here are the opening lines, first in Wycliffe's English and then in modern speech:

In the bigynnyng God made of nouyt heuene and erthe.
Forsothe the erthe was idel and voide, and derknessis weren on the face
    of depthe; and the Spiryt of the Lord was borun on the watris.
And God seide, Liyt be maad, and liyt was maad.
And God seiy the liyt, that it was good, and he departide the liyt fro
    derknessis; and he clepide the liyt, dai, and the derknessis, nyyt. And
    the euentid and morwetid was maad, o daie.

In the beginning, God made of naught heaven and earth. Forsooth, the earth was idle and void, and darkness were on the face of depth, and the spirit of God was borne on the waters. And God said 'Light be made!' – and light was made. And God saw the light that it was good and He departed the light from the darkness. And he klept the light day and the darkness night. And the eventide and morrowtide was made, one day.

That passage is straightforward. But in many places it is not an easy translation. Yet many familiar phrases do have their English origin in this translation: 'woe is me', 'an eye for an eye' are both in Wycliffe, as are words such as 'birthday', 'canopy', 'child-bearing', 'cock-crowing', 'communication', 'crime', 'to dishonour', 'envy', 'frying-pan', 'godly', 'graven', 'humanity', 'injury', 'jubilee', 'lecher', 'madness', 'menstruate', 'middleman', 'mountainous', 'novelty', 'Philistine', 'pollute', 'puberty', 'schism', 'to tramp', 'unfaithful' and 'zeal'

– all these and many more were read first in Wycliffe's Bible. Once again we see not only additions to the English word-hoard but new ideas being introduced or current ideas being given a name – 'humanity', 'pollute', which then, as words often do, took on a larger and more complex life. New words are new worlds. You call them up and if they are strong enough, they keep in step with change and along the way describe more and more, provide new insights, evolve on the tongue and on the page. How many nuances and therefore meanings attach to the multiple uses of the world 'humanity'? In the cause of bringing his greatly revered faith to the English, Wycliffe not only widened the ecclesiastical vocabulary – 'graven', 'Philistine', 'schism' – he also let loose words which over the next four centuries would net meanings far removed from the perilously translated texts of medieval Oxford.

The criticism of Wycliffe's Bible is that it is too Latinate. So in awe were they of the authority of the Latin version that they translated word for word, even keeping the Latin word order, as in 'Lord, go from me for I am a man sinner' and 'I forsoothe am the Lord thy God full jealous'. Another result was that the text itself is shot through with Latinate words, some directly imported, some of which came through the French, such as 'mandement', 'descrive', 'cratch'. There are over one thousand Latin words that turn up for the first time in English whose use in England is first recorded in Wycliffe's Bible, words such as 'profession', 'multitude' and 'glory' – a good word for this Bible.

By the standards of the day it was a bestseller and at first the Church merely condemned Wycliffe. They complained that he had made the scriptures 'more open to the teachings of laymen and women. Thus the jewel of the clerics is turned to the sport of the laity and the pearl of the gospel is scattered abroad and trodden underfoot by swine.'

The swine were to be fed, by Wycliffe and, zealous, alight with his mission, he began to organise and train what amounted to a new religious order of itinerant preachers whom he despatched around

England. Their typical garb was a russet-coloured woollen robe. They carried a long staff. Initially most were those fearless Oxford scholars, though they were quickly joined by 'the low born' in extraordinary numbers. Their avowed inspiration, through Wycliffe, were the seventy evangelists whom Jesus had sent out to convert the world. Their purpose was to spread the Word, literally, in English.

It had the characteristics of a guerrilla campaign. They were out to bring God back to the people through the language of the land. We read that they were in the highways, byways, taverns and inns, on village greens and in open fields preaching against the Church's wealth and corruption and proclaiming Wycliffe's anti-clerical ideas. They were spied on, they were observed. They were taking their lives in their hands, but Wycliffe drove them on. They became known as the Lollards, the name deriving from 'lollaerd', mumbler, from 'lollen', to mutter or mumble. They called themselves Christian Brethren.

Most alarmingly of all, they cut out the priests.

Here is part of Wycliffe's version of the Beatitudes:

Blessid ben pore men in spirit, for the kingdom of heuenes is herne.
Blessid ben mylde men, for thei schulen welde the erthe.
Blessid ben thei that mornen, for thei schulen be coumfortid.
Blessid ben thei that hungren and thristen riytwisnesse, for thei
    schulen be fulfilled.
Blessid ben merciful men, for thei schulen gete merci.

  . . .

Ye ben salt of the erthe.

Blessed be poor men in spirit, for the Kingdom of heaven is theirs.
Blessed be mild men for they shall wield the earth.
Blessed be they that mourn for they shall be comforted.
Blessed be they that hunger and thirst rightwise, for they shall be
    fulfilled.
Blessed be the merciful men, for they shall get mercy.

  . . .

You are the salt of the earth.

The Bible, through English, now called out directly to the people. This could not be tolerated. On 17 May 1382, in Blackfriars in London, on a site now boasting a Victorian public house whose tiled décor remembers Wycliffe's time, a synod of the Church met to examine Wycliffe's works. There were eight bishops, various masters of theology, doctors of common and civil law and fifteen friars.

It was a show trial.

Their conclusions were preordained and on the second day of their meeting they drafted a statement condemning Wycliffe's pronouncements as outright heresies. Wycliffe's followers were also condemned. The synod ordered the arrest and prosecution of itinerant preachers throughout the land. Many of those caught were tortured and killed.

Perhaps most significantly of all as far as the English language is concerned, the synod led, later, to a parliamentary ban on all English-language Bibles and they had the powers to make this effective.

Wycliffe's great effort was routed. He had taken on the power of the Church and he had been defeated. His Bibles were outlawed. The doors of the Church, from the greatest cathedrals to the lowliest parish churches, were still the monopoly of Latin.

On 30 May, every diocese in the land was instructed to publish the verdict. Wycliffe became ill. He was paralysed by a stroke. Two years later he died on the last day of 1384.

In 1399, Henry IV was to accept the crown in English. Chaucer delighted readers and appreciators of English everywhere with *The Canterbury Tales*. But the Church slammed the door.

Yet the Lollards risked their lives and carried on, meeting in hidden places, we are told, especially in Herefordshire and Monmouthshire. One contemporary chronicler wrote that 'every second man' he met was a Lollard and they 'went all over England luring great nobles and lords to their fold'. It is very unlikely they were so numerous or so influential among the nobility although, in a different context, in the Peasants' Revolt in 1381, English was proving its worth as a language of protest against central authority and certain restless nobles and lords might well have welcomed that.

William Langland was a Lollard and his religious poem, *Piers Plowman*, was published in 1390. It was the most popular poem of its day, and it shows how deeply Wycliffe's ideas had bitten in. Langland wrote in the West Midlands dialect and while Chaucer's base was London and the cognoscenti, *Piers Plowman* gathered in the provincial and the strongly religious-minded rural population with whose often desperate plight he sympathised wholly.

His poem is written in alliterative verse; Chaucer had used a regular natural structure and rhyme schemes breaking away from the older tradition. Langland reaches back across the centuries to *Beowulf* as he explains how the poem came to him on the Malvern Hills:

> In a somer seson, whan softe was the sonne,
> I shoop [wrapped] me into shroudes [garments] as I a sheep
>   were . . .
> Ac [but] on a May morwenynge on Malverne hilles
> Me bifel a ferly, of Fairye me thoghte.
> [I had a marvellous dream as if by supernatural intervention]

He refreshes alliterative verse and uses it as a root, making his dreams − of Christian life, of the plight of the poor and of the corruption of the clergy − more believable for being so plainly painted. In Langland's verse:

> Ac I beheelde into the eest an heigh to the sonne,
> I seigh a tour on a toft, trieliche ymaked . . .

In Modern English:

> I looked to the East towards the rising sun
> And saw a tower on a hill, wonderfully built.
> A deep dell beneath, a dragon inside
> With a deep ditch dark and dreadful to look at.

In between I found a fair field full of folk
Working and going about their business.
. . .
Some laboured at the plough with no time for pleasure.
Planting and sowing and sweating with effort.
. . .
I found there friars of all four orders
Preaching to the people to profit themselves
Glossing the gospel just as they liked.
. . .
For the parish priest and the pardoner
Share in the silver
That the parish poor would have
If they were not there.

This is meant to sound like the language of the people and in that language Langland continues the work of Wycliffe. This language and the poetry of it prefigures *Pilgrim's Progress* and other works central to the Protestant English language of the Reformation. Yet there was only so much, in truth comparatively little, that a poet could do.

After Wycliffe's death and despite the condemnation and harshness of the Church, copies of Wycliffe's Bible continued to be produced and circulated – even when it became a mortal crime to own any of Wycliffe's works. With astonishing courage, Catholics who spread the English language were prepared to defy the Pope and take a chance with their lives and their eternal souls in order to read the word of God to the English in their own language.

But the hierarchy could not bear it. In 1412, twenty-eight years after Wycliffe's death, the Archbishop of Canterbury ordered all of Wycliffe's works to be burned and in a letter to the Pope entered a list of two hundred and sixty-seven heresies 'worthy of the fire' which he claimed to have culled from the pages of Wycliffe's Bible. He is quoted as having said, 'That wretched and pestilent fellow, son of the Serpent, herald and child of Antichrist, John Wycliffe, filled up the measure of his malice by divining the expedient of a new translation of Scripture in the mother tongue.'

Today, in a much more secular age, the question arises – why all this fury? What had he done? Perhaps he would have been pardoned if he had been the Oxford classical scholar content to concentrate solely on translating the Bible? Perhaps if he had not gone for the Church's throat, challenged its worldly existence, stirred his theological criticisms into the social upheaval which followed the Black Death? Then would he have managed to slip English through the west door, down the nave and on to the imperial lectern holding the Bible? It is doubtful. For reasons sincere and cynical, Latin was held to be the language of the Holy Book and ever more must be kept inviolate. Wycliffe had threatened the very voice of the Universal Church of the One Invisible God. It is a terrible example of the power in language.

The Church was not finished with him yet. The Emperor Sigismund, King of Hungary, called together the Council of Constance in 1414. It was the most imposing council ever called by the Catholic Church. In 1415 Wycliffe was condemned as a heretic and in the spring of 1428 it was commanded that his bones be exhumed and removed from consecrated ground.

With the Primate of England looking on, Wycliffe's remains were disinterred and burned, thus, presumably, it was thought, depriving him of any possibility of eternal life. For when the Last Judgement came and the bodies of the dead rose up to meet those souls chosen to live with God, Wycliffe would be unable to reunite body and soul and so, if he had not already perished in hell, as they prayed for and hoped, he would certainly perish at the last.

The Bible remained in Latin and Wycliffe's failed attempt was an implacable and damning lesson to anyone foolish enough to attempt to mount another unholy attack on the side of English.

Wycliffe's remains were burned on a little bridge that spanned the River Swift which was a tributary of the Avon. His ashes were thrown into the stream. Soon afterwards a Lollard prophecy appeared:

> The Avon to the Severn runs,
> The Severn to the sea.
> And Wycliffe's dust shall spread abroad
> Wide as the waters be.

In English.

8

English and the Language of the State

Thwarted on one front, English turned its energy on another. It had lost the battle for the soul, now it would take on the body politic. It was a struggle catalysed by one of the greatest of all technological inventions, printing. Its English master, Caxton, would do more to regularise a Standard English than his bestselling author, Chaucer. It was a struggle in which anonymous clerks in the civil service of the day would exercise more power than kings. This was England coming through the Middle Ages, battle-weary and battle-hungry in a seemingly endless war against France, an England in which kings led from the front and it was one of the greatest of these warrior-kings, Henry V, who, like Alfred the Great, used English to unite the English.

A key moment was in his letters home from Agincourt – here in Modern English. 'Right trusty and well beloved brother,' he wrote, after that famous victory, 'right worshipful fathers in God and trusty and well beloved, for as much as we know well that your desire were to hear joyful tidings of our good speed touching the conclusion of peace between the two realms, . . . we signify unto you that . . . our labour has sent us a good conclusion.' In Henry's own English, it reads: 'Right trusty and welbeloved broþer Right worschipfull and worschipfull faders in god and truest and welbeloved ffor as muche

as we wote wele þat youre desire were to here Ioyfull tidings of oure
goode spede touching þe conclusion of pees betwixt þe two Rewmes
. . . we signiffie vnto yow þat . . . of oure labour haþ sent vs a goode
conclusion.'

A letter may seem a small thing but the cliché of little acorns and
oaks is appropriate, especially as it was the English bowmen with
their hearts of oak who turned the battle. In writing his despatches
home in English, Henry V broke with three hundred and fifty years of
royal tradition. This proved an astute move. Under his father, Henry
IV, English kings had begun to speak English but all court documents had hitherto been written in French as they had been since
1066. Henry's letters can be seen either as the final acceptance of the
tongue of the land by those who ruled it or as deliberate propaganda,
written in the vernacular the easier to be spread throughout the land.

Here he writes about the peace treaty in 1420:

upon moneday þe 20th day of þis present moneþ of May we arrived in
þis town of Troyes . . . and þaccorde of þe said pees perpetuelle was þere
sworne by boþe þe saide Commissaires . . . And semblably by us in oure
owne name. And þe letters (þerupon) forwiþ enseled under þe grete seel
of oure saide fader to us warde and under oures to hyum warde þe copie
of whiche lettres we sende you closed yn þees to þat ende: þat ye doo þe
saide accorde to be proclamed yn oure Citee of london and þorowe al oure
Rewme þat al oure pueple may have verray knowledge þereof for þare
consolacion . . . henry by þe grace of god kyng of England heire and
Regent of þe Rewme of ffrance and lorde of Irelande

Upon Monday the 20th day of May we arrived at this town Troyes . . .
and the accord of the peace perpetual was here sworn by the Duke of
Burgundy and semblably by us in our own name, the letters forthwith
sealed under the Great Seal, copies of which we send to be proclaimed
in our City of London and through all our realm that our people may
have knowledge thereof for their consolation . . . Signed. Henry, by the
grace of God, King of England.

He was on the side of public opinion as anti-French fervour was once again at a high pitch. Victories over those who had conquered 'us' and then become part of 'us' carried a complicated sweetness. But when he returned from his campaigns, Henry Plantagenet continued to write in English. He even used it in his will. In doing so he made the first major step towards the creation of an official standardised English that everyone could read. For where the king led, his people followed, in peace as in war.

The principal residence of the monarchy was the Palace of Westminster – today better known as the Houses of Parliament. The enormous hammer-beamed Hall survived the great fire of 1834, and in that Great Hall would have been the first circle of government which would have included the Signet Office.

This office wrote personal letters on behalf of the monarch, which carried the royal seal. Henry decreed that the Signet Office should use English. This provided at last a breach in the walls guarding the citadel of French; English poured through it. French was dispossessed of the language of office. It must have felt itself to be as invulnerable as one of its deep-walled Norman castles or its high unscalable keeps. Now the French language was routed as significantly as the French cavalry had been slain at Agincourt. English became the language of rule and English clerks got control.

But which English was it to be? Across the country a great number of dialects were spoken and people would still have had trouble understanding each other. The obstinacy of the English dialects is as impressive as the capacity of English to standardise, to absorb and to spread around the world. Almost one thousand years after the Anglo-Saxons had arrived with what was the fundament of the language, a man from Northumberland could still have the greatest difficulty in understanding a man from Kent. This local tenacity and loyalty continued for centuries and in certain areas it perseveres. It is like an ineradicable counterpoint. We have a world language but a Geordie can still baffle a resident of Tunbridge Wells a mere three hundred miles away, as he did in Caxton's day.

The word 'stone' in the south was 'ston', not 'stane' as in the north. 'Running' was spoken in the north as 'runnand'. It appears as 'runnende' in the East Midlands and as 'runninde' in the West Midlands. Runnand, runnende and runninde: add the singular twang of a local accent and it is possible to imagine even words as close as this coming out confusingly different.

But the pronunciation was nothing compared with the variety of spelling in use. If you look at a spelling map of the day it reads – spell as you speak. Because England had used Latin traditionally and French for over three hundred years as the written languages, there had never been any need to agree on a common linguistic standard for its native tongue or even how to spell particular words. Now there was.

The variety was profligate. Take the word 'church' for instance, one of the most common in the language. In the north of England at that time it was commonly called a 'kirk' while the south used 'church'. However, according to the *Linguistic Atlas of Late Mediaeval English*, 'kirk' could be spelled 'kyrk', 'kyrke', 'kirke', 'kerk', 'kirc', 'kric', 'kyrck', 'kirche' and 'kerke'; 'church' was variously 'churche', 'cherche', 'chirche', 'cherch', 'chyrch', 'cherge', 'chyrche', 'chorche', 'chrch', 'churiche', 'cirche'. And then there were 'schyrche', 'scherch', 'scherche', 'schirche', 'schorche', 'schurch', 'schurche', 'sscherch'.

This magnificent fertility of English spelling was everywhere. There were over five hundred ways of spelling the word 'through' and over sixty of the pronoun 'she', which is quite hard to imagine.

The word 'people' could be spelled 'peple', 'pepule', 'pepul', 'pepull', 'pepulle', 'pepille', 'pepil', 'pepylle', 'pepyll', 'peeple', 'peopel', 'poepull', 'poeple', 'poepul', 'puple', 'pupile', 'pupill', 'pupyll', 'pupul', 'peuple', or 'pople'. The word 'receive' appears as 'rasawe', 'rassaif', 'rassave', 'recave', 'receave', 'receawe', 'receiuf', 'receve', 'receyf', 'receive', 'reciffe', 'recive', 'recyve', 'resaf', 'resaif', 'resaiff', 'resaive', 'resave', 'resawe', 'resayfe', 'resayff', 'resayve', 'resywe', 'rescaive', 'rescayve', 'resceive', 'resceve', 'rescewe', 'resceyve', 'reschave', 'reschayfe', 'rescheyve', 'rescyve', 'reseve', 'reseyve', 'ressaif', 'ressaive', 'ressave', 'ressawe', 'ressayf', 'ressayve', 'resseve', 'resseyve', and 'reycive'. For local pride it was a glorious proof of individuality. For central authority it was a nightmare and worse, beyond control.

The scribes of Westminster took it on in the Chancellery, the big engine of state, shortened to 'Chancery'. This was a huge office responsible for the paperwork involved in running the kingdom. It was a cross between today's Law Courts, the Tax Office and Whitehall, and the scribes knew that it was crucial that a document produced in London could be read three hundred miles north in Carlisle as Latin and French had been.

A common written language was needed and Chancery was well equipped to provide one. It was strictly hierarchical. There were twelve senior clerks, the 'first form', known as the Masters of Chancery. The 'second form' had another twelve clerks. Below them were twenty-four cursitors, and below them an army of sub-clerks who copied documents but had no power to initiate, draft or sign them. It was the birth or, if we reach back to Alfred's not dissimilar set-up, the rebirth of English governmental bureaucracy.

If you visit the Public Record Office today you can see thousands of official documents kept from the fifteenth century. In these dry scrolls written English was fashioned. Hundreds of decisions had to be made about which form of word and which spelling to adopt. The final decisions were most likely in the hands of the Masters. The fact that many of these documents had legal status reinforced the necessity for consistency. Evidence had to have sound words widely understood. Even the most commonplace words – 'any', 'but', 'many', 'cannot', and 'ought' – had to be given a consistent form which in all these cases and thousands more is the modern form. 'I' became 'I'; previously 'ich' (and many other variants) had also been allowed. 'Suche' was preferred to 'sich', 'sych', 'seche', 'swiche' and, again, many other variants. 'Lond' became 'land', although this took a long time to be settled. During the decade 1469–79 alone, for instance, the modern word 'shall' appears in the peculiarly East Anglian form of 'xal', then 'schal' before settling into the word we all use now.

'Righte' became 'right'. 'Hath' and 'doth' were retained until the nineteenth century, but their eventual replacements appear as 'has' and 'does'. The Masters of Chancery had no qualms about taking on literary genius either: they preferred 'not' to Chaucer's 'nat', 'but' for his 'bot', 'these' for 'thise', 'thorough' for 'thurgh'. The men from Westminster knew best. This standard still admits of a lot of variation and we are not going to see a spoken standard until much later, but English was being square-bashed into its first drilled lines.

Chancery English, partly, it appears, because of the flow of people into London from the Midlands and the employment of a number of them as scribes, shows the influence of the Central and East Midlands dialects as well as that associated with London. So it could claim, when it emerges as the material of a literary language after about 1500, that it drew on a bigger reservoir than that of the metropolitan poets, even the author of *The Canterbury Tales*. London, with forty thousand people, was by far the biggest city in the country. But forty thousand people could be seriously affected by a determined group of immigrants. 'Chancery Standard' became the English word standard and once again we see the continuous democratic element in the growth of the English language. This first great disciplining into standard was achieved by scores of anonymous men, attempting to clarify and refine the way we used the words we spoke when we transferred them to writing.

Nor was it only in official documents that English was welling over the land. In the fifteenth-century letters of a Norfolk family, the Paston Letters, of which there are over a thousand, we see how the native language has become second nature to educated persons. It is difficult to decide whether such widespread usage came because of the example set at the top or the top took its cue from widespread usage. English was not only the language of state but the written and preferred language of the class of people most expected to be the state's closest supporters.

Yet just because the spelling was being regularised did not always mean that it was being simplified or made to follow rules of common sense. There is a scroll of doggerel in many school classrooms today which reads:

> We'll begin with a box and the plural is boxes.
> But the plural of ox should be oxen not oxes.
> Then one fowl is goose, but two are called geese.
> Yet the plural of mouse should never be meese.
> You may find a lone mouse or a whole lot of mice.
> But the plural of house is houses not hice.
> If the plural of man is always called men,
> Why shouldn't the plural of pan be called pen?
> The cow in a plural may be cows or kine,
> But the plural of vow is vows and not vine.
> And I speak of foot and you show me your feet,
> But I give you a boot . . . would a pair be called beet? . . .

This reflects the survival of old plural forms (ox, oxen), historical sound changes in Old English words (foot, feet), and loan words adopting 's' as a plural (vows). Broadly, there were reformers who wanted to spell words according to the way they were pronounced and traditionalists who wanted to spell them in one of the ways they always had been.

There was another party, however. We could call them the Tamperers. In a desire to make the roots of the language more evident and perhaps give it more style, more class, some words that had entered English from French were later given a Latin look. The letter 'b' was inserted into 'debt', and 'doubt', the letter 'c' equally unnecessarily into 'victuals'. Words thought to be of Greek origin sometimes had their spelling adjusted so that 'throne' or 'theatre' acquired their 'h'; 'rhyme' on the other hand was awarded its 'h' just because 'rhythm' had one. On a similar principle or whim, an 'l' was inserted into 'could' because it was still present – as a silent 'l' – in 'should' and 'would'. In the sixteenth century this became a fad designed to winnow out the under-educated, stump children and fox foreigners.

Yet some of the English have come to an exasperated love and pride for these illogical irregularities as the doggerel concludes:

> The masculine pronouns are he, his and him
> But imagine the feminine she, shis and shim!
> So our English, I think you'll all agree
> Is the trickiest language you ever did see.

The Tamperers were attempting in their way to bring reason to bear on the development of the language. English has never been very partial to reason and as if to prove it, at the same time as the 'b's and the silent 'l's and 'h's were being smuggled into perfectly sound words, the Great Vowel Shift occurred which resulted in many of the English pronouncing most things differently anyway.

The Great Vowel Shift can take a lifetime to investigate and another to explain. As I understand it, new and important studies are under way into its true causes and effects – one of several areas of mystery in medieval linguistics now in hot debate. But the main point, I trust, is this. Printing had largely fixed spelling before the Great Vowel Shift got under way. So to a large extent our modern spelling represents a pre-GVS system, whereas the language as a result of the GVS had changed enormously. Spelling fixed: spoken in turbulence: result – out of sync.

It is thought to have happened between the end of the fourteenth and the end of the sixteenth centuries. Before the Great Vowel Shift, English was pronounced in a way that sounds foreign to us. 'I name my boat Pete' would have sounded 'Ee nahm mee bought Peht'.

Writing eventually brings uniformity to language and the invention and spread of printing brought great power to writing. The first modern press was invented by Gutenberg in Mainz around 1453. England was slow into print – Caxton's press only went into service in 1476. Printing marked the beginning of the information age. Because it became so easy to manufacture books in large numbers it became more difficult to control the spread of ideas. The flatbed press was a liberator.

William Caxton was born in Kent somewhere around 1420. He was apprenticed to a textile dealer and went to Bruges in the 1440s where he did well. In 1462 he was appointed governor of the English Trading Company there, the Merchant Adventurers. Caxton was a man of learning as well as being a merchant and in 1469 he began work on a translation of a French account of the Trojan War. It was while working in Cologne that he learned about printing and once back in Bruges he set up a press to print his seven-hundred-page translation: *The Recuyell* [French – 'compilation'] *of the Historyes of Troye*, the first book printed in English. In 1476 he set up his press near Westminster Palace and before his death he had published ninety-six items, some in several editions.

The first dated book printed in England in English was *Dictes or Sayengis of the Philosophres* in 1477. Caxton printed romances, books of conduct and philosophy, history and morality and the first illustrated book in English, called *The Myrrour of the Worlde*, in 1481. He printed *The Canterbury Tales*, two editions, as well as other works by Chaucer, Malory's *Morte d'Arthur* and work by Gower and Lydgate and his own translations.

Caxton worried about how to achieve a common standard that would be understood and read by all. The prologues and epilogues to some of his translations reveal an anxiety similar to that expressed by Chaucer in the verse beginning 'Go, litel bok'. 'Certaynly,' he writes, 'it is harde to playse every man by cause of dyuersite & chaunge of langage. For in these dayes euery man that is in ony reputacyon in his countre [country], wyll vtter his commynycacyon and maters in suche maners and termes that fewe men shall vnderstonde theym.'

In the same passage he then gives what became a famous example of people from one part of the country, as Caxton said, 'failing to make themselves understood in another'. Caxton tells us that he is translating the Latin poet Virgil from a French version but he does not know which English word to use for 'eggs'. He tells a story of some merchants who are away from home and who visit a house to buy food. One asks the woman for 'eggys' – the Old Norse form, common in the north and east. She tells him that she doesn't speak French, at which he takes offence. Another asks for the same thing with a different form, 'eyren', which is Old English, still probably current in much of the south of England, and she understands. Caxton chooses 'eggs'. It must have been the case many, many times that like the Masters in Chancery, the masters of the printing press became the arbiters of what would become standard and correct English spelling. Caxton gave himself what I regard as an encouraging rule of thumb: 'In my Iudgemente,' he wrote, 'the comyn termes that be dayli vsed ben lyghter to be vnderstonde than the olde and auncyent englysshe.'

And the common daily terms he uses and chooses are generally those he hears around him, the speech of London and the south-east, though more heavily influenced by the Central and East Midlands than was once thought. That mongrel dialect through the printed book and the diktats from Chancery slowly takes precedence over the dialects of other regions, gradually becomes the common written language, anomalous spellings and all.

The King had set an example; Chancery followed; the printing press reinforced the importance of a common written language. By the end of the fifteenth century, English was the language of the state and equipped to carry messages of state in an increasingly uniform spelling north, south, east and west, its manuscripts and later its books rolling over the old dialects which nevertheless stayed stoutly on the tongue.

There was only one more kingdom for English to conquer. The keepers of this eternal kingdom, the Roman Catholic hierarchy, were being threatened by popular movements, like that of Wycliffe, all over Europe and their reaction was to dig in deeper and fight with all the natural and supernatural means they thought and were thought to have at their command. Latin was their armour believed to be blessed and made invulnerable by God Himself. Any assault on the Latin Bible was an assault on the spirit, meaning and purpose of the Church.

In Little Sudbury, in Gloucestershire, in 1521, a young Oxford-educated tutor came out of the large household in which he was employed and began to preach 'in the common place called Saint Austen's Green' in front of the church. He was to write a book which became the most influential book there has ever been in the history of language, English or any other.

9

William Tyndale's Bible

The prediction of the Lollards, that Wycliffe's Bible would live on, was not a vain prophecy. Early in the reign of Henry VIII, the new king was still promising the Pope that he would burn any 'untrue translations'. By these he meant Wycliffe's Bible which, despite all the efforts of the court and the Church, was still relentlessly circulating in the land in hand-copied editions.

Henry VIII set his powerful and efficient Lord Chancellor, Cardinal Wolsey, to hunt down heretical books. Wolsey, aware that Martin Luther had shaken the Roman Catholic Church in 1517 with the demands he had nailed on the church door at Wittenberg, and as anxious as his master to please the Pope, instituted a nationwide search. On 12 May 1521, a bonfire of confiscated heretical works was made outside the original St Paul's Cathedral. The flames, it was said, burned for two days. The great book-burning was clearly a foretaste of what could and would happen to those who insisted on challenging the Pope's authority.

This was the year in which William Tyndale began his public preaching on St Austen's Green and set out on the path which was to bring about a radical change both in the English language and in English society.

It is not always easy fully to comprehend or even imagine what was at stake. It was a great power battle. The reach of the Roman Catholic Church across many countries, states, principalities and peoples was unique. It was wealthy and a sought-after ally in war. It demanded obedience through its monopoly of the one true faith. Its parish priests covered almost every acre of ground, heard confessions, had the power to absolve sins, enforced attendance at church, the paying of Church taxes and conformity with the Church's rulings on all matters of public and of private morality; even sex was a Church matter. Its great cathedrals, splendid artefacts, dazzling robes, processions and festivals provided a backdrop of glamour and excitement to what was very often a bleak and meagre existence. Above all, and key, the Church had unique access to God and so to eternal life. Only through the Roman Catholic Church could anyone contact God and have any chance of resurrection.

Wycliffe, Luther and Tyndale challenged that. They wanted ordinary people to have direct access to God, and a Bible in the language of the people was the way to make that happen. The battle over language became outright rebellion against the Roman Catholic Church as the gatekeeper to God, the claim to be His sole representative on earth, whose earthly laws all Christians must obey every bit as much as they obeyed the laws of heaven. This had proved intolerable to different groups over the centuries and now the river of protest was swelling. The rebellion was led by deeply religious men and women. They too believed in the virgin birth, in the divinity of Christ, above all in the Resurrection. They were light years away from atheism or even agnosticism. They wanted the souls of the people to be saved but not through orders and sermons handed down from a central Latinate control in Rome for whose authority they found no evidence in the Bible. And to the rebels, the fate of the soul was the most vital matter in life: it was worth dying for.

Centuries later there would be those who would feel much the same about liberty, but even they could not have been more zealous, even fanatical, more totally convinced of the rightness of their cause as men such as William Tyndale were of theirs. After all, Tyndale was doing no less than serve the one true God, the maker of all things, the Creator, the Almighty, the giver and taker of life, the judge of all men and women, the harvester of the good, the slayer of evil. There could be no greater service in life than to do His work.

To Tyndale, English was, in effect, the way in which God could best reach the people of that language and the way in which they could best reach Him. The fight for the English Bible was a battle for salvation through the scriptures. To a priest who challenged him, Tyndale replied, 'Ere many years, I will cause a boy that driveth a plough to know more of the scriptures than thou dost.'

Like Wycliffe, Tyndale was an Oxford classical scholar and like Wycliffe he wholly contradicts the idea that such a scholar who was also, as Tyndale was, an ordained priest, was fated to be a mild, place-seeking conformist. Tyndale took risks and lived a life comparable to that of any twentieth-century revolutionary 'hero', and met an end worse than most of them.

It is interesting that the large household in Gloucestershire in which he was tutor was owned by a wealthy family, a new breed of successful wool merchants who called themselves 'Christian Brethren', the polite and politically safer name for Lollards. They built a private chapel in their garden dedicated to St Adeline, the patron saint of weavers, and they appear to have been happy secretly to fund Tyndale's plans. This quality of support so early in his life must have given Tyndale any extra encouragement he might have needed.

But like Wycliffe, he appears to have been a man totally driven by an idea. In 1524, at the age of thirty, William Tyndale left England to pursue his work outside the repressive spy-state set up by Henry VIII and Cardinal Wolsey. He would never return.

He met Erasmus and later Luther, the two key men in the movement towards what became Protestantism. He settled in Cologne and began single-handedly to translate the New Testament not from Latin but from the original Greek and Hebrew. It was this, no doubt, coupled with Tyndale's genius for language, which made his translations so telling and memorable.

Two years later, six thousand copies had been printed abroad – evidence of the substantial nature of the patronage Tyndale must have received from the wool merchants of Gloucestershire, and of the speed and efficiency of print. The new Bibles were packed and sent to the coast ready to be smuggled into England. Yet again English comes to England from across the sea, this time written English, some of the most sublime ever put on paper.

But Henry VIII and Wolsey's spies informed them of this invasion. It now seems quite extraordinary, but the whole country was put on alert. In order to prevent the word of God in English landing in the land of the English, naval ships patrolled the coastal waters, boats were stopped and searched, men were arrested and a great many Bibles were intercepted. The action taken was indistinguishable from being on a war footing and to Henry VIII and Wolsey it was just that. Latin was the only word of God allowed by the state and now the state came out in full armed force to defend its most loyal ally, the Church.

At first tens and then hundreds got through the lines. The Bishop of London then tried another tack: he sought to buy the entire print run through an intermediary.

'O he will burn them,' Tyndale is supposed to have said when he heard of this. 'I am the gladder,' he went on, 'for these two benefits will come thereof. I shall get money of him for these books to bring myself out of debt and the whole world shall cry out upon the burning of God's word.' And that is what happened. The bishop bought and burned the books and Tyndale used the money to rework, prepare and print a better version, as it were at the Church's expense.

Tyndale's aim was simple: 'I had perceived by experience,' he wrote, 'that it was impossible to stabilise lay people in any truth unless the scripture were to be plainly set before their eyes in their mother tongue so that they might see the process, order and meaning of the text.' He did this in a plain, conversational style as in this passage from Genesis:

But the serpent was sotyller [subtler] than all the beastes of the felde which ye Lorde God had made and sayd vnto the woman, Ay syr [sure]

God hath sayd ye shall not eate of all maner trees in the garden. And the woman sayd vnto the serpent, of the frute of the trees in the garden we may eate, but of the frute of the tree that is in the myddes of the garden (sayd God) se that we eate not, and se that ye touch it not; lest ye dye. Then sayd the serpent vnto the woman: tush ye shall not dye.

But the glory of Tyndale is in his soaring poetic which is yet always earthed, you feel, in the truth as in the Beatitudes from the Gospel According to St Matthew:

Blessed are the povre in sprete: for theirs is the kyngdome off heven.
Blessed are they that morne: for they shalbe comforted.
Blessed are the meke: for they shall inherit the erth.
Blessed are they which honger and thurst for rightewesnes: for they
    shalbe filled.
Blessed are the mercifull: for they shall obteyne mercy.
Blessed are the pure in herte: for they shall se God.
Blessed are the peacemakers: for they shalbe called the chyldren of
    God.
Blessed are they which suffre persecucion for rightwenes sake: for
    theirs ys the kyngdome off heven.
Blessed are ye when men shall reuyle you and persecute you and shall
    falsly say all manner of yvell saynges against you ffor my sake.
Reioyce and be glad for greate is youre rewarde in heven. For so
    persecuted they the prophets which were before youre dayes.
Ye are the salt of the erthe.

It is impossible to over-praise the quality of Tyndale's writing. Its rhythmical beauty, its simplicity of phrase, its crystal clarity have penetrated deep into the bedrock of English today wherever it is spoken. Tyndale's words and phrases influenced between sixty and eighty per cent of the King James Bible of 1611 and in that second life his words and phrases circled the globe.

We use them still: 'scapegoat', 'let there be light', 'the powers that be', 'my brother's keeper', 'filthy lucre', 'fight the good fight', 'sick unto death', 'flowing with milk and honey', 'the apple of his eye', 'a man after his own heart', 'the spirit is willing but the flesh is weak', 'signs of the times', 'ye of little faith', 'eat, drink and be merry', 'broken-hearted', 'clear-eyed'. And hundreds more: 'fisherman', 'landlady', 'sea-shore', 'stumbling-block', 'taskmaster', 'two-edged', 'viper', 'zealous' and even 'Jehovah' and 'Passover' come into English through Tyndale. 'Beautiful', a word which had meant only human beauty, was greatly widened by Tyndale, as were many others.

It is too fanciful to believe that the words themselves were so powerful and illuminating that Henry VIII and Wolsey redoubled their efforts to kill off the man and all his works, but these English words do have an instant memorability and authority that must have shaken the Latinate establishment. Tyndale was not only bringing the word of God to the people, he was also, within that process, bringing in words which carried ideas, described feelings, gave voice to emotions, expanded the way in which we could describe how we lived. Words which tell us about the inner nature of our condition; words which, as in the Beatitudes, express as never before or since, the great loving dream of a moral life which applies to everyone and challenges every ruling description of society from the beginning until today. Writer after writer, in the UK, in the USA, in Australia, on the Indian subcontinent, in Canada, in Africa and the Caribbean, has absorbed Tyndale's rhythms, appropriated and played with his words and been enriched by the opportunities his language provided, the vocabulary for thought.

Before long England was ablaze for Tyndale's Bible, this time on fire to read it. Thousands of copies were smuggled in. In Tyndale's own happy phrase, 'the noise of the new Bible echoed throughout the country.' Produced in a small pocket-sized edition that was easily concealed, it passed through cities and universities into the hands of even the humblest men and women. The authorities, especially Sir Thomas More, still railed at him for 'putting the fire of scripture into the language of ploughboys' but the damage was done. The

English now had their Bible, legal or not. Eighteen thousand were printed: six thousand got through.

Tyndale spent his life on the run. Constantly hounded by Catholic spies he moved secretly around the Protestant-sympathising lands of northern Europe. In 1529, off the coast of Holland, his ship was driven on to the rocks and the entire manuscript of his new translation of the Old Testament was lost. Yet in the following year he is printing it in Antwerp.

> In the begynnynge God created heven and erth.
> The erth was voyde and emptie and darcknesse was vpon the depe
>   and the spirite of God moved vpon the water.
> Than God sayd: let there be lyghte and there was lyghte.

It was in Antwerp that Tyndale became friendly with two English-men. They were hired assassins. They trapped him and took him to Vilvorde Castle where he was imprisoned in the dungeon. They had got their man and though the Bible was out and circumstances in the politics of the Church were changing dramatically, the vengeance of Henry VIII would not be denied.

In his last letter, Tyndale asked that he might have 'a warmer cap, for I suffer greatly from the cold . . . a warmer coat also for what I have is very thin; a piece of cloth with which to patch my leggings. And I ask to have a lamp in the evening, for it is wearisome to sit alone in the dark. But most of all I beg and beseech your clemency that the commissary will kindly permit me to have my Hebrew Bible, grammar and dictionary, that I may continue with my work.'

And continue, for a short while, he did, bringing us phrases, poignantly, heart-breakingly, like 'a prophet has no honour in his own country', 'a stranger in a strange land', 'a law unto themselves', 'we live and move and have our being' and 'let my people go', and there would have been yet more, but in April 1536 Tyndale was found guilty of heresy by a court in the Netherlands. The way they chose to kill him was to strangle him, to cut him off at the voice which they did on 6 October 1536.

Finally this sublime master of language, this heroic Christian scholar and the begetter of so much of our English language, was burned at the stake. His last words were: 'Lord, open the King of England's eyes!'

Two years before Tyndale's execution, Henry VIII, who had earlier been given the title 'Defender of the Faith' by Pope Leo X for denouncing Luther's ideas, had left his wife Catherine and secretly married his pregnant mistress Anne Boleyn. A new Pope, Clement VII, threatened him with excommunication. In 1535, Miles Coverdale, using Tyndale's text wherever possible, published a complete Bible dedicated to the king, the first legal Bible in English. That was a year before Tyndale's execution. Needing allies, Henry entered negotiations with some Lutheran princes in Germany in 1536, the very year of Tyndale's execution, but there is no record of him giving a thought to the man whose words would now help him seal a hold on a new Protestant England. In 1537, the Matthew Bible – an amalgam of Coverdale's and Tyndale's – was allowed to be printed in England. In 1539 we have the Great Bible – the official version.

After centuries of suppression, the walls came tumbling down and three Bibles were approved and published inside six years. And it went on: the Geneva Bible in 1560, the first in Roman type; the Bishops' Bible in 1568, a revised version of the Great Bible; and the Douai-Rheims Bible of 1609–10.

The English language flowed into religion. It had already returned to the court and into the state and begun to be the language of a vivid and vigorous national literature. Now with the split from Rome, it conquered the last and highest bastion, the Church.

It was a principle of Protestantism that the Bible be available to everyone. In 1530 Sir Thomas More had complained bitterly about the shame of the Bible in English in the language of ploughboys. But the Great Bible of 1539 came with an introduction by More's successor, Cranmer, which commended it to all: it was to be placed in every church in the land. A translation reads:

Here may men, women; young, old; learned, unlearned; rich, poor; priests, laymen; lords, ladies; officers, tenants and mean men; virgins, wives; widows, lawyers, artificers, husbandmen, and all matter of persons of what estate or condition soever they be learn all things, what they ought to believe, what they ought to do, as well as concerning Almighty God as themselves and all other.

It was unconditional surrender. It was defecting en masse to the side of the enemy. It was purging the past out of memory. It was now the King's Bible's English.

Where the medieval Catholic Church and Henry VIII most violently up into the 1530s had kept the Bible from the people, Henry's new Church set out to get the Bible to as many as possible. It has had an incalculable influence on the spread of our language. For centuries it was heard week in week out, sometimes day in day out, by almost all English-speaking Christians wherever they were and its precepts, its images, its proverbs, its names, its parables, its heroes, its promises, its words and rhythms sank deep shafts into the minds of the men and women who heard it. It went to the heart of the way we spoke, the way we described the world and ourselves. Its English bound the English together.

By the beginning of the seventeenth century there were so many competing versions that seven hundred and fifty reformers from within the Church of England requested James VI of Scotland, who had become James I of England, to authorise a new translation. Fifty-four translators were chosen from the Church and the universities to produce an edition which would be submitted to the bishops. The work took about five years and it cannot go unremarked that this tremendous endeavour makes the achievement of Tyndale appear all but superhuman.

To go back to the Beatitudes, Tyndale writes:

When he sawe the people he went up into a mountayne and when he was set, his disciples came to hym and he opened hys mouthe, and taught them, sayinge, 'Blessed are the povre in sprite: for theirs is the Kyngdom of heven . . .'

In the Authorised, the King James Version, it reads:

And seeing the multitudes, he went vp into a mountaine: and when he was set, his disciples came vnto him. And he opened his mouth, and taught them, saying, Blessed are the poore in spirit: for theirs is the kingdome of heauen . . .

Tyndale had the final say.

The fifty-four translators made very little attempt to update his language which was now eighty years old. Even though by 1611, English had undergone further revolution, the King James translators would still use 'ye' sometimes for 'you' as in 'ye cannot serve God and Mammon', even though very few said 'ye' in common speech any more. They used 'thou' for 'you', 'gat' for 'got', 'spake' for 'spoke' and so on. Either they were too struck by the beauty and power of Tyndale's prose to want to interfere with it, or this was a deliberate act of policy. They may have chosen to keep archaic forms. They made the Bible feel ancient, mysteriously spiritual, out of the past, imbued with deeply rooted traditional authority.

We are told that the men who made the final drafts read them aloud over and over again to make sure that they had the right rhythm and balance, matters which Tyndale, a preacher as well as a scholar, knew about well. The English Bible has often been called a preacher's Bible. Written to be spoken, written to spread the word in the language of the land, a cause for which Wycliffe and Tyndale and hundreds of other English Christians had lived and died.

> In the beginning was the Word, & the Word was with God, and
> the Word was God.
> The same was in the beginning with God.
> All things were made by him;
> And without him was not anything made that was made.
> In him was life, and the life was the light of men.
> And the light shineth in darknesse,

And the darknesse comprehended it not.
And the Word was made flesh, and dwelt among vs.

English at last had God on its side. The language was authorised
by the Almighty Himself.

10

A Renaissance of Words

To write of the English Renaissance without putting Shakespeare at the centre of it is indeed *Hamlet* without the Prince, but Shakespeare must wait for a couple of chapters while we prepare the ground.

In the thirty or forty years that bridged 1600, the English language could lay fair claim to being reborn, yet again, but with a self-conscious luxuriance and a world reach quite new. It is as if its appetite, far from being sated by the feast of French which it had digested and turned into English, was whetted and enlarged by it and looked around greedily for more nourishment.

As so often in the history of English the new chapter came by water. It is worth remembering that Spanish could have settled here. Philip II's formidable Armada of 1588 should have brushed aside the English opposition on the seas. His armies, the best trained and most successful in Europe, would almost certainly have found little to match them on a march to a largely undefended London. It seemed no contest. We know that God or bad weather, superior English seamanship or a combination of all three checked his attempt, but at the time the danger was acutely felt, so much so that Elizabeth I – a monarch by divine right – took to horse and went to the port of Tilbury near the mouth of the Thames.

There, before a great crowd and the ships and crews who would determine the future of her kingdom, she used English to raise their confidence, lift up their spirits, in superb rhetoric, the art of which she had been taught by her Cambridge tutor, Roger Ascham. Mounted on her horse, in the middle of the army, she spoke in inspirational English. This is the version as reported in 1654:

My loving people, we have been perswaded by some, that are careful of our safety, to take heed how we commit our self to armed multitudes for fear of treachery: but I assure you, I do not desire to live to distrust my faithful, and loving people. Let Tyrants fear, I have always so behaved my self, that under God I have placed my chiefest strength, and safeguard in the loyal hearts and good will of my subjects. And therefore I am come amongst you as you see, at this time, not for my recreation, and disport, but being resolved, in the midst, and heat of the battaile to live, or die amongst you all, to lay down for my God, and for my kingdom, and for my people, my Honour, and my blood even in the dust. I know I have the bodie, but of a weak and feeble woman, but I have the heart and Stomach of a King, and a King of England too . . . We shall shortly have a famous victorie over those enemies of my God, of my Kingdomes, and of my People.

England had indeed a famous victory, blessed by some luck, over a much superior enemy.

And English had a famous escape. For Spanish too was a marauding and conquering language.

After 1588, the naval effectiveness of the comparatively small island grew even stronger and opened up the world to trade. This brought a massive injection into the language. As England imported a huge cargo of goods, English imported a huge cargo of vocabulary. Another ten to twelve thousand new words entered English in this Elizabethan and Jacobean period and delivered a new map of the world and new ideas.

At the time of the Spanish Armada, England was well behind other European powers in the reach of its colonial conquests and English inevitably lagged badly in the influence it exerted abroad. Portuguese had already made its mark in Brazil and was biting deeply into southern America; Spanish had been spoken in Cuba and Mexico for more than half a century and Spain was taking its trade, its religion and its culture and its language all around the New World. Over eight hundred years earlier, Arabic had raced through the Middle East and North Africa and could still be called an imperial language, while Hindi was comfortably establishing itself as a vernacular if not a literary language throughout the populous Indian region.

On a very much smaller scale during the sixteenth century, English had begun to spread more widely to parts of Wales, Scotland and Ireland. Yet even in its more limited scope, English showed its voracity for new words and its power to enfold them almost instantly into the mother language.

France still provided rich pickings. In they came, the new loan words: 'crew' (creue); 'detail' (détail); 'passport' (passeport); 'progress' (progresse); 'moustache' (moustache); 'explore' (explorer). Other words from or via France include 'volunteer', 'comrade', 'equip', 'bayonet', 'duel' and 'ticket'. English sailors and traders could not get enough of them. It was a national appetite, a national sport, asset stripping foreign word banks. 'Embargo' (embargo), 'tornado' (from tronada, 'thunderstorm'), 'canoe' (canoe) from French and Spanish; 'port' (port) though, which seems to come from or via Spanish and Portuguese, is Old English. Spain and Portugal brought 'armada' and 'banana', 'desperado', 'guitar' and 'hammock', 'hurricane', 'mosquito' and 'tobacco'. Nor were the Dutch left out: 'keelhaul' (kiehalen), 'smuggle' (smokkelen), 'yacht' (jaghte), 'cruise' (kruisen), 'reef' (rif), 'knapsack' (knapzak) and 'landscape' (landschap) all come from the Dutch. So does the exoneration of Anglo-Saxon, for so long thought the source and origin of our favourite swear words. It has been suggested that it was English sixteenth-century sailors who brought in 'fokkinge', 'krappe' and 'buggere' (though that is ultimately 'Bulgarus', Latin for Bulgarians), which they had found irresistible in Low Dutch. Even when they are found in earlier English, these words are not swear words. 'C—t' is not taboo; 'bugger' does not mean sodomite until the period we are talking about.

Again and again even in those brief lists we can see how the words not only increased the vocabulary but set in train lines of thought which went way beyond the original descriptive function of the word and bred shoals of new English meanings and thought. 'Progress', for instance, from the French; 'embargo' from Spanish and Portuguese; 'smuggle' and 'landscape' from the Dutch – all of these have grown and multiplied inside English.

When English sailors encountered new foods and fruits and barrelled them up to try their luck in the riverside markets of England, they brought the names or an Anglicisation of the original names with them: 'apricots' and 'anchovies', again from or via Spain and Portugal. 'Chocolate' and 'tomato' from French: though, a good example of the melting pot of language, 'tomato' could also be from the Spanish.

About fifty other languages joined the cargo of new words brought back in this period and swiftly integrated into English. In some cases there was an intermediary language. The language of the Renaissance bristled with imported words. 'Bamboo' (Malay); 'bazaar' (via Italian) and 'caravan' (via French) both Persian; 'coffee' and 'kiosk' (Turkish via French); 'curry' (Tamil); 'flannel' (Welsh); 'guru' (Hindi); later there would be 'harem' and 'sheikh' and 'alcohol' (Arabic); 'shekel' (Hebrew); 'trousers' (Irish Gaelic). Off they went, English ships all over the world, trading in goods, looting language.

But this game or addiction was not confined to men on ships. It was a time when English artists, scholars and aristocrats began to explore Europe. Their preferred destination was Italy, the dominating culture of the time. There they were awestruck by the architecture, the art, the music, and brought back words which described what they saw and once again provided a platform for new ideas, in this case ideas about a cultural explosion, which England so far had heard mostly from an islanded distance. But back they came, flashing off their purchases from abroad: 'balcony', 'fresco', 'villa' (from Latin), 'cupola', 'portico', 'piazza', 'miniature' and 'design' – all from Italian – as are 'opera', 'violin', 'solo', 'sonata', 'trill', 'cameo', 'rocket' (which could also be French) and 'volcano': 'soprano' and 'concerto' came later.

Yet the biggest and most important seam of all at that time was mined in England itself, chiefly in Oxford and Cambridge.

It is another twist in the adventure of English that the heirs of those classical scholars whose learning and courage had pushed through the translation of the Bible from Latin into English and toppled Latin's supremacy for ever, now led the movement to revive the study of Latin. It was, I think, this growing addiction to uncover new words which was the driving force in this revival.

Renaissance scholars at the two universities founded schools teaching pure and literary Latin. Roger Ascham, Elizabeth I's tutor, was just one of those Renaissance scholars. Classical texts written by Seneca, Lucan and Ovid, for example, were sourced from the medieval manuscripts into which they had been copied and translated into English. The scholars, or humanists as they came to be known, saw Latin as the language of classical thought, science and philosophy, all of which were gathering interest as the Renaissance rolled through the minds of Europe. It was also the universal language, with which they could communicate with other European scholars. Thomas More wrote his *Utopia* in Latin in 1517 – it was only translated into English in 1551. Isaac Newton, in 1704, published his *Opticks* in English. It was translated into Latin in 1706, since Latin remained the language of international debate and controversy. Milton's usefulness to Oliver Cromwell in the 1650s was greatly to do with his skill in putting forward Cromwell's arguments in a Latin which would impress his enemies in Europe.

It is tempting to think that part of this impetus came from the victory of English in the Bible. Latin was no longer associated with suppression. It was no longer first and most emphatically thought of as the acknowledged word of God. All these scholars were religious; they had to be, to be allowed to study as scholars in the first place. There would have been differing degrees of belief but Christianity was the unchallengeable belief system. Yet Latin was no longer primarily the servant of the Church. It could come out of the west doors and play, be explored for other than religious purposes, be used to discover old ideas and name them new. Now that it had won through, English could afford to and wanted to plunder the old enemy.

Thousands of Latin words came into the English vocabulary of educated people. In the rush to co-opt them, the scholars made scarcely any effort to change them. They were gobbled up, raw and whole. 'Excavate' (excavare), 'horrid' (horridus), 'radius' (radius), 'cautionary' (cautionarius), 'pathetic' (patheticus), 'pungent' (pungentum), 'frugal' (frugalis), 'submerge' (submergere), 'specimen' (specimen), 'premium' (præmium). And the words 'manuscript', and (from the Greek) 'lexicon' and 'encyclopaedia' were absorbed into English.

The new English words soon found their place in pamphlets, plays, poems, slotting in as if they had always been there, bringing yet more distinction and fine distinctions into the home tongue, and again bringing a spring of ideas in a few syllables. 'Absurdity', for example, came in at this time and both then and since it has spiralled into innumerable uses and nuances, bringing in the description of absurd situations and absurd circumstances and absurd people all of whom had been just as absurd before the word came in but were now classified accurately as such although to use the word 'classify' of a characteristic in a human being is rather absurd in itself. And, from Latin and Greek, we have 'chaos' or 'crisis' or 'climax', words seized on by everyone who loved exaggeration as most of us do, who enjoyed the scary side of life, the darker, the melodramatic. Once again the words soon began to spin their own story, spread like an infection, increase their territories of meaning so that 'climax' becomes sexual as well as dramatic, a resolution as well as a final confrontation, or just a happy lazy way to pep up daily life by introducing a little excitement through a big word. And 'chaos' now has a range of applications from chaos theory to a rather disorganised day at the office.

The Renaissance was a time when scholarship, the arts and intellectual pursuits in many areas were re-energised basically by the rediscovery of the classical past, much of it transferred to western Europe by Arabic translations and scholars. Science was once more of legitimate concern and as new worlds were discovered on the planet so new worlds were discovered above, inside and around the planet. Medicine too awoke in Europe from the sleep of over a thousand years. It was to Latin and Greek that the scholars often went to initiate their studies and it was to these ancient languages they went to describe what they found. From Latin, or from Greek via Latin, we borrowed 'concept' and 'invention' and 'technique'.

A closer look at the words borrowed from Latin and Greek in the developing area of medicine gives us a snapshot of the time. So successful was the classical branding of medical terms during the Renaissance that it has gone on ever since. Among the hundreds of words that arrived from Greek via Latin were our 'skeleton', 'tendon', 'larynx', 'glottis' and 'pancreas'. From Latin we also inherit 'tibia', 'sinuses', 'temperature' and 'viruses' as well as 'delirium' and 'epilepsy'. Our 'parasites' and 'pneumonia', even our 'thermometers', 'tonics' and 'capsules' are all words of classical origin. We talk of our bodies in ancient tongues.

Even today we use Latin and Greek for our medicine and technology. The Greek-derived 'plutonium' came in the nineteenth century, but got its current meaning in the twentieth. The Latin 'insulin', 'id', 'internet', 'audio' and 'video' are all twentieth-century inventions. One of the most recent additions to the *Oxford English Dictionary* in 2002 was the phrase 'quantum computation' which is purely Latin in origin. Every day in the sixteenth century we spoke Latin, Greek, French – Norman, Francien and Parisian – Dutch, Anglo-Saxon and Norse and sprinklings of languages from Celtic to Hindi, all alchemised into English. And it has multiplied greatly since then.

The word-grab into Greek and Latin for the new science and medicine of the Renaissance might have had elements of apprehension and snobbery about it. Respectability is often craved by the new kid on the block and the classical languages certainly helped. Reassurance is often another necessity when coming in out of the blue and what could be more reassuring than languages with thousands of years of achievement. Great and lasting empires had been built, learning had flourished, laws been laid down in Greek and Latin. There was also, perhaps, a little snobbery, which grew as time went on. To give something a Greek or Latin name gave it an exclusivity, made it something of a cult, meant that you had to have at least the smatterings of a superior education to be on terms with it, took it away from the common tongue, as had happened in the Church. Some Latin scholars thought that English was simply not up to certain tasks. Francis Bacon, for instance, wrote in Latin on subjects in which he thought that English would 'play the bankrupt with books'.

The late Roy Porter, when Professor of the History of Medicine at the Wellcome Institute, was eloquent about this:

Suddenly you find that there are thousands of plants and elements and stars and things that nobody quite knew what to call. When, at the end of the eighteenth century, the astronomer William Herschel discovered a new planet, he had to find a name. But what do you call a new planet? He wanted to call it 'George's Planet' after King George. That however was considered rather too vulgar . . . they worried that the French wouldn't like it very much if a whole planet was called after England. So in the end they Latinised it and called it 'Uranus' instead . . . It was one of the great claims of so many nineteenth century scientists when they were naming the elements that they weren't just scientists in the lab, but they were scholars of Greek or Latin. And therefore they were very proud of themselves when they thought of words like 'paleolithic' instead of saying simply 'dawn of time'. Paleolithic gave everything a higher status . . . So when you found particular sorts of rocks in Mid-Wales, instead of calling them 'slaty rocks' or 'grey rocks' or 'hard rocks' or 'friable rocks', you called them 'Silurian'. Silurian was based on the Latin name of the tribes who'd lived there – a word taken from the writings of Caesar.

Yet there is something attractive and even poetically apposite about a Welsh tribe who had fought the great Julius Caesar living on as a name in those slaty, grey, hard, friable rocks. Most of these

Graeco-Roman names are memorable, sui generis, and often accurate.

Power play, snobbery and cherished distinctions in style, in class, in accent have played an entertaining role in the adventure of English. 'Speak as we speak or you will show that you are inferior' has been a refrain of the controlling elite throughout languages, I would guess, and there is a mountain of proof for this seemingly inevitable element – ownership – in the development of English.

Many of those factors were brought into play during the Inkhorn Controversy, named after the horn pot which held ink for quills. Inkhorn words were new, usually elaborate, classically based terms. This controversy was the first and probably the greatest formal dispute about the English language. In a sense it became a thing of its own, leaving behind snobbery and power play and ownership. It became an exuberance, a spouting, an intoxication with words which in Renaissance England grew into a fever. There was a rush to invest in bubbling and fashionable new stock on the word exchange.

The honeycombing of English with these Latin and Greek terms disturbed some scholars: there seemed no stopping it. Latin, they feared, had the potential to eliminate some Old English words. For not only were the Latinists mining the classics, Latinate words that had already been borrowed from the French under the Normans were borrowed again, in their original Latin form, adding duplicates and choice. So now 'benison' stood with 'benediction', 'blame' with 'blaspheme', 'chance' with 'cadence', 'frail' with 'fragile' and 'poor' with 'pauper'.

The Inkhorn Controversy was intense, public and serious and men felt that they were defending and defining the breath of life itself. Curious or even ridiculous as it might seem today, there arose guardians of what they claimed as the True, the Old English, who were every bit as determined to repel the invaders as Drake and his fellow captains to repel the Armada. These were serious scholars, men of stature, zealots, fearful that their language would be overwhelmed by immigrant words.

Like Francis Bacon, the scholars often used monetary terms to describe their feelings in what became a bitter debate. New words were currency. Supporters of the new terms used words like 'enrich' and 'credit'; opponents, supported by a strong Puritan strain, talked about 'bankruptcy' and 'counterfeiting'.

One of the key defenders of the influx was Sir Thomas Elyot (1490–1546) who published *The Boke Named The Governour*. He worried, he even apologised for new words like 'maturity' which he termed 'strange and darke' but which, he assured his readers, would soon slot in, soon be as 'facile to understande as other wordes late commen out of Italy and Fraunce'. He saw borrowings from Latin as part of 'the necessary augmentation of our langage'.

Another supporter of lexical expansion was George Pettie (1548–89), who was pithy: '. . . it is not unknowen to all men how many wordes we have fetcht from thence within these few yeeres, which if they should be all counted inkpot tearmes, I know not how we should speake anie thing without blacking our mouthes with inke: for what word can be more *plain* than this word *plain*, and yet what can come more neere to the Latine?' (my italics)

This potential knock-out punch was ridden quite easily by the defenders of true English. Thomas Wilson (1524–81) wrote: 'Among all other lessons, this should first be learned, that wee never affect any straunge ynkehorne termes, but to speake as is commonly received: neither seeking to be over fine, nor yet living over-carelesse, using our speeche as most men doe, and ordering our wittes as the fewest have done.'

The Inkhorn Controversy is interesting because it set up a discussion which still goes on as to the most effective, the most poetic, the most honest, even the 'truest' way of writing English.

The leading opponent of the increasing invasion of Latin and Greek words was Sir John Cheke (1514–57), Provost of King's College, Cambridge. He argued strongly that English should not be polluted by other tongues. Ironically, Cheke was a classicist and the first Regius Professor of Greek in Cambridge. Nevertheless, Cheke believed that English should be reappraised as a Germanic language.

It had to go back, uncover and build on its Anglo-Saxon roots. During his time the history of English became a fashionable subject and manuscripts copied from Anglo-Saxon texts were read aloud among the anti-Inkhorn tendency. To prove a point, Sir John even went so far as to translate the Gospel of St Matthew using English lexical resources for new words. He invented 'gainrising' for 'resurrection', 'ground-wrought' for 'founded' and 'hundreder' for 'centurion' and used 'crossed' for 'crucified'.

He wrote: 'I am of this opinion that our own tung shold be written cleane and pure, unmixt and unmangeled with borowing of other tunges, wherin if we take not heed by tiim [by time], ever borowing and never payeng, she shall be fain to keep her house as bankrupt.' It is significant that, as Francis Bacon was to do in the time of Shakespeare, Cheke should seek out the analogy with money, with the wealth of man, with the financial stability of the state. Words, like money, must be kept in credit, no National Debt, balanced books. Yet the words Cheke used – like 'bankrupt' and even 'pure' itself – are not of Anglo-Saxon or Germanic origin. They are from the Latin-based languages, Italian and French. He disliked what he called 'counterfeit' words – though 'counterfeit' itself was not of Anglo-Saxon origin.

Cheke found a formidable ally in the poet Edmund Spenser, whose work was thought at that time to soar above all others in the English tongue. Spenser too argued that we should attempt to revive obsolete English words – what were sometimes called 'Chaucerisms'! – and to make use of little-known words from English dialects: 'algate' for altogether, 'sicker' for certainly, 'yblent' for blinded.

A minor victory for Cheke was achieved in his own Cambridge college. In his time there were, and they still exist, the Protocollum books which contain the records of admission to King's College since its foundation. The name of the book is Latin and it is written in Latin. But written beneath Cheke's entry, for the very first time in this book, is a text in English. This short English note was the first chink in the classical shutter that had protected scholarship and isolated it from everyday people. The passage begins: 'First of all I do protest and declare that otherwise I do not swear or promise anything thereby that should bind me contrary to the true doctrine of the Church of England.' It was undoubtedly a step forward for English.

But however hard he tried to promote a pure English, however much Spenser's great authority weighed in the balance and Thomas Wilson brought cannons of sarcasm to bear against Latinisation in *The Arte of Rhetorique* (1553), Cheke had no chance. No one could control the appetites of the English language. By the end of the sixteenth century, after more than fifty years of influx and controversy, the building blocks had been laid to create a language that we can still understand today and that we call Modern English. It is shot through with Latinate words.

Some of those which seemed oddest at the time have survived — words like 'industrial', 'exaggerate', 'mundane', 'affability', 'ingenious', 'celebrate', 'dexterity', 'discretion', 'superiority', 'disabuse', 'necessitate', 'expect', 'external', 'exaggerate' and 'extol' — all thought most curious in the sixteenth and seventeenth centuries.

However, Cheke may have taken some comfort from the fact that some of the thousands of Latin and Greek words coined during the great Inkhorn Controversy did not survive. Natural selection had its way and 'obtestate' (to bear witness) and 'fatigate' (to make tired) have been lost, as have been 'illecebrous' (enticing) and 'deruncinate' (to cut off). 'Abstergify' (to cleanse), 'arreption' (a sudden removal) and 'subsecive' (spare) have all slipped out of use. 'Nidulate' (to build a nest), 'latrate' (to bark like a dog) and 'suppeditate' (to supply) have also disappeared. Whilst a word like 'impede' survived, its opposite, 'expede', did not. It is fun to mock these creations but they demonstrate the intense interest the English language inspired among the educated English. It is arguable that in that period they explored language with more enthusiasm and rigour than they explored the sciences or the globe itself.

New formations came in from prefixes: 'disabuse', 'disrobe', 'nonsense', 'uncivilised'; from suffixes: 'gloomy', 'immaturity', 'laughable'; from compounding: 'pincushion', 'pine-cone', 'rosewood'; and conversions from verb to noun as in 'invite' and 'scratch' and from noun to verb as in 'gossip' and 'season'. Confidence could be seen everywhere.

Richard Mulcaster (1530–1611), the headmaster of Merchant Taylors' School, promoted the idea of using Latin words in conjunction with English words and wrote: 'I do not think that anie language, be it whatsoever, is better able to utter all arguments, either with more pith, or greater planesse, then our English tung is . . . I honor the Latin, but I worship the English.' He spoke for an increasing, intelligent, often word-obsessed number of men and women to whom the language was not only a necessity but a delight, to be embellished, groomed, increased and multiplied.

English was now poised to grow into a richness, a subtlety and complexity which would enable it to become a world language.

II

Preparing the Ground

Yet, for all its gathering confidence, English in the sixteenth century still felt itself in the shadow of other European languages. One source of evidence for this is the number of glossaries that were compiled in the form of bilingual Italian to English, French to English and Spanish to English dictionaries.

England had to wait until the dawn of the seventeenth century, 1604, to get its own dictionary. This represents the first indication of a challenge to the rest of Europe as it was eight years ahead of the first Italian dictionary, and thirty-five years before the French. Although, to put it in a rather longer perspective, it was eight hundred years after the first Arabic dictionary and nearly a thousand years after the first Sanskrit dictionary in India.

The word 'dictionary' is first used in its Latin form, 'dictionarius', around 1225. In many ways a dictionary is particularly well suited to the English language, a language that has absorbed so many others.

The first English dictionary was put together in 1604 by Robert Cawdrey. He called it *The Table Alphabeticall*. The copy I examined – the only surviving copy – is in the Bodleian Library in Oxford. It is a small, slim volume, about the size of the palm of an average hand. It is a list of English words, mainly though by no means wholly, of Latinate origin, with a brief explanation of the meaning of each.

So the first word in this first dictionary is 'abandon' – 'cast away or yeelde up, to leave or forsake'. 'Maladie' we find is 'a disease', 'summarilie' is 'briefly' or 'in fewe words'. 'Argue' is 'to reason' and 'geometrie' is 'art of measuring the earth'. 'Elegancie' is 'finesse of speech' and 'empire' is 'governement or kingdome'. 'Quadrangle' is 'foure-cornered' and 'radiant' is 'shining or bright'.

There are only two thousand five hundred and forty-three words in this dictionary. It was a meagre word-hoard but a first attempt at a collection. You don't find everyday words here, like 'shoe', 'cold' 'food' or 'house', 'cow', 'wet', 'rain', 'dress', 'fish' or 'love'. More than anything, this little book was a recognition of the new status of the English language. As it declared on its first page, it was: 'full of Hard Usuall English Wordes borrowed from the Hebrew, Greeke, Latine or French &c.'

Cawdrey intended his dictionary to be used by those who might not understand words 'which they shall heare or read in Scriptures, Sermons or elsewhere'. This was not a book for scholars. It was a book for the gentlefolk and for intellectually ambitious people to catalogue new words and to explain the new ideas connected with those words. The English population was growing, and growing more educated. One estimate is that by 1600, half of the three and a half million population – at least in towns and cities – had some minimal education in reading and writing. Their minds were hungry, wanting to be fed.

It was the aristocracy and the gentry who were at this time self-consciously determined to cultivate and satisfy the appetite for the finer words of life.

By the middle of the sixteenth century, French had already had the poems and works of Villon, Du Bellay and Ronsard to rival or at least challenge those of Petrarch. Italian's earlier literary Renaissance had also produced Dante, Machiavelli and Ariosto, while Spanish could boast Juan del Encina and Fernando de Rojas. Although English could already claim Chaucer and his contemporaries, their works were written in an English which had become to a great extent defunct. Because of changes in pronunciation and in forms of speech

– like the loss of the final 'e' – the Tudors could not hear Chaucer's music in his lines. Compared with other countries, and despite Spenser, English did not have a national literature written in its new language. Gentlemen of England were eager to take on the task of inventing one.

The educated and upper classes were travelling in greater numbers to the Continent, especially to Italy, and they returned baggage laden with old artefacts, borrowed fashions, new words and wider ambitions. In Italy they admired the way language was being explored in poetry. Poetry refined and advanced the language in a way the English admired and were determined to emulate.

To write in your own language, to play with it and mould it – these all became aims to which the educated wished to aspire. English literature became the vogue. Roger Ascham, Elizabeth I's tutor, said that his colleagues would much rather read Malory's mid-fifteenth-century tale *Le Morte d'Arthur* (in English) than the Bible. They began to copy and experiment. Henry Howard, Earl of Surrey, beheaded by Henry VIII, had used blank verse when translating Virgil's *Aeneid*.

One of Surrey's fellow poets, the humanist and courtier Sir Thomas Wyatt, was acquitted of treason and escaped Henry VIII's execution machine, then travelled to Italy, France and Spain. In the French and Italian courts he found a form that would shape and fit English for its unparalleled poetic future: the sonnet. The sonnet was a fourteen-line poem written in iambic pentameters which had been in use since the thirteenth century. Wyatt – like so many others – looked towards the great Italian Petrarch's sonnets and noted also the love motifs which inhabited so many of them, for which indeed they seemed made. He took the sonnet into English.

It might seem hard to argue that the English sonnet that developed from Wyatt's raid on Europe was crucial to the development of the English language. But many do. The English language by now was a thickly plaited rope, a rope of many strands, still wrapped around the Old English centre, still embellished with Norse, lushly fattened and lustred with French, and it was now a language serving many demands. It was a language for religion, a language for law, a language for the court, a language for the fields, a language for war, for work, for celebration, for rage, for rudery and puritanical prudery, a language for all seasons but not yet confidently and fully a language exquisitely honed for the expression of the finest emotions and tuned to perfect pitch for feelings, strung to the heart. The sonnet took it along that way.

Although its rigid rules of order and arrangement might seem limiting, the sonnet became a proving ground for poets. It was the place where you could burnish the language, polish every word, dazzle your rivals. And in polishing their own work, these gentlemen poets also polished English.

Queen Elizabeth I has a fair claim to be the best educated monarch ever to sit on the throne of England. Apart from her mastery of rhetoric – demonstrated at Tilbury – she spoke six languages and translated French and Latin texts. Furthermore, she enjoyed writing poetry:

> I grieve and dare not show my Discontent;
> I love and yet am forc'd to seem to hate;
> I do, yet dare not say I ever meant;
> I seem stark mute but Inwardly do prate.

England was seeking a literature to reflect its newly enriched status and it was to the courtiers, the knights of Elizabeth's entourage, that the role fell to turn the English language into literature. The gentleman-poet was called up, he who could handle the pen with as much skill as the sword; it was his turn now to play his part in the adventure of English. The courtier wrote for pleasure, for show and for the love of writing; it was his plumage, playing with the language, seeking lines belonging only to him, looking for immortality in verse.

The perfect embodiment of the courtier-poet was a heroic nobleman born in one of the great houses of England, Penshurst Place, in 1554,

1. Bede, English monk and scholar, wrote the first ever history of the English-speaking people in Latin, completed in 731. He proposed that the English language should also be used in books.

2. The only surviving manuscript of *Beowulf*, dating from the tenth century, the first great poem in the English language, begins 'So: the Spear Danes in days gone by/ And the Kings who ruled their clan were a legend. . .

3. By the mid-ninth century the marauding Danes threatened to take over the English language.

4. The Alfred jewel bears the inscription – in English – 'Alfred had me made'. By defeating the Danes, Alfred had saved the English language.

5. After William's victory at Hastings in 1066, depicted in the Bayeux Tapestry, the French language of power and authority ruled the land.

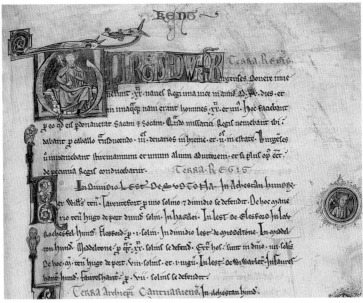

6. Twenty years later, William sent out his officers to take stock of his kingdom. The result, the Doomsday Book, was written in Latin. Detail from the shorter illustrated version.

7. The Peasants' Revolt, 1381: Richard II, the boy king, met Wat Tyler at Smithfield and addressed his subjects in English, the language of the people.

8. When Henry IV was crowned in 1399 he made his speech in what the official history calls 'His Mother Tongue' – English.

9 and 10. In 1415 Henry V broke with 350 years of royal tradition in writing his dispatches (*below*) from Agincourt in English instead of Latin or French.

Of eche of hem so as it semed me
And whyche they were and of what degre
And in what aray eke they were ynne
And at a knyght thenne I wyl begynne

A Knyght ther was a worthy man
That fro the tyme that he first began
To ryden out / he loued chyualrye
Trouthe & honour fredom and curtesye
Ful worthy he was in hys lordis werre
And therto hadde he ryden noman ferre
And as wel in crystendom as in hethenesse
And euer honoured for hys worthynesse
At alisaundre he was whan it was wonne
Ful ofte tyme he hadde the boord begonne
Abouen alle nacions in pruce
In lettowe hadde he reysed and in Ruse

11. Prologue to *The Canterbury Tales*, from the printed version by Caxton c. 1485. Before the end of the fifteenth century Caxton had printed two editions and *The Canterbury Tales* has never been out of print in English since.

CÆTERA FAMA E D

A
Table Alphabeticall, conteyning and teaching the true
vvriting, and vnderstanding of hard
vsuall English wordes, borrowed from
the Hebrew, Greeke, Latine,
or French. &c.

With the interpretation thereof by
plaine English words, gathered for the benefit &
helpe of Ladies, Gentlewomen, or any other
vnskilfull persons.

Whereby they may the more easilie
and better vnderstand many hard English
wordes, vvhich they shall heare or read in
Scriptures, Sermons, or elsvvhere, and also
be made able to vse the same aptly
themselues.

Legere, et non intelligere, neglegere est.
As good not read, as not to vnderstand.

AT LONDON,
Printed by I. R. for Edmund Weauer, & are to be sold at his shop at the great
North doore of Paules Church.
1 6 0 4.

12. Sir Philip Sidney painted in 1576, the perfect embodiment of the courtier poet.

13. Title page of Robert Cawdrey's *A Table Alphabeticall*, 1604, the first English dictionary.

and dead a mere thirty-one years later on a battlefield fighting the Spanish in the Netherlands: Sir Philip Sidney. He achieved lasting fame for giving his water bottle to another wounded soldier with the words 'Thy need is greater than mine.'

By his mid twenties, Sidney had already worked as Elizabeth's ambassador abroad and had written and published the finest collection of love poems of his age. He had the leisure, the wealth, the education, the wit and the will to make English itself the subject of some of his poetry and his treatise about language, *A Defence of Poesy*. He composed music and songs, he was the very perfect courtier-poet.

One of his sonnets made a conversation about the English language itself. It is a dialogue between the poet and his inner doubts, about whether writing poetry can ease the pain of love, and what other people will make of his words. In line eleven, he tells his wit (his inner voice) to be silent, because his thoughts (also wit) are spoiling his ability to write (wit again). But the poet still has doubts, and wonders whether his writing is just a waste of ink – though he hopes that some of his words may express the qualities of Stella, the woman he loves, and the cause of all this anguish.

> Come, let me write. And to what end? To ease
> A burthen'd heart. How can words ease, which are
> The glasses of thy dayly-vexing care?
> Oft cruel fights well pictur'd-forth do please.
> Art not asham'd to publish thy disease?
> Nay, that may breed my fame, it is so rare.
> But will not wise men thinke thy words fond ware?
> Then be they close, and so none shall displease.
> What idler thing then speake and be not hard?
> What harder thing then smart and not to speake?
> Peace, foolish wit! With wit my wit is mard.
> Thus write I, while I doubt to write, and wreake
> My harmes in inks poor losse. Perhaps some find
> Stella's great pow'rs, that so confuse my mind.

Poetry and the innovation it brought in became the benchmark for what might be called High English. In his *Defence of Poesy*, Sidney praises a 'sound stile' that cannot allow 'an old rustike language'. He argues that poetry should reach for the ideal as opposed to imitating the reality. The poet can make a world more beautiful than nature did: words can change the world. This was an intoxicating challenge to the educated young gallants and would-be gallants of England and they took it up. The testing ground for English was now in its poetry.

Sidney had set a daunting example in his life. The intensity and high-flying drama of the life seemed somehow a springboard for his writing. There are two thousand two hundred and twenty-five quotations from Sidney in the *Oxford English Dictionary*. Numerous first usages are attributed to Philip Sidney: 'bugbear', 'dumb-stricken', 'miniature' for a small picture. He was fond of adding words together to form evocative images ranging from 'far-fetched' to 'milk-white' horses, 'eypleasing' flowers, 'well-shading' trees, to more unusual ones like 'hony flowing' eloquence, 'hangworthy' necks and 'long-with-love-acquainted' eyes.

He could make a clichéd story new by the boldness of his words and his employment of fresh new terms. Thus the well-worn classical story of Cupid shooting someone with the arrow of love becomes a dark criminal event:

> Fly, fly, my friends. I have my death wound, fly;
> See there that Boy, that murthring Boy I say,
> Who like a theefe hid in dark bush doth ly
> Till bloudy bullet get him wrongfull pray.

Professor Katherine Duncan-Jones, the leading authority on Philip Sidney, has said of the poet and of the time that

I think there was this sense that very modern things, things of absolutely the present moment could be done with the language, that this was a language that was both very historical and carried many relics of Latin and Greek and French and Saxon and yet was absolutely streetwise. Sidney believed that English and English culture could be as rich as French, Italian, and, even to name the enemy, Spanish culture. Sidney was very well informed about Spanish literature and culture too, he was actually Philip of Spain's godson, named after him. So he had a confidence in the English language as a medium in which great works of art could be produced and also everyday transactions could be carried on. They didn't have to be in Latin or in the kind of French used by diplomats. The English language could actually be used for important matters of state.

He brought into the language words and phrases across the spectrum. 'My better half' for a much-loved spouse which, Professor Duncan-Jones points out, 'in its context in Sidney is tragic and now is a sort of sitcom cliché – "I'll have to see what my better half thinks about that". And "conversation" which used to mean just having dealings of an undefined kind with other people but the specific application to having dealings through language was Sidney's.'

Sidney wrote: 'But for the uttering sweetly and properly the conceite of the minde ... Which is the ende of thought ... *English hath it equally with any other tongue in the world*' (my italics).

There is a sense of triumph, even victory, in that last sentence. Partly because of Sidney, poetry, not royal commands or sermons or even the Bible itself, poetry became the benchmark for English. By the 1600s, poets like John Donne, Thomas Campion, Michael Drayton, Ben Jonson, George Herbert and many more were writing lines such as Jonson's 'Drinke to me, onely, with thine eyes' and Donne's 'No man is an Iland' which have become everyday expressions. And in enriching their writing technique, poets also enriched English as a language, fit for the most testing poetic and dramatic endeavours.

After his death on the battlefield, Sir Philip Sidney, the young man who had become the star of this movement, was borne back across to England from the Netherlands as the first English itself had been more than a thousand years before him.

*

Perhaps as a consequence of all this, the language of the courtier was drifting even further from the language of the people. Attitudes towards regional varieties of speech and their accents were hardening. Class was discovering a fertile home in speech differences. But by this time to be at the top table was not to speak Latin or French but English of a particular variety. The Received Pronunciation of the day was that of London and the Home Counties.

In 1589, George Puttenham, the author of the rhetoric manual *The Arte of English Poesie*, wrote that:

ye shall therfore take the usuall speach of the Court, and that of London and the shires lying about London within lx myles, and not much above. I say not this but that in every shyre of England there be gentlemen and others that speake but specially write as good Southerne as we of Middlesex or Surrey do, but not the common people of every shire to whom the gentlemen, and also the learned clarkes, do for the most part condescend.

Puttenham's distinction between written English – which could, he says, be of quality in whatever part of the country – and spoken English outside the charmed spell of Middlesex and Surrey is an early and acute insight.

How does that compare with English today? In terms of newspapers, magazines, essays, books of scholarship, and most poetry, drama, film and fiction, the language has been largely consolidated as 'that of London'. Yet the written word in television drama has decisively broken away from that and often with success: *Coronation Street* is Britain's most popular soap over its forty years even though its writers use a heavily accented northern tongue. *EastEnders* poses an intriguing problem. Though London based, it is not written in the sort of London language George Puttenham was describing in 1589. Yet it also reaches out to millions of understanding English speakers.

There are similar exceptions in poetry, fiction and drama, but fewer. On the whole, Puttenham's world is already recognisably our contemporary literary world and yet our most overwhelmingly popular medium is television, whose writers can claim audiences per episode of twelve to eighteen million compared with, say, the two hundred to three hundred thousand who eventually read a successful literary novel or the fifty to a hundred thousand who will read well-reviewed modern poetry. So whose English has it?

The easy way out is to dismiss television writers as 'popular'. It might be relevant to note that the early East End novels of Daniel Defoe were also designated by the status-setters of the time as merely popular. Perhaps because they were poor novels. And *EastEnders*, like other soaps, cannot, I think, compare with the best plays, novels and films being written now. But it has never been a clever bet to disregard the potential energy in what is so very popular. Defoe went on to be one of the founders of English journalism and the English novel with *The Journal of the Plague Year* and *Robinson Crusoe*. Surely that could never happen with soaps? Yet Estuary English creeps in and shows no sign of ebbing.

Until quite recently, the Puttenham thesis would have been wholly unchallenged. Sir Thomas Elyot, of the Inkhorn Controversy on the side of tolerance and inclusiveness, advises in his *Governour* that the nurses who look after the children of noblemen in their infancy should speak an English which he says should be 'cleane, polite, perfectly and articulately pronounced, omittinge no lettre or sillable'. Rather as medieval commentators had enjoined that the women who looked after the Norman-French children should speak to them only in good French. Everybody knew what the ruling tongue was – and on the whole they knew they had to ape it to succeed. It is not quite as clear-cut today.

The struggle for the 'right and proper' ways to speak was and is a continuing debate. Sir Walter Raleigh's Devonshire accent was strongly remarked on. Local accent was a matter of comment for a long time. Wordsworth's Cumbrian accent was noted at the end of the eighteenth century; D.H. Lawrence's Nottinghamshire (and his dialect in poems and short stories) at the end of the nineteenth and the beginning of the twentieth centuries; William Faulkner's southern

American in the mid twentieth; Toni Morrison in the late twentieth century. But on the whole these were exceptions: the standard was established in London, in New York, in capitals everywhere.

The Renaissance saw the beginning of the great writing rift, the splitting away of literature from everyday speech. Dialect words and terms often made an appearance in the work of major mainstream writers – Mark Twain, Rudyard Kipling and Thomas Hardy, for instance – but dialect writing was and is still, largely, thought to be below the salt. On the whole, literature still belongs to the high table, as George Puttenham indicated in 1589, and realists of the sixteenth century saw this and identified it. Writing had its own web to spin, its own written rhythms to discover, its own silent world to plumb and most of it was thought and aimed to be above common speech.

In the sixteenth century, dialect began to be considered uncouth, while at the same time it was admitted to contain energy. The story has not changed much since. In the late sixteenth century the dialect in southern Kent was possibly considered the most clumsy. It was used to indicate ignorance and foolishness on stage. Some of the early comedies like *Ralph Roister Doister* (about 1550) have characters using 'ich' for 'I', 'chill' for 'I will' and 'cham' for 'I am'. It was considered positively rustic – and therefore funny and to be condescended to – to say 'zorte' for 'sort' and 'zedge' for 'say'.

But the juice in the dialects and local tongues did not dry up because of the laughter of London. They were to dig in for an astonishing number of years, over four centuries in some cases and a few, even today, are going strong. Scotland provides the most vivid examples.

For centuries the streets of London had developed their own street slang. Crown and finance were centralised in London: so were rogues, thieves, prostitutes and criminals. There was so much interest in the language of vagabonds and thieves that a number of glossaries were published, such as John Awdely's *The Fraternyte of Vacabondes* (1575). So we know that 'cove' meant man, 'fambles' meant hands, 'gan' was mouth, 'pannam' was bread and 'skypper' was barn.

Shakespeare was to use courtly English, street slang and his own local dialect. For much of the sixteenth century troupes of actors had been travelling England, performing plays and easily incorporating local dialects to heighten the effect and please the local audiences. These performances could be dangerous events and near riots are recorded at some of them. But it was these men (all men then) who knew that the mix, the spoken mix of high and low, of the beautiful high flow of Sir Philip Sidney, set alongside Ralph Roister Doister and the fast gang slang of Southwark, was combustible on stage.

Eventually these acting troupes settled in open-air theatres in London, the first in 1576. From 1583, the court had its own troupe of players, called The Queen's Men, who also toured the country. Those players were not speaking the new upper-class language of the poets, nor were they concentrating on the language of the streets. They had found a theatrical language, a way to address people across class and educational lines, to reach the majority. For wherever they played they were such a unique event in that town's history that it was the majority who turned up and paid and wanted to be pleased.

They roared into London and set up their theatres in Southwark. It was the principal nest of crime in the capital, it was filthy, crowded and dangerous, but it was cheap and next to the river for the convenience of those afraid to walk. It was also outside the City of London and hence the jurisdiction of the City Fathers who tended to deal with actors under the harsh laws against vagrancy. The Globe was built there in 1599. On these popular communal stages, something extraordinary happened which was to ornament, deepen, mine and charm English into a language capable, it seemed, of taking on anything, any thought, any action, any story, any feeling, any drama.

These stages became a public crucible of English and the playwrights of the period transformed the turbulent mixed and still unsettled English language that they were reading and hearing. They combined the rich vocabulary and poetry and charmed voices of the courtiers with the slang and sensation and vulgar quick-fire action of the commoners. Because the theatres of the time had no scenery and barely any props, language was the means of choice on the stage to captivate the audience. The scene was set for Shakespeare.

The plays that were written by Shakespeare as well as those by his contemporaries, Marlowe, Jonson, Marston and Chapman, and later Webster and Middleton, attracted a truly incalculable proportion of the population of London. The Globe could hold between three thousand and three thousand five hundred people – and there were five other theatres in London which could rival the Globe. A ten-day run for a play counted as a long run and the London population of merely two hundred thousand inhabitants demanded constant novelty, especially as theatre-going became such a craze that most of those who wanted to had seen the play in the ten days. It has been estimated that a box-office hit like Shakespeare's *Titus Andronicus* would have been seen by one in two men in London.

English's seeding of words was no longer restricted to the courtier-poets and the scholars. In the theatre it had come into the open and now it faced the people. It was ready to take on the world. All the world was now, for English, a stage.

12

Shakespeare's English

Amateur scholars may have their uses but they need special indulgence in writing about Shakespeare. So much has been written about him and so well, from his contemporaries, Ben Jonson and Thomas Freeman, to our contemporaries, Harold Bloom and Sir Frank Kermode. Not only have fellow poets and playwrights written about him, but so have historians, psychologists, politicians, philosophers, sociologists, scientists, novelists, satirists, screenwriters, composers, columnists, linguists of many shades of meaning, antiquarians, actors and amateurs of many persuasions and delusions. He is not only thought to be the greatest writer the world has seen but the most written-about writer the world has ever known for his chroniclers and commentators spill over global tongues, German, Italian, Spanish, French, Dutch, Russian, Japanese, Hindi; unroll the map. He is in more than fifty languages. He was not for an age but for all time, was the boast and the prophecy, and so far it has been fulfilled.

In the eighteenth century, Dr Johnson took a calmer perspective and a broader sweep:

From the authors which rose in the time of Elizabeth [he wrote], a speech might be found adequate to all purposes of use and elegance. If the language of theology were extracted from Hooker and the translation of the Bible; the terms of natural knowledge from Bacon; the phrases of policy, war and navigation from Raleigh; the dialect of poetry and fiction from Spenser and Sidney; and the diction of common life from Shakespeare, few ideas would be lost to mankind for want of English words in which they might be expressed.

No one could deny the truth of that and yet time has eroded interest in some of those disciplines and swollen interest in others, as fashion has changed and the selectivity of our hindsight scythes down the contenders. Only Shakespeare of those mentioned remains as pre-eminent in our consciousness, as the others have faded or at best held steady in the case of Spenser and Sidney. It is sufficient, I hope, to look at the works of Shakespeare in order to see, at this hinge time of English, where the language had come to since the Frisian invasion of the fifth century and what shape it was in as it set out west again, to America.

Shakespeare was born in Stratford-upon-Avon in 1564. His father, John, was a glover (there are more than seventy detailed and accurate references to gloves in his works); his mother, Mary Arden, came from a farming family. He was the eldest of three sons and four daughters and was educated locally until he was fifteen or sixteen. What happened to him until he landed in London in around 1591 is unclear, save that in 1582 he married Anne Hathaway (he was eighteen) and they had three children. Did he work for his father? Did he join a group of strolling players? Did he go off to the war in France or the Netherlands? Did he become a tutor in a large Roman Catholic and subversive household in Lancashire? Was his father secretly a Catholic which was extremely dangerous under Protestant Elizabeth with all the Popish plots against her? His principal teacher in the local grammar school was part of a Catholic circle which shadowed Stratford – but like much else this scrapes together fragments and jigsaws them into pictures constantly challenged by other conjectures.

At the beginning of the 1590s he arrived in London as an actor-writer. It was the year in which the still lamented English aristocratic hero-poet Sir Philip Sidney's *Astrophel and Stella* was posthumously published and the gallants and the university wits were caught in a fever of sonneteering. Shakespeare, who without coy misrepresentation, can I think be described at this time as just another young man up from the sticks, who had left wife and family behind to chance his arm in the booming city, subject to sneers by the university wits for his lack of an Oxbridge education, unleashed sonnets to match and beat the best of them at their own game. Sonnets were his duelling ground, his language laboratory and his visiting cards. He was new, from Warwickshire, 'uneducated', a ragtaggle actor, but, in print, a poet.

> Shall I compare thee to a summer's day?
> Thou art more lovely and more temperate:
> Rough winds do shake the darling buds of May,
> And summer's lease hath all too short a date:
> Sometime too hot the eye of heaven shines,
> And often is his gold complexion dimm'd.
> And every fair from fair sometime declines,
> By chance, or nature's changing course untrimm'd;
> But thy eternal summer shall not fade,
> Nor lose possession of that fair thou ow'st;
> Nor shall Death brag thou wander'st in his shade,
> When in eternal lines to time thou grow'st;
> So long as men can breathe, or eyes can see,
> So long lives this, and this gives life to thee.

This sonnet strikes a very confident note about the author's view of his talent. He is writing 'eternal lines': and as long as anyone can breathe or see, they will read what he has written. Perhaps the remark of that university wit, Richard Greene, playwright, that Shakespeare was, among other things, 'an upstart Crow' came not only from envy but from a certain exasperation with the new star's cockiness. A cockiness which was justified, which made it worse! For other of Shakespeare's contemporaries were very soon cheering him on.

'Honey-tongued Shakespeare,' John Weever wrote in 1599 when Shakespeare had been in London for less than a decade. 'When I saw thine issue, I swore Apollo got them, and none other.' Apollo, the sun god, was appropriate: Shakespeare claimed himself as 'A man on fire for new words'. The association between fire and words is expressed most tellingly at the beginning of *Henry V*:

> O! for a Muse of fire, that would ascend
> The brightest heaven of invention.

Most scholars today attribute thirty-eight plays, one hundred and fifty-four sonnets and other major poems to Shakespeare. He brought us characters who describe those we know: Falstaff, Kate, Polonius, Iago; figures from history, more memorable than their 'true' historical counterparts: Richard III, King Lear; dramas and plots still produced and as dramatic today: *Macbeth*, *Othello*, *Hamlet*. You can scale Shakespeare by many routes: here we concentrate on his contribution to English. Well over two thousand of our words today are first recorded by him, either plucked out or invented by him.

Although he may or may not have invented them, the words 'obscene', 'accommodation', 'barefaced', 'leap-frog', and 'lack-lustre' are just a few of those which make their first appearance in his work. Again we can see how words like 'obscene' and 'accommodation', for instance, once identified and put in print, bred many lines. It is as if a new word, if it strikes a deep chord in our minds, is immediately rooted to feed itself, to grow, to seek out more and more areas and nuances of expression, to bring back news to the mother-ship, to release a part of the brain just waiting for that word. Other words that make their first appearance include 'courtship', 'dextrously', 'indistinguishable', 'premeditated' and 'reliance'.

Over four hundred years ago, Shakespeare had a vocabulary of at least twenty-one thousand different words: some have estimated that with the combination of words, this could have reached thirty thousand. Comparisons are entertaining: the King James Bible of 1611 used about ten thousand different words. The average educated man today, more than four hundred years on from Shakespeare with the advantage of the hundreds of thousands of new words that have come in since his time, has a working vocabulary of less than half that of Shakespeare.

The language at that time was in flux: Shakespeare must have made it dizzy. He 'out-Heroded Herod'; 'uncle me no uncle,' he said, he would 'dog them at the heels' – just one of the astonishing, simple transferences of a common observation, a dog at someone's heels, into a phrase which could be menacing, funny, admirable, pestering: and it is clinchingly memorable.

Shakespeare shoved into bed together words that scarcely knew each other before, had never even been introduced. He coupled 'ill' with 'tuned' – 'ill-tuned' it was and is and ever more shall be. 'Baby' suddenly found itself hitched to 'eyes' and 'baby-eyes' hit the page. 'Smooth', unaware of its new mate, was joined with 'faced' and the 'smooth-faced' appeared among us. 'Puppy' met 'dog'. In the sixteenth century people began to start their sentences with 'oh', 'why' and 'well' as 'pray', 'prithee' and 'marry' began to die off. Shakespeare was on to them. Almost every word could be used as almost any part of speech. There were no rules and Shakespeare's English ran riot.

If the stature of a writer depends on his quotability then Shakespeare appears to be unmatchable. 'To be or not to be, that is the question' is known around the world. It is probably the best known quotation in any language ever.

'What the dickens?' has nothing to do with Charles but makes its first appearance in *The Merry Wives of Windsor*; 'as good luck would have it' – that does too. It 'beggar'd all description' and 'salad days' are two of many still alive lines from *Antony and Cleopatra*. He coined so many of the expressions we use today but 'brevity is the soul of wit', so I won't play 'fast and loose' or refuse to 'budge an inch', but 'in one fell swoop' let this paragraph like 'all our yesterdays' vanish into 'thin air'.

Hamlet, as has been observed, is full of quotations, more than any other of his plays: 'the play's the thing', 'in my mind's eye', 'though this be madness yet there is method in it'. We can be 'cruel only to be kind', serve up 'caviar to the general' and 'hold the mirror up to nature'. But 'more in sorrow than in anger' this 'primrose path of dalliance' must come to an end and 'the rest is silence'.

It is not the purpose of this book to examine the ideas in Shake-speare any more than it is to investigate his historical research or his relationship with other writers of the time. But as has been men-tioned, words can stand for ideas. Words are both an expression of and a report on the human condition. Shakespeare abundantly exemplifies and demonstrates this. In *Hamlet*, for example, one phrase 'to thine own self be true' began to explore the notion of personal identity, the study of which has intensified since his day to an extent that even he might not have been able to predict. The great soliloquies express dynamic shifts in states of mind. Drama can be internal. He is saying no less than – this is how we think and how we think is itself dramatically rich. In Greek drama, the long soliloquies were expositions of a fixed state or an argument. Here Shakespeare is turning the mind into itself and making discoveries materially paral-leled in the 'opening up' of the world by the West Europeans. He takes on thought as a subject.

Emerson wrote: 'What point of novels, of manners, of economy, of philosophy, of religion, of taste, of the conduct of life, has he not settled? What mystery has he not signified his knowledge of? What office, or function, or district of man's work, has he not remembered? . . . What maiden has not found him finer than her delicacy? . . . What sage has he not outseen?'

And there are those like Harold Bloom who even argue that the whole of the English-speaking sensibility, even the whole of modern sensibility since Shakespeare, has been moulded by him and from him it fed into all the other Renaissance languages.

In many ways Stratford-upon-Avon itself defined Shakespeare's use of the English language. In the second half of the sixteenth century, it had fifteen hundred inhabitants and as the son of a local businessman involved with everyone in the place, Shakespeare from the start would have known about the high and the low and lived among the middle. The local language would still have been rough-tongued, uttering its Old English openly: the roots of English would have been in his ears in his infancy.

At the local grammar school which, despite one of those absences of hard evidence so frustrating to Shakespearean scholars, it can safely be assumed he attended, he would have studied the masters of classical Latin literature, Cicero, Virgil, Horace and Ovid. He would have been taught in English by teachers whose own vocabulary would be drenched in the classics and streaked throughout with the thousands of words from the French. In the Upper Form, where to this day and in that same room, students at Stratford School learn their Latin, it would have been forbidden to speak in English, only Latin. Ovid's *Metamorphoses* was especially influential and the alleged description by Jonson of his having 'small Latine and lesse Greek' seems a bit harsh with regard to the Latin. It appears that he picked up some French and Italian later in his life: with his ear for mimicry, the cosmopolitan nature of the London he moved in, and facing up to, perhaps goaded by, the swagger of those who had visited those countries, that would seem very likely.

He would also have heard written English and at length from the Bible. His father was publicly criticised for being lax in his church-going, but for a boy of Shakespeare's age and background attendance at church, which was compulsory, could scarcely have been ducked for long if at all. At home it seems the family would have had the Bishops' Bible and then the Geneva Bible. The Great Bible was placed in every parish church. It was based on the Matthew Bible which was based largely on Tyndale's translation. Thomas Cranmer wrote a preface to it and it became known as 'Cranmer's Bible'. He would also have known the Book of Common Prayer.

Perhaps scholars can track to their Bible source some of the expressions and attitudes in Shakespeare. For a youth so evidently sensitive to language, it must have been influential. Especially as, newly liberated into English, the words might have been read with passion and freshness and authority. It was prepared as a preacher's Bible – a book of drama as well as of truth. This was a language to reckon with. It could be that this unacknowledged education was as important as anything learned on the hard school bench. In Holy Trinity Church in Stratford, it is good to think that in some measure Tyndale was speaking directly to Shakespeare.

Lacking the university education that mattered a lot to the dedicated poets of fashion, Shakespeare had to be outstandingly responsive to poetry and to fashion and he was. It appears that he was well aware of the Inkhorn Controversy and, as usual, he waded in. He used new words which had appeared from the middle to the end of the sixteenth century, like 'multitudinous', 'emulate,' 'demonstrate', 'dislocate', 'initiate', 'meditate' and 'allurement', 'eventful', 'horrid', 'modest' and 'vast'. He invented and was also very fond of composite words: 'canker-sorrow', 'widow-comfort', 'bare-pick't', 'halfe-blowne'. Some, like 'dislocate', 'horrid' and 'vast', are first recorded in Shakespeare.

On the other hand, he could back losers too. Everyday language might sound rather different if we were saying 'appertainments', 'cadent', 'questrist', 'tortive', 'abruption', 'perisive', 'ungenitured', 'unplausive' or 'vastidity'. His longest word, 'honorificabilitudinatibus', which means 'with honour', has also fallen out of fashion.

He ransacked everywhere for words. He used his own Midlands dialect to bring in regional words like 'baton', which means cudgel, 'batlet' which was still used around Stratford-upon-Avon until the mid twentieth century to mean the bat to beat clothes in the wash; there's 'keck' for 'fool's parsley' and 'honeystalks' for 'white clover'; 'mobled' for 'muffled'; 'gallow' from 'gally' – to frighten and 'geck' for 'a fool'. He wrote: 'Golden lads and girls all must/As chimney-sweepers come to dust'. Until recently in his home county the golden-faced dandelions were called 'golden lads and lasses' and they do turn to dust, and in the shape of a chimney-sweeper's brush. Children still blow them to find out if 'she/he loves me, she/he loves me not'.

Shakespeare's accent would have sounded rather like some current regional accents as used today by older speakers – unsurprising given the stubborn grip of the dialects of England which retain pronunciations older than those in 'educated' English. He would have used a rolled 'r' in words like 'turn' and 'heard'. 'Right' and 'time' would be 'roight' and 'toime'. Alert as any, though, to the passages leading to power, Shakespeare declared the court dialect of London to be the 'true kind of pronunciation'.

There was little in the landscape of speech that escaped him. In *Henry V* he sets down what must be the first of a hundred thousand jokes about the accents of the Welsh, the Scots and the Irish, and even at this distance and in these few sentences, he catches the caricature:

CAPTAIN MACMORRIS (Irish): . . . tish ill done: the work ish give over, the trompet sound the retreat . . .

CAPTAIN FLUELLEN (Welsh): Captain Macmorris, I beseech you now, will you voutsafe me, look you, a few disputations with you, as partly touching or concerning the disciplines of the war . . .

CAPTAIN JAMY (Scots): It sall be vary gud, gud feith, gud captains bath: and I sall quit you with gud leve, as I may pick occasion; that sall I, marry.

Shakespeare reached out to include everything and so of course he had an ear for the coarse, for 'country matters', as in *Hamlet*.

John Barton, who has worked with the Royal Shakespeare Company in Stratford-upon-Avon for almost half a century as scholar, historian and expert on speaking Shakespeare, can deliver Henry V's great speech beginning 'Once more unto the breach, dear friends, once more' in an accent which cries out as authentic. The best that can be managed on this page is to say that it is partly to do with where the stress is placed – in 'aspect', it is the second syllable which is hit, as-*pect* – partly to do with the length of the vowels and the 'r', so war becomes 'waarr', partly to do with using the full word, so ocean becomes 'o-cee-on', but mostly to do with something as rough, gruff, and tough as the most growly of our remaining country dialects.

Shakespeare rhymed 'tea' with tay, 'sea' with say, and 'never die' with memory. 'Complete' has the stress on the first syllable in *Troilus and Cressida*: 'thousand *com*-plete courses of the Sun', but on the second in *Timon of Athens*: 'Never com-*plete*'. '*An*-tique', '*con*-venient', '*dis*-tinct', '*en*-tire', and '*ex*-treme' would all have the stress on the first syllable. 'Ex-*pert*', 'para-*mount*', and 'par-*ent*', on the last. There was a great deal of what might be termed 'poetic licence'.

'Shakespeare was very free with words,' John Barton says, 'and he would scan the same word differently within the same scene or speech.' As we can see with '*com*-plete' or 'com-*plete*'. 'I think we tend to look down the wrong end of the telescope if we don't allow they were not quite settled in their spelling; that they were free to play games with words and language and it was in dispute.'

John Barton made a stunningly simple point about Shakespeare's language:

It's the monosyllables that are the bedrock and life of the language. And I believe that is so with Shakespeare. The high words, the high phrases he sets up to then bring them down to the simple ones which explain them. Like 'making the multitudinous seas incarnadine, making the green one red.' First there is the high language, then the specific clear definition. At the heart of Shakespeare, listening to it for acting, the great lines, often the most poetic, are the monosyllables. Deep feeling probably comes out in monosyllables. He teemed with word invention but in some way the living power of the language comes from the interplay of the two.

Is it pushing this to point out that the monosyllables are or are nearest to Old English? That the deepest, most earthed of the languages in our many-layered tongue carry the deepest, most basic meanings? It is as if the foreign elaborations, the wonderful artifice of the new and the inserted words only really strike fire when they hit the flint of the old. Since Shakespeare's time, one way to divide writers is between the embellished, the high extravagant stylists – Charles Dickens, James Joyce – and the more earthed – George Eliot,

Samuel Beckett. Of course there was crossover in these as in others, but the two strands are clearly here in Shakespeare and he gorges on both.

His inventiveness was almost a disease. To take just one insult, 'knave', Shakespeare produces fifty different instances of it in his plays. I've set a few of them out as dialogue, as a long insulting rally:

A: Foul knave!

Z: Lousy knave!

A: Beastly knave!

Z: Scurvy railing knave!

A: Gorbellied knave!

Z: Bacon-fed knave!

A: Wrangling knave!

Z: Base notorious knave!

A: Arrant malmsey-nose knave!

Z: Poor cuckoldly knave!

A: Stubborn ancient knave!

Z: Pestilent complete knave!

A: Counterfeit cowardly knave!

Z: Rascally yea-forsooth knave!

A: Foul-mouthed and calumnious knave!

Z: The lyingest knave in Christendom!

A: Rascally, scald, beggarly, lousy, pragging knave!

Z: Whoreson, beetle-headed, flap-ear'd knave!

A: Base, proud, shallow, beggarly, three-suited, hundred-pound, filthy, worsted-stocking knave; a lily-livered, action-taking knave; a whoreson, glass-gazing, superserviceable, finical rogue; one-trunk-inheriting slave; one that wouldst be a bawd, in way of good service, and art nothing but the composition of a knave, beggar, coward, pandar, and the son and heir of a mongrel bitch! Pah!

It is his contemporary Ben Jonson who caught him best. Writing a few years after Shakespeare's death he used terms which might have been thought hyperbolic and now seem prophetically accurate. It was 1623, the year in which Shakespeare's *First Folio* was published.

> Thou art a monument without a tomb
> And art alive still while thy book doth live
> And we have wits to read and praise to give.

Jonson ranks his contemporaries well below him; even the Greeks, Aeschylus, Euripides and Sophocles, are called on to honour him. Jonson takes great pride in Shakespeare's nationality. Since the joining of Scotland with England and Wales under James I, the word 'Britain' had come into play:

> Triumph, my Britain, thou hast one to show
> To whom all scenes of Europe homage owe.
> He was not for an age, but for all time . . .

In *The Tempest*, Shakespeare's last play, the main character, Prospero, uses a staff that is often seen to be an image of Shakespeare's quill. Shakespeare called Prospero's magic 'a potent art'. And Shakespeare himself used the power of language to conjure up a multitude of enduring phrases and images. When, in Prospero's last speech, he breaks his staff, Shakespeare could be laying down his pen, as he did when he moved from London with the intention of living out a long hale life as a country gentleman in Stratford-upon-Avon.

> . . . But this rough magic
> I here abjure, and, when I have required
> Some heavenly music, which even now I do,
> To work mine end upon their senses that
> This airy charm is for, I'll break my staff,
> Bury it certain fathoms in the earth,
> And deeper than did ever plummet sound
> I'll drown my book . . .

He did put down his staff but his books refuse to drown. Editions of his works have appeared uninterruptedly since that *First Folio* seven years after his death. The *Oxford English Dictionary* lists more than fourteen thousand Shakespeare quotations. There were more than three hundred film adaptations of Shakespeare in the twentieth century and almost every person brought up in the United Kingdom will have read or seen at least one of Shakespeare's plays. At any given moment a Shakespeare play is being performed or read somewhere from London to Broadway to an amateur theatre group in Nepal. And for the first time in English history, with Shakespeare and his contemporaries, language supports the professional writer, the man of letters.

In his time, English was also beginning one of the greatest voyages in its adventure: to America, where English would discover and make a new land of words. The Plymouth Pilgrims took with them flags, Bibles and this remarkable language.

Shakespeare gave us a new world in words and insights which would colour, help, deepen, lighten and depict our lives in thought and feeling. He had to the known limit exercised that most important and mysterious faculty, the imagination. At the end of *A Midsummer Night's Dream*, Theseus says:

> And as imagination bodies forth
> The forms of things unknown, the poet's pen
> Turns them to shapes, and gives to airy nothing
> A local habitation and a name.

13

'My America'

English went west once more on its most fateful journey since the fifth century. A weighty proportion of the early settlers came from East Anglia, the land of the Angles where Englalond became England. The *Mayflower* families and those who followed them were, on the whole, people of above-average literacy, moral certainty, religious passion and, possibly, among the most stout-hearted. It was the first mass exodus from a very small country – about three and a half million (a fifth of the population of France at that time) – and the beginning of centuries of considerable emigration, of seeding of continents with the English and the 'British' and with the English language. This emigration was at the expense, many feared, of the size and quality of the English 'stock' in England itself.

But there was no stopping it.

In the last year of the sixteenth century, Samuel Daniel, the court poet, inebriated on English and intoxicated about its powers, speculated:

> And who in time knows whither we may vent
> The treasure of our tongue, to what strange shores
> This gain of our best glory shall be sent,
> T'inrich unknowing nations with our store?

America and Americans became the prime inheritor of the English tongue which they made their own. From Britain to America it went on to the ends of the earth, where nations were often enriched with our stores though sometimes impoverished of their own. At the beginning of the seventeenth century the English adventure took to the ships once more and sailed out for what it thought of as fertile, free and conquerable land just as it had done more than a thousand years before.

It is appropriate to begin at Plymouth Rock in New England, where the Pilgrim Fathers landed in November 1620. At the end of the sixteenth century, the English had already made two settlements further down the coast. The total population in one of the settlements, at Roanoke Island, left to fend for themselves while fresh resources were brought from the mother country, had vanished completely and without trace. In the next colony, at Jamestown in Virginia, the settlers had actually been on their way back to England when a ship arrived with supplies to keep them alive. There are acknowledged claims to American-English paternity in the Jamestown area and on Tangier Island, where a quarter of America's oysters and much valued crabs still keep alive a community of less than a thousand people whose accent is pickled in an English Cornish dialect almost four hundred years old. But as America's biggest holiday is Thanksgiving, in November, a celebration of the harvest and other blessings of the year 1620, the Pilgrims do not seem to be an unreasonable starting point.

The *Mayflower* group were religious separatists with a powerful and sustaining belief in the word of God. The Bible in English was the foundation of their faith and their works. They wished to create a new community in which they could worship as freely as they wanted. In this they were wholly different from their fifth-century Frisian ancestors, who had moved west across the sea to seize inadequately defended farming land. On the other hand, the consequences of settlement soon brought similarities into play. The Pilgrim Fathers – with all that phrase implies about seeking a promised land and mastering it once there – bound themselves by an oath, the Mayflower Compact, swearing to found a colony for the glory of God and the advancement of the Christian faith.

They were not the first people on that continent. Native Americans had been there for about thirty thousand years and there were hundreds of different, often complex, languages. And, much more recently, the Spanish had been in South America since 1513 and spread as far as Florida, and the French had established trading posts up the St Lawrence. These would soon grow into such large swathes of the continent that for many years the English settlement appeared no more than a sliver, the rind on the edge of a large chunk of the Franco-Spanish land mass. Even the Dutch, secure in New Amsterdam on the rock of Manhattan, seemed much better dug in. There must have been a sense in which those interminable European wars, Spain versus England versus France versus Spain versus Holland had simply gone across the Atlantic to find a bigger field to fight in. Whose language would prevail? Would any? There were hundreds of languages already in place which were in good shape and giving good service to those who used them.

In terms of the European 'competition', the English Protestants were to score heavily because they came primarily not to plunder, which had been the gleeful purpose of the Spanish, the Portuguese, the French and the Dutch and the English before them, nor even to trade; but to settle and build a new world in accordance with God's law and above all following God's word. They came to stay.

And it is difficult to overemphasise the fact that they came with the Bible in English and they lived every hour of their days by that Bible. For the word of God in English, their predecessors – as we saw with Wycliffe and Tyndale – had suffered exile, persecution, torture and death. They went to America to find a better place. They wanted to stay English and they sought a true England in which to plant their courageously and obstinately claimed English Bible. They were not going to yield its language to anyone.

By what could be called a miracle they just escaped total extinction. They arrived in winter and found not Eden but what they saw as a desolate and dangerous wilderness, 'wild beasts, wild men', winter. William Bradford, first governor of the Plymouth colony and chronicler of the Pilgrims, wrote in his journal:

And for the season it was winter, and they that know the winters of that country know them to be sharp and violent and subject to cruel and fierce storms, dangerous to travel to known places, much more to search an unknown coast. Besides, what could they see but a hideous and desolate wilderness, full of wild beasts and wild men? And what multitudes there might be of men they knew not.

One of these wild men would be the miracle.

Cold, hungry, weak, sick, unable to understand how to feed themselves in this foreign land, nearly half of that God-fearing company of a hundred and forty-four had died within weeks.

There is an impressive reproduction of the first Mayflower settlement at 'Plimouth Plantation' a few miles out of Plymouth in Massachusetts. The stockaded habitation has not only been rebuilt in accurate detail – the small dark cottages, the little fort on top of the small hill, the pens and barred gates – but the place is now permanently populated by actors, each of whom has studied and impersonates one of the original settlers. They cook, they farm, the preacher preaches and they take great trouble to adopt the known English dialects of the early seventeenth century, like that of Mistress Standish, 'Barbary is my name', who came, summoned as a second wife, unusually from the north, from Ormskirk in Lancashire, and had to get used to 'butchery and slaughtering'.

Yet the original village might never have survived but for Squanto.

William Bradford caught the moment. 'Whilst we were busied hereabout, we were interrupted, for there presented himself a savage which caused an alarm. He very boldly came all alone and along the houses straight to the rendezvous, where we intercepted him, not suffering him to go in, as undoubtedly he would, out of his boldness. He saluted us in English and bade us "welcome".'

What odds against the first word the Pilgrim Fathers met with in America, and from a 'wild man', would be 'welcome'? That having travelled three thousand miles and hit a spot on the continent they had not aimed for, they should be met in English?

The man who came out of the woods had picked up some words from English fishermen along the coast. But he was not the miracle. He introduced them to Tisquantum, abbreviated to Squanto, and it was Squanto who saved the settlement. He is a most important man in this chapter of the adventure of English.

Squanto had been kidnapped by English sailors fifteen years before and taken to London where he was trained to be a guide and interpreter and learned English. He managed to escape on a returning boat. By chance, or through God's providence, the Pilgrims had hit America next to the tribal home of the Native American who was certainly the only fluent native-English speaker for hundreds of miles around and arguably the most fluent English speaker on the entire continent: and he had been delivered into their hands, or they into his.

Bill Bryson, author of books on the English language, *Made in America* and *Mother Tongue*, is in no doubt about the key importance of Squanto:

The Pilgrim Fathers were extremely fortunate to find a person who was both sympathetic and could communicate with them in an efficient manner. You couldn't have had a more helpless group of people to start a new society. They brought all the wrong stuff, they didn't really bring people who were expert in agriculture or fishing. They were coming with a lot of faith and not a great deal of preparation. They were nearly wiped out with the hardship of it. With Squanto they just squeaked through. He taught them not only which things would grow but also how to fertilise corn seed by adding little pieces of fish – the fish would rot and actually fertilise the seed – and he taught them how to eat all kinds of things from the sea.

Squanto engineered the survival of the Pilgrim Fathers and it was because of his help that an English-speaking society eventually prevailed there. Their own language had saved them. Now they not only survived, they multiplied. By 1640, another two hundred ships had brought fifteen thousand more settlers to New England. Twenty-five thousand inhabitants had spread out into settlements around the area. They found new plants, new animals, new geographical features and they needed new words to describe them. Some came from local languages, others from new combinations of English words or from familiar names applied to unfamiliar animals and birds.

New words for geographical features which defied close comparison with the English landscape known to the early settlers who came largely from the flatlands, include 'foothill', 'notch', 'gap', 'bluff', 'divide', 'watershed', 'clearing' and 'underbrush'. Native words for natural things included 'moose', 'raccoon', 'skunk', 'opossum' and 'terrapin'; for native foods 'hominy' and 'squash' for the variety of pumpkin grown there. 'Squaw' came in, as did 'wigwam', 'totem', 'papoose', 'moccasin' and 'tomahawk'. William Penn remarked on the beauty of the native language. He wrote: 'I know not a Language spoken in Europe that hath words of more sweetness and greatness, in Accent and Emphasis, than theirs.' And many place names came from Indian words, as do numerous rivers, including the Susquehanna, the Potomac and the Miramichi.

The language of the Native Americans is on the map and in the conversation but given their overwhelming numbers, given the beauty of the language as described by William Penn and the Indians' ownership of the land, it is more surprising that their words are not there in great numbers. English and those who spoke and wrote it stuck to their own wherever possible.

So they would coin new English words for natural things as often as they could, as with 'mud hen', 'rattlesnake', 'garter snake', 'bull-frog', 'potato-bug', 'ground-hog' and 'reedbird'. They preferred their own words even when describing Native American life, as with 'war-path', 'pale-face', 'medicine man', 'peace-pipe', 'big chief' and 'warpaint'. English seemed more comfortable with its own.

It could be argued that what is really remarkable is not that Indian words came into the English vocabulary – what could be more natural or necessary? – but that so few of them were admitted. Norse had made serious attacks on English grammar in the ninth and tenth centuries and made such a deep thrust into English that in the north three centuries after the Pilgrim Fathers went to America, the effect of their accent and vocabulary was still recognisable. Latin had never let its spring be blocked, coming in through the Church at the time of Bede, via French, via Italian, and again through the exuberance of the Renaissance scholars; Latin brought thousands of words. And the inundation of French has been repeated often enough. But in America, faced with hundreds of languages, English took on words only in handfuls. In the writings of the Founding Fathers there are fewer than a dozen borrowed Indian words.

Perhaps they were so word crammed, so smitten by the word spell of the Bible and whatever phrases of Shakespeare and his contemporaries had by then entered common currency that they felt no need for more. The bounty of the Bible and the Renaissance would take time to digest. Or perhaps Squanto spoiled them. He did their dealings with the natives for them, he was a willing interpreter, a blessed short cut. And the Indians, it seemed, enjoyed picking up English partly to baffle less cosmopolitan tribes, partly for the fun of it. Another reason not to try so hard. Moreover, the English found Indian languages very difficult. The word 'skunk', for instance, began as the uneasy 'segankw'; 'squash', much more alarmingly, was 'asquutasquash'; 'raccoon' was one of many which originally had several native names: 'rahaugcum', 'raugroughcum', 'arocoune', 'arathkone', 'aroughcum' and 'rarowcun'. Perhaps the struggle to reproduce the native pronunciation was just too much and they settled for raccoon.

Again and again, the colonists seem to have refused to grapple with local words and preferred their own. The text of Wood's *New Englands Prospect* reads in part:

Of the birds and fowls both of land and water . . .

The eagles of the country be of two sorts, one like the eagles that be in England, the other is something bigger with a great white head and white tail . . .

The hum-bird is one of the wonders of the country being no bigger than a hornet.

The old-wives be a fowl that never leave talking day or night, something bigger than a duck. The loon is an ill shaped thing like a cormorant, but that he can neither go nor fly.

The turkey is a very large bird, for he may be in weight fifty pound. He hath the use of his long legs so ready that he can run as fast as a dog and fly as well as a goose.

That was largely how English named what it saw in the New World. 'Hum-bird', 'old-wife' and 'loon' make their first appearance in print here: turkeys and eagles are unfamiliar birds called by familiar names. America is full of examples of such anglicised birds, beasts, trees and flowers. 'Robin' has a red breast but it is a type of thrush; American 'rabbits' are English 'hares'.

Perhaps it was fear of the unknown which made them reach for the comfort of old familiar names. They certainly did this with place names. Ipswich, Norwich, Boston, Hull, several Londons, Cambridge, Bedford, Falmouth, Plymouth, Dartmouth – there are hundreds in New England. New England, those two simple words, say a very great deal. Insofar as they could, these stern fathers wanted to recreate the place they had left behind, knowing full well it was New but wanting for many reasons to hold on to the old.

Scott Attwood at the Plimouth Plantation had this to say:

I think their instinct was that the English language would take over. They were very proud of being Englishmen. They had their differences with the Reforms in the church and other matters under the rule of King James I, but they were still very proud to be Englishmen and considered it just the natural way that people should speak. There were much greater attempts to make the natives learn English than there were for anyone to learn native tongues. In the second generation after the Pilgrims, Christian schools were set up for the natives to teach them English, with the single perception that this was a better way to speak.

They were of course men and women with a mission. Those who see the skull beneath the flesh will conclude that to ignore or virtually to ignore the language of so many peoples, with whom you would eventually fight, over whom you will finally rule, is the first step in plotting their subjugation. Others would say that the zeal of the Christian was such that the word of God and the spreading of the word of God so that souls could be saved and salvation brought to those hitherto outside the Christian fold was a paramount imperative. The Indians had to learn English to understand about God and be saved.

Those and other factors feed into the mix of reasons which became the set truth, that English prevailed as often as possible; that English looked at this enormous continent on which it had the merest toehold and claimed it, as its, as 'my America'.

It seems that from quite early on there was an erosion of original regional accents. Being crammed into a single boat and forced into cramped intimacy might have speeded this up. The central and essential features of life were reading aloud from the Bible and listening to very long sermons. Rhetoric, the delight of Elizabeth I, was not encouraged. As the preface to the *Bay Psalm Book*, the first book published in English in America in 1640, said, 'God's altar needs not our polishings.' A standard accent began to appear reasonably quickly.

These people were obsessively aware of the power of words. Improper speech was a crime. Blasphemy, slander, cursing, lying, railing, reviling, scolding, swearing and threatening were all offences. Curse God and you were in the stocks for three hours. Deny the scriptures and you would be whipped or you could be hanged. Language was what they lived by: language was what they lived for, provided it was the right language.

They set out to control it and control began in the schoolroom.

The *New England Primer* sold over three million copies in the seventeenth and eighteenth centuries, including copies to schools, which means that every English-speaking family in America must have worked their way through this clear, well-constructed teaching aid. It was totally grounded in the positive view of the religious life, its duties, its goals, its commandments. This was a society with a very high regard for literacy. Every settlement of fifty people had to provide a teacher to ensure that children could read and write.

The *Primer* – for reading and spelling – was simple and to the point. Every child was to get it by heart.

> A: In Adam's Fall, we sinned all.
> B: Heaven to find, the Bible mind.
> C: Christ crucify'd, for sinners dy'd.
> D: The Deluge drown'd the earth around.
> E: Elijah hid by ravens fed.
> F: The judgement made Felix afraid.
> G: As runs the Glass, our life doth pass.
> H: My book and Heart must never part.
> J: Job feels the rod, yet blesses God.

There will be commentators who might call this religious propaganda, but context is vital. It was the strength of their religious convictions which had led the Pilgrims to take terrible risks in their own country. They valued greatly what they had bought so dearly and it was a prize they were committed, divinely commanded, to pass on.

> K: Proud Korah's troop was swallowed up.
> L: Lot fled to Zoar, saw fiery Shower on Sodom pour.
> M: Moses was he who Israel's host led thro' the Sea.

By the end of the seventeenth century, English was being heard and taught along more than a thousand miles of the eastern coast, and the first colonies in Massachusetts and Virginia had been joined by Maryland (1633), Rhode Island (1636), Connecticut (1636), New Hampshire (1638), North and South Carolina (1663), New Jersey (1664) and Pennsylvania (1682). Georgia came on board in 1732 and all but two of these – Massachusetts and Connecticut – take their names from people and places in England and not from Native American terms.

War brought other colonies under British rule. New Amsterdam was taken and became New York in 1664. New Sweden became New Delaware. Dutch terms remain in Breukelen (Brooklyn) and Haarlem, and in 'waffle', 'coleslaw', 'landscape' (as it had done back in England), 'caboose', 'sleigh', 'boss' (to become very important as a way in which slaves and servants could address their employers or owners without calling them 'master'), 'snoop' and 'spook'.

There was rivalry with the French of course. Why should that incessant enmity be given up just because they had moved thousands of miles west and to a continent which had room enough for France and England tens of times over? When the New World old-style war ended in 1763, England was given the rights to all the territory between the coast and the Mississippi and took a hold to the north in Canada. Meanwhile, the word-flow from French continued. 'Toboggan' and 'caribou' came from native to French to English, as did 'bayou', 'butte' and 'crevasse' describing landscape features. There was the 'depot' and 'cents' and 'dimes' were kept in a 'cache'. There would be words from French New Orleans – 'praline' and 'gopher'. 'Chowder' from the Breton, and 'Picayune', a small coin, came to mean anything small. Borrowings from the Spanish were on a very big scale – Spanish is still the biggest feeder into American English: 'barbecue', 'chocolate', 'stampede', 'tornado' and 'plaza'.

American English was gathering its own forces although there are those who argue that its vocabulary does not become distinctively American until some decades after the Declaration of Independence. Before this, however, words appeared which are new to the English language and are found during the seventeenth and eighteenth centuries. They derive their popularity from the development of the American political system: 'congressional', 'presidential', 'gubernatorial', 'congressman', 'caucus', 'mass meeting', 'state-house', 'land office'. (Again, the English habit of looking to Latin to validate the new.) And steadily, remorselessly, the new way of life was finding its own English: 'back country', 'backwoodsman', 'log cabin', 'clapboard', 'cold snap', 'snow-plough', 'bob-sled'.

A more extended mix of accents was now arriving from the old country. William Penn founded Pennsylvania in 1681, Philadelphia in 1682. It was then a mixed population of English Quakers, Welsh, Scots, Irish and Germans. After 1720 many Ulstermen (about fifty thousand) arrive on the east coast, find the land occupied and go west and south and by 1750 Pennsylvania is one-third English, one-third Scots and one-third German. The Germans too were escaping religious persecution and their hybrid language, Pennsylvania Dutch (Deutsch), still survives through association with the Amish and the Mennonites. A generation after Culloden (1746) as a result of Scottish landowners evicting their tenants, thousands of Scots go west. The population is coming from different areas of Britain, but the advance of English is uninterrupted.

What gave English primacy over the other languages of Britain besides that sense of mission was the force of numbers and the sense of occupation. What gave it a stronger presence than the other European languages, French and Spanish in particular, came through the ploughshare. On the whole the Spanish had sent armies and priests and taken gold. The French sent fur trappers and looked for trade. The English came to settle and that finally ensured that it was the language of Tyndale and Shakespeare which would be heard in the mid eighteenth century from the Atlantic coast to the Appalachian Mountains.

As English spread, it began to chafe at the bonds and then to cut loose from the language spoken in England. In some cases meaning had shifted. The English 'shop' became the American 'store'. 'Lumber' was rubbish in London, on the east coast it was and is 'cut timber'. An English 'biscuit' was an American 'cracker'. An American 'pond' could be as big as an English 'lake'; an American 'rock' could be as small as an English 'pebble'. In America a piece of land became a 'lot', named after the method of drawing lots to determine which new owner received which new territory.

It was also developing a sound of its own. The blend of dialects begun on the ships quickly came to mean that no single accent dominated. The accent today around the north-eastern corner of

America is largely uniform and beguiling in its crisp distillation of dialects. And across America, to this day, there is a comparatively small variation of accents compared to the deep differences still rooted in Britain. English upper-class visitors to America noted the absence of regional pronunciation with approval. In 1764 Lord Gordon wrote: 'The propriety of language here surprised me much, the English tongue being spoken by all ranks, in a degree of purity and perfection, surpassing any but the polite part of London.' Another visitor observed: 'We hear nothing so bad in America as the Suffolk whine, the Yorkshire clipping or the Newcastle guttural. We never hear the letter 'h' aspirated improperly, nor omitted to be aspirated where propriety requires it. The common pronunciation approximates to that of the well-educated class in London and its vicinity.'

In 1781, John Witherspoon, a Scotsman who was President of Princeton, wrote, convincingly:

The vulgar Americans speak much better than the vulgar in Great Britain for a very obvious reason viz. that being much more unsettled, and moving frequently from place to place, they are not so liable to local peculiarities either in accent or phraseology. There is a greater difference in dialect between one county and another in Britain than there is between one state and another in America.

Even *The Last of the Mohicans* author, James Fenimore Cooper, joined in: 'The people of the United States speak . . . incomparably better English than the people of the mother country.' This opinion was repeated over and again. The Americans did not just speak good English, they spoke it better than the English back in England. They were delighted, even hubristic, about this: they stood apart and had no need of English tuition on anything.

In 1775, on the bridge at Concord in Massachusetts, a gun was fired. It was, Emerson said, a 'shot heard around the world' and the American Revolution began. A year later, thirteen colonies declared their independence. The language for the great moment was at hand. It was perfect classical English, a masterpiece of English prose.

When in the course of human events, it becomes necessary for one people to dissolve the political bands which have connected them with another, and to assume among the powers of the earth, the separate and equal station to which the Laws of Nature and of Nature's God entitle them, a decent respect to the opinions of mankind requires that they should declare the cause which impel them to their separation. We hold these truths to be self-evident, that all men are created equal, that they are endowed by their Creator with certain inalienable Rights, that among these are: Life, Liberty and the pursuit of Happiness.

After independence, some Americans it is said were swept away by enthusiasm and agreed that America should cut off completely from Britain and adopt another language altogether – French, Hebrew, even Greek, were suggested. This is most likely a myth. Ninety per cent of the white population was of English stock in a population of about four million.

What they did do, though, the grand old men of the new country, was to decide to attempt to make their English the best in the world. They would both separate from England and in the process take over its greatest achievement. They were quite clear and determined about this.

John Adams, who would become the second President of the United States, wrote a letter in 1780:

English is destined to be in the next and succeeding centuries more generally the language of the world than Latin was in the last or French is in the present age. The reason of this is obvious, because the increasing population in America and their universal connection and correspondence with all nations will, aided by the influence of England in the world, whether great or small, force their language into general use, in spite of all the obstacles that may be thrown in their way, if any such there should be.

It may have read then, and read now, as an exuberant boast: but he was right. And he liked to rub it in to the former masters. 'England,' he wrote, 'will never have any more honour, excepting now and then imitating American.' About that he was wrong.

Adams took the English language into the destiny of America not unlike Henry V and Elizabeth I had done in England itself. He wrote of a future in which no one would be excluded because of the way they spoke. The plain speaking of English would underpin the American democratic ideal. It was no longer the King's English, it was the people's English. He even attempted to set up the first public academy for refining and improving English but it never got going.

Liberated Americans were enthralled by what their new country could and would do with what they now saw as 'their' language. Noah Webster wrote: 'North America will be peopled with a hundred millions of men, all speaking the same language ... the people of one quarter of the world will be able to associate and converse together like children of the same family.'

This visionary, Noah Webster, was a schoolteacher who wrote a little book, known as the *American Spelling Book* or the *Blue Backed Speller*. It sold in general stores at fourteen cents a copy and in its first hundred years it sold sixty million copies, more than any book in America with the exception of the Bible. It is one of the most influential books in the development of English.

> She fed the old hen.
> The cow was in the lot.
> She has a new hat.
> He sits on a tin box.

Spelling began early, simply, at school, through Noah Webster. Monosyllables were easy. Polysyllables were made to appear easy by breaking them down and also by emphasising all the syllables:

A.L. – al P.H.A. – pha B.E.T. – bet I.C. – ic. Alphabetic.
C.E.M. – cem E. – e T.E.R. – ter Y. – y. Cemetery.

It's still in use and that chanting of syllables by millions of children in tens of thousands of schools over two centuries changed and set the sound of much of American English. Americans pronounce poly-syllables with a far more even emphasis than the English. Webster was not an admirer of the English aristocratic clipped vowel and his classroom drill could have been especially designed to oppose it. Where the English say 'cemet'ry', Americans have 'cemetery', English 'laborat'ry', American 'laboratory'.

Webster had other ambitions. He wanted to teach America to spell. Correct spelling came to be seen as the standard of a good education throughout America and the famous American spelling bee was born and became part of the social and self-improvement life of every town and village in the land.

This nationwide embrace of spelling as a way to have a night out is remarkable. It shows Americans at their self-help best. It shows that they treat their language with care and seriousness. It continues the John Adams notion that correct speech and spelling is all the vital equipment an American needs to achieve great things. And it was fun; Americans to this day enjoy it. It could also be very serious indeed – shoot-outs are recorded over disagreements down at the local spelling bee.

Like most reformers, Webster appealed to 'logic'. 'Colour' and 'honour' had to get rid of that illogical 'u' and they did. 'Waggon' could roll just as easily with one 'g', so one 'g' went. 'Traveller' lost an 'l', 'plough' became 'plow', 'theatre' and 'centre' were turned into 'theater' and 'center' and so it went on for scores of similar words. 'Cheque' became 'check', 'masque' became 'mask', 'music', 'physic' and 'logic' lost the final 'k' that English gave them. A great number of these made good sense, though like some others I'm always a bit nervous about tinkering with what has worked well enough. But Webster would not be diverted by any anxieties or nostalgia. He cleaned up the spelling and he set out how to speak the words and he carried most of his countrymen, women and children with him.

America became very confident in its own English language. A witty resolution was proposed in the House of Representatives in 1820 suggesting they educate the English in their own language:

Whereas the House of Representatives in common with the people of America is justly proud of its admirable native tongue and regards this most expressive and energetic language as one of the best of its birthrights . . . Resolved, therefore, that the nobility and gentry of England be courteously invited to send their elder sons and such others as may be destined to appear as politic speakers in Church and State to America for their education . . . [and after due instruction he suggested that they be given] certificates of their proficiency in the English tongue.

It could have been instructive.

Every man of intellect, it seemed, was obsessed by the English language. Benjamin Franklin, who by the age of seventeen had become a printer and is known as one of the fathers of the new nation, spent a good deal of his time concerned with American spelling. He read the essays of Thomas Addison in the English *Spectator* to improve his style. Though he was a great defender of American English, when David Hume, the philosopher, criticised his use of 'colonise' and 'unshakable' he withdrew them. Yet he had a radical view of the language and wanted to get rid of letters he thought unnecessary – c, w, y and j – and add six others. He wanted to remove silent letters and reform the whole business. He sent his scheme to his friend May Stevenson in a letter beginning: 'Diir Frind' but May replied that she could 'si meni inkanviiniensis az vel az difikylties'. That stopped it.

By the 1820s, Americans felt that not only did they have the future of English in their hands, not only were they refining and embellishing it, they were also keeping it pure, still using words the former owners had dropped, words like 'burly', 'greenhorn', 'deft', 'scant', 'talented', and 'likely'. And Americans still say 'sick' to mean ill, not just nauseous. They say 'fall' meaning autumn, just as the English once did. The Americans pronounced the old flat 'a' in 'path' and 'fast' – both abandoned in southern England in the late eighteenth century. They use the old 'gotten' not 'got'. They say 'eether', we say 'eye-ther' – America's is the old form. They use 'I guess' as Chaucer did.

Yet there was still a wariness about pressing too hard. Franklin had backed down over the perfectly good and as it turned out long-lived words 'colonise' and 'unshakable'. When Webster published his great dictionary in 1828, for all his anti-Old Englishness, he was quick to protest that the dictionary contained fewer than fifty terms that were new to the country. The east coast still saw itself in the same orbit as Old England.

But the west was different. In the west, English went wild.

14

Wild West Words

In the west, American English escaped the control of the East coast Pilgrim Fathers and their highly educated, competitive, controlling and linguistically accomplished heirs and successors along the Atlantic seaboard. It had a continent to conquer and name, plains and mountain ranges, deserts and forests untouched by its restless adventuring spirit. English would not be confined, not even when it was cosseted and groomed by the formidable progeny of the *Mayflower* and those that sailed in its wake.

Who could have predicted that it would be the French who would have given the opening English needed to flood over North America? But it was the Louisiana Purchase that did it. In 1804, President Jefferson, on behalf of the United States, bought what was then called Louisiana from the French for three cents an acre. It cost them about fifteen million dollars. It more than doubled the size of the country. If ever proof were needed of the difference between the French and the English in North America – that the one came to trade, the other to settle – this was it.

The French grip on the massif central of America had effectively blocked the exploration of the west. The Great Plains were there, endless lands drained by the Mississippi and its tributaries the Missouri, Ohio and Tennessee. It stretched from New Orleans in the south to the Rocky Mountains and what is today the Canadian border in the north.

In its early years on the stage as an independent country the United States was lucky in many of its leading men. President Jefferson, who had not only bought Louisiana, which must be a contender for the bargain of all time, immediately set up an expedition of forty-five men under the leadership of Captain Meriwether Lewis and William Clark (two more English names it is hard to imagine). They were to find a navigable river route to the west coast. The Louisiana Purchase was itself enough to put Jefferson in the chronicles of fame in his new country; the immediate setting up of the expedition was a seizing of the day which only the finest politicians seem able to do. But for this story, for the adventure of English, Jefferson's genius was to insist that the explorers wrote daily journals. They kept their word. The result is a glorious introduction to the often fantastical new worlds which English discovered. To meet these new experiences English invented and stole wholesale.

Lewis and Clark were army-trained frontiersmen, and backwoods specialists. The pure English dreams of John Adams and the proprietorial revisions of Webster and Franklin, the whole Puritan propriety went out of the window in the west when they sat down to compose their journal.

It was after dark before we finished butchering the buffaloe, and on my return to camp I trod within a few inches of a rattle snake but ... fortunately escaped his bite ... late this evening we passed another creek ... and a very bad rappid which reached quite across the river ... a female Elk and its fawn swam down through the waves which ran very high, hence the name of Elk Rappides which (we) instantly gave this place ... opposite to these rappids there is a high bluff and a little above on the lard (larboard) a small cottonwood bottom in which we found sufficient timber for our fire and encampment.

By comparison with the whirlwind that was soon to be reaped in the west, this reads rather tamely. Even so, it is a clear signal that the language of the east and therefore the language of London is not sufficient. In England 'creek' is a tidal inlet, in America it covers all manner of streams. An adjective is turned into a noun – 'rapid' into 'rapids'. 'Bluff' is an American coinage to describe broadfaced cliffs. 'Rattle snake' and 'cottonwood' are examples of the way two English words could combine forces in the face of new material. 'Elk' is one of the words imported from England but applied to a different beast. 'Buffalo', oddly, had been an English word for two hundred years, imported from a Portuguese book about China. And American buffaloes are bison.

Webster in his dictionary had said that it contained not fifty words peculiar to America. In the untutored journals of the two frontiersmen, Clark and Lewis, we discover many hundreds of new words which can claim to be peculiarly American English.

It is significant that these frontiersmen and those who followed their trail were much more open to Indian words. Partly because there was so much to describe and the Indian word was the handiest. But partly I guess because the men were far less engaged in the battle to beat London polite society at its own game or remodel English as a classical language to match Latin, and construct an imperial language to out-Rome Rome.

And perhaps the men on the frontier had a finer democratic instinct when it came to culture. Five hundred Indian words are recorded in those journals for the first time. Not an overwhelming number, but many more than before. Some fell away, some have been mentioned, but words derived from native languages include: 'hickory', 'hominy', 'maize', 'moccasin', 'moose', 'opossum', 'pecan', 'persimmon', 'squaw', 'toboggan', 'powwow' and 'totem', as well as more obscure words such as 'kinnikinnic', a mixture of leaves for smoking; 'pemmican', a preserved mixture of meat, fat and berries; and 'tamarack', a kind of larch. Of the first thirteen states, only Massachusetts and Connecticut are from Indian words. As the country went west, more Indian words were used for the states. For example: Dakota (from Santee 'allies'); Wyoming (Algonquin 'place of the big flats'); Utah (Navaho 'upper land' or 'land of the Uti'); Mississippi (Chippewa 'big river') and Kentucky (Iroquois 'meadow land').

There are often grey areas. Does the 'whippoorwill' bird derive from native Indian or is it an English coinage coming from the sound the bird makes? 'Mocking bird' is definitely an English word coined, or invented, because of the bird's habit of imitating other birds' songs.

These dawn-of-the-nineteenth-century journals also give us, sometimes for the first time in print, names and phrases usually made by combining Old English words, most often by jamming together two syllables: 'black track', 'black bear', 'blue grass', 'box alder', 'brown thrush', 'buck-eye', 'bull-frog', 'blue jay', 'bull snake' and through the alphabet to 'night-hawk', 'sage brush', 'snow-shoe', 'war-party' and 'wood duck'.

Some English words recorded here can be seen to have taken on new meanings: 'braid', 'crab apple', 'dollar', 'fork', 'gang', 'grouse', 'meal', 'mammoth', 'hump' and 'rush'. 'Boil' and 'lick' became nouns; 'snag' and 'scalp' became verbs.

On that expedition English went word-drunk and it was to stay intoxicated out west for decades to come. Lewis and Clark and their men became dab hands at naming: they used physical characteristics – 'Crooked Falls' and 'Diamond Island'; incidents – 'Colt-Killed Creek'; names of members of the expedition – 'Floyd's River', 'Reuben's Creek'; ladies back home were toasted in geography – 'Fanny's Island', 'Judith's Creek'. And Jefferson himself, as was fitting, got a place – 'Jefferson's River'.

One thing this shows, I think, at its simplest, is that language is no respecter of persons in that it will find birth wherever and whenever it can. There is very often something wonderfully anonymous about the whole process: a pimp can coin a word as lasting as that of a poet, a street hawker as a statesman, a farmer as a scholar, a foul mouth as a Latinist, vulgar as refined, illiterate as schooled. Language leaps out of mouths regardless of class, sex, age, or education: it sees something that needs to be said or saved in a word and it pounces. In the American west it pounced for more than fifty years.

This was partly perhaps because people were coming into a new land, full of fear and excitement and hope – all stimulants; determined to make their mark, often finding energy in joining ranks with a language they needed to master in order fully to be part of their new society. Immigrants. The word 'immigrant' is an American invention. Migration of people had occurred in the Old World but in the New it was the single common defining experience.

New settlers brought new linguistic resources, as they still do today. The Pilgrim Fathers had come primarily from the south and east of England. Two hundred years on, new Americans from Britain were more likely to come from Scotland or from Ulster, where they felt driven out by a combination of natural disasters, high rents and religious intolerance. There were also among the Scots and Irish many who came, as others did, in search of a better life and with hope to make one. It has been claimed that half the population of Ulster left for America.

They found the land on the eastern seaboard and the land nearest to it already occupied and staked out. They moved west. They were regarded as good fighters and encouraged to go to the frontier and face the greatest risks. The Ulstermen were unjustly regarded and written about as uncouth and they pushed on from where they were not welcome to the wilder, emptier places they made their own. Their older accents can still be heard among the hillbillies of the Appalachians and in the music that evolved into country and western.

The Scots and the Irish brought their own words with them and saw them turn into American English. 'Scon', the Scottish verb meaning skim over the water, became 'schooner'. And you can still hear old Scots dialect words and pronunciations: 'ingine' for 'engine', 'brickle' for 'brittle', 'donsie' for 'sickly', 'poke' for 'boy' – all eighteenth-century survivals. The Irish were to bring 'speakeasy', 'smithereens', 'shillelagh' – not many actual words but they influenced speech habits: 'shall' for 'will', 'ag'in' for 'against', 'ketch' for 'catch', 'drownded' for 'drowned', 'yes indeedy' and 'yes sirree'.

Lewis and Clark had opened up the west. It was an immense effort and yet they are probably less well remembered for it today than for the journals they had to scribble every night, descriptions and words which have gained for them a sort of immortality. It was the great rivers that became the superhighways and a place like St Louis, the gateway to the west, would be the site of scores of paddle-steamers carrying, as well as everything else, cargoes of words.

The old French presence came into its own along the Mississippi. It's in the place names, New Orleans, Baton Rouge, Lafayette in the south and up north in St Louis, Cape Girardeau and French 'villes' everywhere – Belleville, Abbeville, Centreville, Pineville, Jacksonville. 'Shanty', 'sashay', 'chute' all come in from the French as does one of the great meeting places in the west, the 'hotel'.

In France, a hotel was a grand private house or a municipal building. In America it became – at its best – a palace for the people, meant to be a cut above the taverns and inns of old England, meant to offer style and a secure lodging place in a shifting, growing, booming busty world, offering the best to anyone who could rake up the modest charges. The word can be found in Smollett in 1765, but 'hotel' is a good example of a word that not only changed its meaning but was to take off, first in America and then elsewhere, into a host of other meanings, nuanced, varied, rich, bare: the hotels of Raymond Chandler in downtown Los Angeles, the hotels of Scott Fitzgerald in the 1920s, the rich glitz of Truman Capote in the mid century, places open to all who could pay, an oasis, and in some cases a shot at paradise. In the early days there were some who did indeed refer to hotels as 'People's Palaces'.

Many of the clients at these hotels were businessmen. In eighteenth-century England merchants had been described as businessmen, but once again, in going across to America, the word took on new meanings, from the princes of finance who set up Wall Street and brunched in the Plaza Hotel to the small businessmen whose salesmen came to epitomise the longing to catch the American dream. Later, the progeny of businessmen was to include 'executive', 'well heeled', 'fat cat', 'go-getter', 'yes-man', 'assembly line' and 'closed shop'.

'Rednecks' got the name because of the way their necks were burned in the sun as they bent to work in the fields. The poor travelled on rafts which they steered with oars called 'riffs' – the 'riff-raff' (although a similar phrase, 'rif et raf', had been recorded in France in 1470, meaning 'nothing whatever'). On board the bigger boats the richer travellers were called 'highfalutin' because of the high fluted smokestacks that carried the soot and cinders well away from the passengers. And they gambled.

Paddle-steamers, river boats, the Mississippi and other swathes of slow-moving water shifting traffic around territories brand new to the immigrants: what better stage for gambling? It became the favourite activity among river-boat passengers. Some travelled only to gamble. Some never got off. English was on the cards.

'Pass the buck' and 'the buck stops here' both come from card games. The 'buck' was originally a buckhorn-handled knife passed round to show who was dealing. Gamblers put many fine phrases into the word-kitty. 'Deal' itself became the power behind phrases such as 'new deal', 'square deal', 'fair deal', 'raw deal', 'big deal'; 'you bet!', 'put up or shut up!', 'I'll call your bluff' were first heard around the American card table, perhaps on a river boat gliding down to New Orleans. Thanks to these dedicated gambling men you can today have 'an ace up your sleeve' so you put 'up the ante' and when someone 'throws in his hand' you keep a 'poker face'. Even when the 'chips are down' and 'the cards are stacked against you' you can play a 'wild card' and 'scoop the jackpot'.

They drank while they played. Drink has been good to the English vocabulary. 'Bar-room' and 'saloon' entered the language in the first half of the nineteenth century, soon followed by 'bar-tender' and 'set 'em up!'. A 'snifter', a 'jigger' and a 'finger' – all these measures came from America. So did 'cocktail'. Not from the 1920s but from 1806, on the frontier, when it was a mixture of spirits, sugar, water and bitters. 'Bootlegging', which became an industry, a crime, a social disaster, began when men hid a flat bottle of whisky in the leg of a boot, whisky which would be sold illegally to the natives.

They were good on words for a drunk. Even before the Revolution, Benjamin Franklin listed two hundred and twenty-nine! Here are a

few of them, set out, as a tribute to those who have been intoxicated
(American English), as if they were verse:

> He's casting up his accounts
> He's pissed in the brook
> His head is full of bees
> He sees the bears
> He's cherry merry
> He's wamble crop'd
> He's half way to Concord
> He's kill'd his dog
> He's eat a toad and a half for breakfast
> He's spoke with his friend
> He's groatable
> He's as dizzy as a goose
> He's globular
> He's loose in the hilts
> He's going to Jerusalem
> He clips the King's English
> He sees two moons
> He's eat the cocoa nut
> He's oil'd
> He's been among the Philistines
> He's wasted his paunch
> He's religious
> He's been too free with Sir Richard
> He's like a rat in trouble
> He's double tongu'd
> He's tramel'd
> He's got the Indian vapours
> He's out of the way.

And many more then, and many more since. For such bounty, English
could only say 'Cheers!'

'On the wagon' is only first recorded in the twentieth century.

Perhaps 'on the wagon' meant that when you were driving the wagon, being drunk was not a good idea.

The wagon routes like the Oregon and the Santa Fe trails were bringing the invader and the indigenous people into conflict. 'Scalp' has already been noted: a harmless English noun become a verb fit to make your hair stand on end. In came 'war-path', 'war-whoop', 'war-dance' – the white man identifying the practices of his enemy. There are some grey areas here. Phrases once thought of as translations from Indian languages – 'How?' for 'hello', 'heap' as in 'heap big', 'pale-face', 'happy hunting ground' and others – may have emerged from the frontier pidgin Indians developed or they may have been made up by writers such as Fenimore Cooper, who certainly used them. Phrases like 'no can do', and 'long time no see' seem to be translated from the Indian but they are classic pidgin – they emerge on the Mexican border, too. 'Brave' as in an Indian brave, is French. But whoever introduced 'white man speaks with forked tongue' was describing life on the frontier as it was. Americans made declarations of fair play to themselves before God and sometimes strove to keep them: their promises to the indigenous population, the Native Americans, were worthless. The word 'reservation' adopted a new and miserable meaning.

Meanwhile Americans met landscapes on a scale and of a magnificence they had never before encountered, could scarcely have imagined and were yet undaunted in letting their English loose on it. The frontier rang with the sound of words striking out as loudly as the axe hitting the tree. Frontier English came in like a hungry mountain lion, like a crazed grizzly, like a wildcat full of spit and vengeance – and if you think that a trifle exaggerated, hear the words attributed to that Scots-Irishman, Davy Crockett:

There is times that come upon us like a whirlwind and an airthquake; they are come like a catamount on the full jump! We are called upon to show our grit like a chain lightning agin a pine log, to exterminate, mollify and calumniate the foe . . . ! Pierce the heart of the enemy as you would a feller that spit in yer face, knocked down your wife, burnt up your horses and called your dog a skunk! Cram his pesky carcase full of thunder and lightning like a stuffed sessidge and turtle him off with a old hot poker so that there won't be a piece of him left big enough to give a crow a breakfast and bit his nose off into the bargain . . . !

And while the Stars of Uncle Sam and the Stripes of his country wave triumphantly in the breeze, whar, whar, whar is the craven, low-lived, chicken-bred, toad-hoppin', red-mounted, bristle-headed mother's son of ye who will not raise the beacon light of triumph, storm the citadel of the aggressor and squeeze ahead for Liberty and Glory!

Davy Crockett. Born, as the song says, on a mountain top in Tennessee. His father was a veteran of the Revolution. He became 'the King of the wild frontier', the hero of a series of paperbound books telling stories about him. He read about himself as a legend of the west. He became a famously plain-speaking Congressman and died defending the Alamo in Texas in 1836. He was the first great exponent of a style of speech that seemed to want to be as big as the country. It was called Tall Talk.

The east coast's mission for Americans to become the guardians of a perfected classical English was a long way away. Ornate words were prized. 'Shebang', 'shindy' and 'slumgullion'; 'kerbang', 'kerflop' and 'kerthump'. American English meant that an American need not simply leave hurriedly, he could 'absquatulate' or 'skedaddle'; he didn't just use something up, he 'exfluncticated' it. The language was 'hunky-dory', 'rambunctious' and 'splendiferous'. The comparison with Cambridge in the sixteenth century and all those Latinate Inkhorn words, many of them loved and invented by Shakespeare, is irresistible. But there were not only new words of the ravines and rapids, the forests and the high mountains, there were new words you met on the streets, as in:

It's not my funeral if you fly off the handle because you have a chip on your shoulder and an axe to grind. I won't sit on the fence or dodge the issue. I won't fizzle out. I won't crack up. No two ways about it, I'll knuckle down and make the fur fly, I'll go the whole hog and knock the spots off you and you'll be a goner. You'll kick the bucket. So face the music. You're barking up the wrong tree. You won't get the drop on me. I'm in cahoots with some people with the know-how. So keep a stiff upper lip and have the horse sense to pull up stakes. OK?

All American.

The derivation of OK, okay, allegedly the most used word in the world, is a casebook study in the origin of a word. The theories are so many and so various, so many groups wish to claim it. At one point I thought that it depended entirely on who you were, as different ethnic, political and academic groups fight for the ownership of the number one word.

Here are just a few of the more respectable theories, brought together by Mike Todd. There are hundreds more . . .

The Choctaw Indians had the word OKEH which means 'it is so'. There is a report that Andrew Jackson, during the Battle of New Orleans in 1815, learned this Choctaw word, liked it and used it. Woodrow Wilson also used it when he approved official papers.

Liberia has 'Oke', Burmese has 'hoakeh', and these might have flitted over to America before 1840, by which time it was in familiar use.

Then there are the young bucks in Boston who enjoyed playing with or tormenting the language. 'ISBD' was used to mean 'It shall be done', for instance, SP meant small potatoes. In the *Boston Morning Post*, March 1839, OK was claimed as short for 'all correct', which the young bucks spelled as ORL KORREKT. Which brings it out of Indian hands and back to the descendants of the English.

In 1840, Martin van Buren was standing as the Democratic presidential candidate and he acquired the nickname 'Old Kinderhook' (he was born in Kinderhook). In March 1840 the Democrats opened the OK Club in New York based on his nickname.

The Times in 1939 claimed it was of Cockney origin – Orl Korrec. The French claimed it came from their sailors who made appointments with American girls 'aux quais' (at the quayside). The Finns have 'oikea' which means correct. *The Times* proposed another theory, that Bills going through the House of Lords had to be approved by Lords Onslow and Kilbracken and each initialled them – O.K. Latinists pointed out that for generations schoolmasters would mark examination papers 'Omnis Korecta', sometimes abbreviated. Shipbuilders marked timber for the outer keel as 'OK Number 1', meaning Outer Keel Number 1. The Scots draw our attention to 'Och aye', of which OK may be an adaptation. The Prussians propose that one of their generals fighting for the American colonies in the War of Independence would sign his orders O.K. – his initials. The Greeks come up with a magical incantation from the past, 'Omega, Khi'. When repeated twice it drives away fleas. The American army suggests that in the Civil War the US War Department bought supplies of crackers from a company called Orrins-Kendall: OK appeared on these boxes and came to stand for good quality . . . etc. etc.

It can get exhausting. Wise linguists now speak of 'coincidental coinage' which covers all eventualities. OK by me.

Two generations after the opening up of Louisiana, American English had been kicked and hurled into another dimension. This was the democratic language that Adams had foreseen although it is debatable whether he would have altogether enjoyed everyone's 'two cents' worth'. Decorum and polite taste were not at the table for this feast.

The gold rush brought even more people west and yet again the language was up for it. 'Prospector' was a new word: he 'staked a claim', he could 'pan out' gold dust from the river bed, he might 'strike it lucky', even 'strike it rich' and get a 'bonanza' (which came from the Spanish word for fair weather). A good investment anywhere from now on became 'a gold mine'.

And there was Mr Lévi-Strauss, who made his fortune providing hard-wearing clothes for the miners. He used a cloth called geane fustian, a three-hundred-year-old English name derived from its original manufacture in Genoa. 'Levis' and 'jeans' were born and show no signs of age or ageing as they stride into their third century.

But Mr Lévi-Strauss's products were distinguished by the modesty of their name. It was the time of Tall Talk and talking up, as if words could conjure reality into being. This became the particular fever of the 'booster', whose job was to talk up property, talk up prospects, talk up gold, talk up the west to whip on to fever the tens of thousands tumbling out of the settled cities of the east, headed for El Dorado. A single-room school might be called a college, a flea-pit could be called a hotel, and, in the spirit not of exaggeration but anticipation, a one-street town could be called a city. And what cities! Out in the west there is Rome, Cairo, Paris and Paradise City. Superior ghost towns in Kansas include Alexandria, Athens, Berlin, Calcutta, London, Moscow, Oxford and Sparta. Mining camps could get names like Bonanza, Wealthy City, Gold Hill or Rich Bar. The spirit of Davy Crockett would not be denied, and we have Dead Mule Canyon, Jackson's Gulch, Hardscrabble, Poverty Hill, Hell-for-Noon City, Slumgullion, One Eye and Quack Hill. The vigour comes from speech, the speech of men on a high and in a hurry, loving to land a KO with words.

Newspapers spoke for this gold-rushing people and language and beat a persistent drum. In 1859, in the *Rocky Mountain News*: 'To our Esteemed Readers. It is now being settled beyond dispute that rich deposits of gold exist throughout a great extent of the country . . . Persons desirous of trying their fortunes in the new Eldorado can now safely begin to make their calculations how to act.'

History in the American west in the mid nineteenth century was on the fast track. Not so much change as transformation every decade. Yet another hurricane of activity came when the railroad opened up the country and created an industry that gave the west its most characteristic vocabulary.

Joseph McCoy had the big idea. He would drive his cattle often hundreds of miles to a railhead where they could be carried to the big city markets in the east. Previously they had only been butchered for local use. McCoy became rich. So rich that some of his innumerable imitators tried to pretend they were the great man himself. McCoy developed the habit of introducing himself to strangers as 'the real McCoy'.

So we come to the cowboy. If any one word describes the quintessential ideal of the American male (and subsequent males in many other countries), if any word has influenced the style of the American male manner and manners, has been copied by Presidents and slid helplessly between truth and fantasy in its power to evoke a certain kind of courage, endurance, probity, determination, clean-living, woman-respecting, law-abiding, but always willing and able to take the law into his own hands when that was required, slow to anger but swift in pursuit of justice, it is the cowboy. The word came from eighteenth-century English, where it referred to an illiterate young lad watching over a few docile beasts. In America it became and it remains multi-dimensional, iconic, heroic, a word the country is proud to describe itself by.

Cowboys down on the Mexican border had been picking up Spanish words for years. They took them north and pooled them straight into the deepening reservoir of English. 'Ranch' comes from Spanish, as do 'mustang' and 'bronco' and the 'chaps', 'sombrero' and 'poncho' they might wear. The 'cinch' secured the saddle and they used the 'lariat' and the 'lasso'. They cried out 'Vamoose!' and 'Pronto!' and more than anything they feared a 'stampede'. 'Plumb loco' is a conjunction of the American and the Spanish words. 'Vigilantes' took their name from the Spanish, as did the 'rodeo' and the 'fiesta'.

The American cowboys themselves joined in. 'Cow-poke', 'cow-hand', 'cow-puncher', 'wrangler', 'range-rider', 'bronco-buster', 'hot under the collar' and 'bite the dust' all came from the men on horses themselves. 'Rustler' was an American word from the imitative verb 'rustle': the cowboys pinched it for 'cattle-thief'. Samuel Maverick was unique in his refusal to brand his cattle because he thought it was cruel. (His detractors thought it was because he could thereby claim all unbranded cattle as his own.) The 'maverick' is his legacy.

The cowboys then took over the entertainment business and spread their words, their lives, their history and their fantasies around a dumbstruck world. It began in a circus tent and it was dreamed up and booted into life by a real cowboy, William F. Cody, turned great showman, Buffalo Bill.

Buffalo Bill's *Wild West* was a rip-roaring success across America and Europe for thirty years. It staged dramatic fights with real Indians attacking a stagecoach long after Indian resistance had finally been crushed. Live buffaloes were still pursued around the ring by the Indians and Buffalo Bill on his white horse long after almost all the buffalo had been massacred and the last Indian had been herded on to a dismal reservation. It was nonsense and it was a smash hit. Queen Victoria attended a performance in London, the first British monarch publicly to acknowledge America since the Revolution. Custer's Last Stand at Little Big Horn was the climax.

Soon there were singing cowboys, sharp-shooting cowboys, lassoing cowboys and trick-riding cowboys. Painters, writers, newspaper columnists, all piled into this gold mine. And when the cinema came, the cowboys rode into celluloid, deep into the twentieth century and into the minds and hearts of millions and millions of children who, like myself, galloped down our streets after these films, sat astride imaginary horses, shot imaginary guns at imaginary Indians, trying to look like and sound like our cowboy heroes, being chided for attempts at an American accent, more knowledgeable in some cases about the Wild West than about our own countries, swept into the everyday epic of the American plains.

It was golden. It was our dream as well as theirs. It spoke to us and in our own language, or was it their language now? And it had no problems a decent man with a sure hold on the truth and his Colt 45 could not resolve.

But back on the Mississippi another expression came in: 'sold down the river'. It derives from the way unruly slaves from the plantations would be sold on to owners further downriver where conditions were supposed to be worse. The slaves had their language too.

15

Sold Down the River

If you can imagine a language having a life of its own, exploring new territories as individuals have explored new territories, taking punishment and being blocked, damaged and imprisoned as individuals have been and are; that language after a certain take-off stage becomes a living entity, like water, a spring, a stream, a river; then the reach of English has been oceanic. It had already, by this stage in its history, the middle of the eighteenth century, gone from a splinter dialect of a subdivision of a branch of an Indo-European tongue to the language of Shakespeare and the King James Bible, the language that sailed in the mouths and minds of zealous and dedicated men and women to plant itself in a new world. Yet of all its many triumphs and cunningly rich compromises, there is little, I think, that so singularly characterises its resources as its encounter with the African languages through the slave trade.

That English united and absorbed so many scores of African tongues and so quickly, that it was itself sufficiently pliable and yielding to receive back the raft of words, phrases and insights brought from cultures so very different, is awesome. For English was able to perform an act of symbiosis with tribal tongues from a wholly different language group, even to survive being taken on by an alien grammatical system. This began to gather strength in the eighteenth century and went on to create a new English, black English, which fed back into the mainstream especially in the twentieth century.

The terrible fate and journey of African slaves has been told many times and needs to be: the hundreds of miles they were force-marched across Africa by the African slavers; the inhuman packaging on the ships for the Middle Passage which the western European seaboard nations forced on them to take them as cheaply as possible to the New World; the sales, the deaths, injustices, branding, sale, exploitation, flogging, dehumanisation; the trade was ended by the country, England, which had come to it last, had been, probably, the most prolific in its commerce, but at least left first after 1807 when the British Parliament abolished the slave trade and the British navy spent decades enforcing that ruling.

Black English, against what must have seemed all the odds, had emerged in triumph by the twentieth century, and with breathtaking irony, it became the key vocabulary in many of the arts of pleasure. English today the world over is laced with words and expressions which came from those to whom for centuries words alone 'were certain good'.

The English which came to the eastern seaboard with the *Mayflower* and its progeny was an English determined to settle as the language of the land, proud to be English, ample in the great globe of the language, soon enough challenging London and proclaiming New England the chief guarantor of true English. The less regulated citizens who went west and further west, the Scots and Irish in their assault on the wild frontier, borrowed words from all over the place: from the Indians, the wildernesses, other European nations and above all the necessity to put into words the astonishing new sites and sights in nature itself. They invented new words and brought an Elizabethan trawl to the table. Now in the south, there entered peoples on whose influence on the language nobody would have bet a penny, but they dug into this alien tongue with their own inheritance and the combined language delivered – a common tongue for them and an uncommon fresh word-hoard for English. I suppose I think that if English could do this and have this done to it, if it could become the instrument even of those it sought to suppress and come out of the encounter so much in credit, then it can be called a language fit for world service.

Between a half and two-thirds of the black slaves who were transported to America arrived in Charleston in South Carolina – Sullivan's Island has been called the Ellis Island of black America. Ellis Island is proudly and significantly made iconic by the Statue of Liberty and the movingly inscribed promise of a new life for the tired, the poor and the huddled masses of the world. There is no statue, no great memorial, no magnificent declaration of hope and welcome on Sullivan's Island where tired, poor and huddled masses also came. There is a plaque, put up in 1998.

Near Charleston there can still be heard a local dialect, called Gullah, which is believed to be close to the English spoken by the African forced immigrants soon after they were put to work, generally on the plantations. It is thought that 'Gullah' probably derives from Angola. The Africans came via the West Indies or directly from West Africa where there were several *hundred* local languages, including Hausa, Wolof, Bulu, Bamoun, Temne, Asante and Twi. The policy on borad ship was to break up groups of speakers of any one language; the idea being that if the slaves could not talk to each other in large numbers they would find it difficult to organise effective resistance. Captain William Smith, in 1744, in his book *A New Voyage to Guinea*, wrote that 'by having some of every sort on board, there will be more likelihood of their succeeding in a plot, than of finishing the Tower of Babel'.

In order to communicate with each other, the slaves had to find a common language. There were two on offer. Neither one their own. The first was what could be termed a Mediterranean lingua franca, used by multinational, multilingual naval crews, called Sabir. It dates back to the Crusades, may be French- or Spanish-based and is thought to be the source of West Indian pidgin and English words like 'pickaninny' (pequeno, Portuguese, small) and 'savvy' (most likely from Spanish).

The second language available was English and a pidgin form of

English developed with remarkable speed often on board ship itself, which is hard to credit given the coffined and confined nature of the unspeakable accommodation on the Middle Passage. But as Robert McCrum pointed out, 'most Africans would know at least three languages'. It would not be unusual for them to know six. 'They are,' he claimed, 'among the most accomplished linguists in the world.' And that cramped state yielded a new dialect, a pidgin form of English which developed further when they came on shore. ('Pidgin' is a word derived from the Chinese pronunciation of the English word 'business'. 'Pidgin' is a language with no native speakers, one constructed for communication between people with no common language.)

The pidgin developed into creole which is a language with its own grammar, structures and vocabulary, and out of that came Gullah. The original Gullah is still spoken by about two hundred and fifty thousand people, as preserved in the amber of history as clearly as the Cornish dialect among eight hundred oyster and crab fishermen on the island of Tangier further north. The vocabulary of Gullah is primarily English, very often derived from dialect words – the words most likely to be spoken by the English sailors; West Country especially. However, studies suggest that somewhere between about three thousand and six thousand words are derived directly from African languages, 'gula' for 'pig', for example, 'cush' for 'bread', 'nansi' for 'spider', 'bucksa' for 'white man'. It has some highly idiomatic expressions: for instance, 'beat on ayun' – mechanic, literally 'beat-on-iron'; 'troot ma-aut' – a truthful person, literally 'truth mouth'; 'sho ded' – cemetery, literally 'sure dead'; 'krak teet' – to speak, literally 'crack teeth'; 'tebl tapper' – preacher, literally 'table tapper'; 'daydeen' – dawn; 'det rain' – downpour; 'pinto' – coffin.

Many African-based Gullah words now appear in Standard English. 'Banana' comes from the Wolof language spoken in Senegal, 'voodoo' is traceable to the word for 'spirit' in Yoruba. Others may include the names of animals: the zebra, the gorilla, the chimpanzee; mixed terms such as 'samba', 'mambo' and 'banjo', and the food and plant names 'goober', meaning peanut, 'yam' and 'gumbo', meaning okra. African compound words were translated, giving English terms like 'bad mouth'; 'nitty gritty', it has been claimed, originated as a term for the grit that accumulated in the bilges of slave ships.

Gullah and Afro-American English share some grammatical features that differ from Standard English. We might hear adjective duplication for emphasis: 'clean clean' not 'very clean'; or verb serialisation ('I hear tell say he knows') and 'don' used for the past tense ('I don killed 'em' for 'I killed 'em'). Or the use of 'be'. 'He talkin'' means 'he is talking' now. 'He be talkin'' means he habitually talks. 'We been see' means 'we have seen', 'We *been* see' (with the stress) means something that took place some time ago.

Grammatical changes – dropping 'is', using 'don't' where English said 'does not' – were held up as evidence by some white speakers that the 'blacks' could not get the hang of 'their' language. In fact what was happening was remarkably similar to what happened when the Saxons and the Danes met head-on across the line of the Dane-law in ninth-century England and changed English grammar for ever. Anything, though, that was thought to 'prove' the inferiority of slaves was seized on by the owners who naturally considered that they owned the language just as much as they owned the slaves. It took some time for scholars to realise and then acknowledge that black speech was not inept white speech but a tributary language of its own which could and did in time enlarge the whole language.

In the same prejudiced manner, the influence of black speech on southern whites was denied for many years despite widely recorded evidence that white children often picked up their language from black nurses and nannies – again we go back, this time to the thirteenth and fourteenth centuries when it was observed and often feared that French-born children would pick up English from their Saxon nurses and nannies. In 1849, Sir Charles Lyell (who had noted that Sanskrit was a four-thousand-year-old source of so many languages, including English) visited the USA and, having noted how black and white children were educated together, wrote: 'Unfortunately, the whites, in return, often learn from the Negroes to speak broken English, and in spite of losing much time in unlearning ungrammatical phrases, well-educated persons retain some of them all their lives.' It is a consistent theme – children learning and often loving the native language of dialect, and being forced to rid themselves of it when they made their way 'up' in a society which depended on the natives being 'down'.

It has been argued that the boundaries of southern white dialect are the same as the boundaries of the Confederacy, where slavery was an institution. This was taken to indicate that southern white dialect must be that most heavily influenced by black speech. If true, this gives a fine twist to the racism and the racist language in the slave-owning south. In Georgia, still in 2003, there are words that can be traced back to over twenty African languages.

But generally black speech did not really begin to influence white speech until the great nineteenth-century migrations to northern industrial cities like Chicago. The English language has never been a great respecter of boundaries any more than it takes a great deal of long-term notice of any other attempt to control it. And it was principally through songs and music at the end of the nineteenth and into the twentieth century, as we will describe later, that black culture brought black English into the main arena.

But preparing the way for that came the stories. We know of black poets such as George Moses Horton early in the eighteenth century, but the first real mark made in story-telling were the Uncle Remus stories with their great hero, Brer Rabbit. Uncle Remus, to make life a little difficult, was a white man, 'undersized, red-haired and somewhat freckled', called Joel Chandler Harris. However, according to Mark Twain, in writing about the 'Negro dialect', Harris was 'the only master the country has produced'. (There was also a Charles C. Jones, Jr, whose stories were similar but whose fame has not endured.) Harris himself wrote of 'the really poetic imagination of the Negro'; he spoke of 'the quaint and homely humor which was his most prominent characteristic'. It seems to me to matter very little that Harris was white. What matters is that he was a collector of stories in the 'ling' (his word) on the plantations of the south Atlantic states. Who knows if Homer was Greek? The stories he told tell us about that people.

Harris' stories, judging from the appreciation of generations of African Americans for the Uncle Remus stories, stand for what was being celebrated. The fascinating aspect is that out of the brutality and horror and profound inhumanity came stories full of wit, of humour, of cunning, of light invention, many descended directly from the stories of animal tricksters who featured in African folklore. It is a supreme example of mankind through language rising above crippling circumstances. The greatest of these animal tricksters, and one who above all preserved his freedom whatever the odds, was the immortal Brer Rabbit and another enrichment of English came among us. The basis of the language seems to be from English dialects; there is the effect on spelling of African grammar and the phonetic written speech of those whose natural speech came from a different root: 'for' spoken from a different language group as 'fuh'; 'them' as 'dem', very like dialects in England even today. This is Charles C. Jones, Jr's version of one of the Brer Rabbit stories:

Buh Wolf and Buh Rabbit, dem bin nabur. De dry drout come. Ebry ting stew up. Water scace. Buh Wolf dig one spring fuh git water. Buh Rabbit, him too lazy an too schemy fuh wuk fuh isself. Eh pen pon lib off tarruh people. Ebry day, wen Buh Wolf yent du watch um, eh slip to Buh Wolf spring, an eh fill him calabash long water an cah um to eh house fuh cook long and fuh drink. Buh Wolf see Buh Rabbit track, but eh couldn't ketch um duh tief de water.

One day eh meet Buh Rabbit in de big road, an ax um how eh mek out fuh water. Buh Rabbit say him no casion fuh hunt water: him lib off de jew on de grass. Buh Wolf quire: 'Enty you blan tek water outer my spring?' Buh Rabbit say: 'Me yent.' Buh Wolf say: 'You yis, enty me see you track?' Buh Rabbit mek answer: 'Yent me gwine to you spring. Mus be some udder rabbit. Me nebber been nigh you spring. Me dunno way you spring day.' Buh Wolf no question um no more; but eh know say eh bin Buh Rabbit fuh true, an eh fix plan fuh ketch um.

It is worth an uncomfortable aside just to reiterate some of the odds against this classic of literature. The lash, the bondage, the total ownership and the quickly but deeply ingrained corruption that black was inferior, that the Negro, from nigrum in Latin for black, and nigger, from Latin via nègre in French for black, was not in the light of civilisation. Even Byron, that fine fighter for liberty, wrote: 'the rest of the world – niggers and what not'. Another great literary man, Daniel Defoe, a century before had put Robinson Crusoe on an island. When Man Friday, the native, turned up the first word he was taught by the white owner of the island was 'Master'. And though Wordsworth in 1805 lauded Toussaint L'Ouverture, and though Wilberforce pushed through his reforms two years later, there is no little proof that the prejudice marches on. To answer that with wit, and later to answer that with words in music which hoovered up the young of the world of all ethnic groups was one of the most unexpected pacts ever made between any people and a foreign and a dominating language.

In a not dissimilar way, the African peoples who were transported to America used the Bible to their own advantage. They were part of a long tradition. In the fourteenth century John Ball had used the Bible to attack the monarch and the Catholic hierarchy. Wycliffe and Tyndale had used English to attack the excluding command language of Latin as the tongue of God. In the seventeenth-century civil wars, the anti-Royalists used the Bible to preach a levelling of political power, anti-monarchism, even egalitarianism. The Pilgrim Fathers had been guided to a new land and a new constitution through their interpretation of the Bible. For the African peoples captured and shipped over to America, the English Bible was full of hopes of peace, and above all promises of freedom.

This is seen most clearly in the spirituals. When the black slaves of the south sang 'Steal Away to Jesus' or 'Come out of the Wilderness' they were singing about the longed-for next world, but they were also singing about this world, about the hope of escaping to the north and to freedom.

> Steal away, steal away, steal away to Jesus
> Steal away, steal away home
> I ain't got long to stay here.
>
> My Lord, He calls me
> He calls me by the thunder
> The trumpet sounds within-a my soul
> I ain't got long to stay here.
>
> Green trees are bending
> Po' sinner stands a-trembling
> The trumpet sounds within-a my soul
> I ain't got long to stay here.
>
> Oh, tell me how did you feel when you
> Come out the wilderness
> Come out the wilderness
> Come out the wilderness.
> How did you feel when you
> Come out the wilderness,
> Oh, praise the Lord.
>
> Oh, did you feel like fighting when you
> Come out the wilderness . . .
> Oh, will you walk the line when you . . .
> Oh, will you go to jail when you . . .
> Oh, will you fight for freedom when you . . .

The Bible in English once again became the book of freedom.

The Civil War which began on 12 April 1861 was to change all that and over time it did, though many believe there is still a distance to go. In 1865, the Confederation forces abandoned Charleston and the Union army marched in unopposed, led by the 55th Massachusetts Regiment, a regiment of black volunteers: they broke open the slave pens and inscribed Abolitionist mottoes on the walls.

The Civil War gave us 'hold the fort'; the phrase 'on the grapevine' came from the southern states where telegraph lines strung in the trees became so knotted that they looked like grapevines. And there was an undistinguished Union general, Ambrose Everett Burnside, who set a fashion for facial hair — 'burnsides' they were first called, 'sideburns' they became, and once, just a few decades ago, no cool youthful face was complete without them.

After the 'Civil War four million slaves were freed, given full citizenship and the right to vote. But the south did not let go that easily and 'Jim Crow' laws were introduced to restrict the rights of blacks. The Ku Klux Klan derived their name from the Greek word 'kuklos', meaning circle. They were formed after the Civil War. The Klan gave English the word 'bulldozer', originally 'bull-dose', meaning a dose large enough for a bull. It was a dose of whipping and it was administered to black people, often fatally. 'Uppity' became part of the vocabulary of the south, to describe a black who did not know his place. It was not for at least a couple of generations, even more, that black and white words began to mix freely. And it was deep into the twentieth century before the black vocabulary claimed its place in the dictionaries. Long before that it had hit the street, the clubs, the young and through the entertainment industry, the wider world of English.

In the 1880s and 1890s, segregated education was brought in in the south and the laws prompted a great black migration to the industrial cities of the north.

That would be the natural end to this chapter save for the first American genius of literature, Samuel Langhorne Clemens, who took his pen name from a counting cry of the Mississippi river boatmen: 'Mark Twain'. It was used to signal two fathoms.

He was a river pilot but the Civil War ended that occupation. He mined silver in Nevada, he was a newspaper reporter, a gold miner in California, a reporter again in San Francisco, a correspondent in the Sandwich Islands, in Europe and the East; he took to the lecture circuit and then became an author. Near the end of his life, he wrote: 'I have been an author for twenty years, and an ass for fifty-five.' All along the way he had picked up language: 'heap', which he called 'Injun-English' for very much; 'strike it rich' and 'you bet' from the prospectors and miners; and slang phrases like 'dead broke', 'take it easy', 'get even', 'gilt edged' and 'close call'. In his preface to *Huckleberry Finn*, he lists the varieties of speech that he uses – Missouri Negro, 'the extremist form of the backwoods Southwestern dialect' and five varieties of Pike County dialect, all alchemised through and into a new English, but still based on Old English and rifted with Latin and French.

The author whose active life in the world and range of tongues rather resembles him is Chaucer. Again, a man who had been out in the world of work and business, in new territories, negotiating what seem to be experiences wildly inappropriate for the modern literary man. And like Chaucer, Mark Twain stands out at the fountain-head of an English: in Chaucer's case, London Middle English; in the case of Mark Twain, American southern English. And the vital thing for our story here is that this Mark Twain English was powerfully laced with black English. He wrote *Huckleberry Finn* in 1885. Like *The Canterbury Tales*, it has never been out of print.

Mark Twain wrote that 'a Southerner talks music'. This is Huck Finn describing life on the river:

It's lovely to live on a raft. We had the sky up there, all speckled with stars, and we used to lay on our backs and look up at them, and discuss whether they was made or only just happened – Jim he allowed they was made, but I allowed they happened: I judged it would have took too long to make so many. Jim said the moon could a laid them; well that looked kind of reasonable, so I didn't say nothing against it because I've seen a frog lay most as many, so of course it could be done. We used to watch the stars that fell, too, and see them streak down. Jim allowed they'd got spoiled and was hove out of the nest.

This is one of the calmer moments. Even here, though, we are far away from the sober serious Bible's truth English of the Pilgrims. This is different in sound and different in character. It is the language of the huckster, the trickster, the liar, the booster and the cheat, but equally of the naif and the dreamer. It is also, through Huck's own words and through Jim, who is uneasy at the prospect that he might be sold down the river, the sound and the words of black English coming into great literature.

The east coast establishment was not amused. Back in Concord, the cradle of the Revolution, the civilised members of the library committee banned *Huckleberry Finn* for its vernacular words. It was, they said, 'the veriest trash, rough, coarse and inelegant; more suited to the slaves than to intelligent, respectable people'. It had not taken all that long for English in America to be used for conflict between states, between classes, between backgrounds, between individuals; just as it was back home. But English itself, like Ole Man River, just kept rolling along.

As the sun sets on the Mississippi, Huckleberry Finn should have the last word on this almost incredible colonisation of a continent with what was once an isolated and minor dialect:

. . . there ain't nothing more to write about, and I am rotten glad of it, because if I'd a knowed what a trouble it was to make a book, I wouldn't a tackled it and ain't agoing to no more. But I reckon I got to light out for the Territory ahead of the rest, because Aunt Sally she's going to adopt me and sivilize me and I can't stand it. I been there before.

16

Mastering the Language

In the east of America English stiffened the sinews of the most cultivated public expression of an act of independence ever known and was conscripted to classicism for the new country which eventually became a potential empire. Further west, the language bucked and reared its way through spectacular landscapes and adventures and fights and fusion with British dialects, new sights and Indian languages of great complexity. In the south it provided a new link language between scores of African tongues. English in the old HQ, England itself, could seem tame by comparison. But that would be to underestimate the passion of thought and the melodrama of intellectual debate. Not only 'true-born' Englishmen but equally true-born Irish and Scots men waded into battle: it was a battle for the ownership of the words both on the page and on the tongue.

Broadly, as the Enlightenment spread – in select, rarefied but influential areas of life – so ideas of order, rationality and mastery grew stronger. The mid-seventeenth-century Civil War had shocked the body of Britain and words like 'commonwealth', 'restoration', 'revolution' and 'iconoclast' were for many scars of a time that must never return. The wheel of the country turned and so did the English language. It took on natural philosophy (science), previously the realm of Latin, and the great Isaac Newton, who wrote his *Principia* in Latin, chose to write his *Opticks* (1704) in English. Those governing

199

the language wanted to bring order, stability, clarity and even permanence to what seemed to some an over-mighty subject.

First, though, a digression which I think illustrates how deeply the idea of language as the key to all understanding had bitten in to the scholars and thinkers of the time. In the seventeenth century attempts grew to discover the 'original' language, the language prior to the Tower of Babel as described in the book of Genesis, when all men spoke the same language. It was thought that this 'Adamic' language had been spoken in the Garden of Eden and that its purity had illuminated all things and all thoughts perfectly. Lost by the sinful behaviour of Adam and Eve and become the Babel of tongues that followed the Fall, it was thought that it could be rediscovered, perhaps by the study of ancient Hebrew. It should be noted that this search went alongside the equally serious search of minds as fine as that of Newton to discover the essential secrets of matter through a study of alchemy. In the second half of the seventeenth century, the Royal Society commissioned one of its members, John Wilkins, to create a universal language. This was a highly regarded undertaking.

In his book *An Essay Toward a Real Character and a Philosophical Language* (1668), Wilkins argued that since the minds of everyone functioned in the same way and had a similar 'apprehension of things', there was no reason to believe there could not be one universal language. This language would not only make international co-operation on every level simpler than ever before, it would also 'prove the shortest and plainest way for the attainment of real knowledge, that have yet been offered to the world'.

Wilkins' solution was complicated and worked by symbols. Of one symbol which 'doth signifie the Genus of Space', he wrote, 'the acute angle on the left side to the top, doth denote the first Difference, which is Time. The other affix signifies the ninth species under this Difference, which is Everness. The Loop at the end of this affix denotes the word to be used adverbially: so that the sense of it must be the same which we express by the phrase, For ever and ever.' 'For ever and ever' in this symbol form did not catch on. Despite being recommended by John Locke, favourably mentioned by Newton, admired by Erasmus Darwin and the anthropologist Lord Monboddo and later much praised by Roget of the *Thesaurus*, it did not meet with the acceptance of the public. Its recorded use remains only in two laborious letters between friends of Wilkins who were also members of the Royal Society. Wilkins, who became a bishop, delivered a treatment of the alphabet and of phonetics considered authoritative for many generations after his death and recently his work has been rediscovered by those involved in the study of symbolic logic and semantics. Yet, as a language for the page, despite its brilliant shot at universality, it failed to make it.

Nevertheless it shows how powerful a key to the better and firmer understanding of life language was now thought to be, not only by poets and dramatists and religious translators but by those who wished to master the universe of learning. A century later, for instance, Lavoisier in France used a 'non-natural' language which did work and was used and has been used ever since in the area of chemical notation.

John Locke, in his most influential *Essay on Human Understanding* (1690), took on this idea that a clarification of language would reap the greatest benefits to mankind. 'I desire it may be considered and carefully examined,' he wrote, 'whether the Disputes of the world, are not merely verbal, and about the signification of words; and whether ... reduced ... to determined collections of the simple ideas they do or should stand for, those disputes would not end of themselves and immediately vanish ...'

It is a prime example of rational idealism. Did Locke, a man of such supreme intelligence, really believe that by getting the language clear and the arguments stripped to basic simplicities then 'disputes would ... end of themselves'? Clearly he did. It seems to me that there is what can only be called blind faith at the heart of what seems pure reason. For, looking back on the civil wars of the seventeenth century, which so many did for generations afterwards, he would have had to discount a battalion of human grievances, power struggles, religious resentments, repressed regional and national furies and viscerally held ideologies to believe that even the most forceful word purge would have ended such a disruption. It is a fascination in this story, though, that men of Locke's calibre did think that in effect language ruled and that they could and should make it rule everything. And that once the language was 'pure' and set, all would be well.

There appeared to be a growing and general confidence in the state of English. Printing presses were no longer licensed and they had spread and proliferated throughout Britain. Grub Street had arrived with its newspapers and its coffee houses. And the greatest intellectual institution of them all (which had commissioned John Wilkins) stepped in much more influentially to argue that the English prose of its natural philosophers (the word 'scientist' was not invented until the nineteenth century) should be stripped of ornamentation and emotive language. A writer must 'convey a sense of his own fallibility . . . he never concludes but upon resolution to alter his mind upon contrary evidence . . . he gives his reasons without passion . . .'. Rhetoric, the ancient craft of persuasion, was to be abandoned; in this enlightened new world, words were for dispassionate truth. Everything should aspire to be as clear and regular as clockwork, the great Newtonian image of the time, the solar system as a clockwork machine overseen, in Newton's belief, by the Great Clockmaker, God.

In 1652, the first coffee house opened in England. The Lloyds Coffee House arrived in 1688 and lingered on to become for some time the world's biggest insurance company. Coffee houses were known as 'penny universities'; a penny was the charge for admission and a cup of coffee and if you wanted a touch of privilege you could toss a coin into an artfully placed tin and give a tip – To Insure Prompt Service. Grub Street lived in and out of coffee houses and its demand was for writers, quickly known as hacks. This came originally from hacking 'a person hired to do routine work', extended to horses for hire, then 'broken-down nags', then 'drudge'. By 1749, it is registered as 'one who writes anything for hire', 'hackneyed', 'trite'. The greed for essays, opinions, for verse, fiction and books of an indecent character seemed unappeasable and the term 'hack', often rather proudly assumed now that journalism is so established, had then no great cachet. Henry Fielding wrote:

> How unhappy's the fate
> To live by one's pate
> And be forced to write hackney for bread.

Fielding was just one of several of the best writers in the language – Dr Johnson and Goldsmith were others – who served time as hacks in Grub Street. The idea of a public and professional writer was spreading and hundreds of hopefuls poured in even though the majority ended up rather like Samuel Boyse, skint, writing wrapped in a blanket with his arms thrust through two holes, or like Richard Savage, under the pen name of Iscariot Hackney, who described how he wrote for the notorious fraud and pornographic publisher Edmund Curll 'obscenity and Profaneness under the [assumed] names of Pope and Swift . . . Mr John Gay . . . or Addison. I abridged histories and travels from the French they never wrote and was expert at finding out new titles for old books.' Curll was made to stand in the pillory for publishing *The Memoirs of John Ker of Kersland*. But he was unstoppable. So was print. English was taken to the streets in sheets hot off the press. The language was gorged up by new and excited readers who were delighted to see their language pry into as many crannies of life as was legally possible.

But coexisting with that exuberance, possibly as a result of it, there was a deep anxiety about the state of the language and that anxiety was expressed not by a bunch of busybodies but by those who used the language with the greatest force and elegance.

Chaucer is important here. The poets and other writers recognised and bowed to his greatness but the harsh truth was that his words were very hard to read (they have become much easier, ironically, over the last few generations with the organised study of old varieties

of language and the increased interest in dialects) and events like
the Great Vowel Shift seemed to have robbed them of song. Chaucer,
the writers feared, would very soon be lost to posterity. And if
Chaucer was in danger, what could they hope for? It is feared by the
greatest. In his *Essay on Criticism* Pope wrote: 'And such as Chaucer
is, shall Dryden be?' The writers believe that this can be prevented
only if they themselves take action to prevent 'the corruption' of the
language. 'Corrupt', 'corrupted', 'corruption' occurs again and again
and will continue to do so for the next two hundred and fifty years.
It is very clearly expressed in 1824 by Anon, *On The Dialect of the
Craven*, which speaks for the centuries which precede and follow it:
it looks for purity in the country and in the past:

Pent up in their native mountains and principally engaged in agricultural
pursuits, the inhabitants of this district had no opportunity of corrupting
the purity of their language by adopting foreign idioms. But it has become
a subject of much regret that since the introduction of commerce, and in
consequence of that, a greater intercourse, the singularity of the language
has, of late years, been much corrupted.

The late sixteenth century, which had ransacked the world for
words, coined them, traded in them, made new words a fashion,
poured a golden vocabulary into the word-hoard of English, was not
an example these men wanted to follow. They wanted language to
be fixed. And their confidence, even in the middle of the fury of new
print, was ebbing away: Shakespeare had written in his Summer's
Day Sonnet that writing (his at least) lasts for ever:

> Nor shall Death brag thou wander'st in his shade,
> When in eternal lines to time thou grow'st;
> So long as men can breathe, or eyes can see,
> So long lives this, and this gives life to thee.

Edmund Waller, in *Of English Verse* as early as 1645, was both
expressing and setting the scene for a crucial change of mind and
mood:

> But who can hope his lines should long
> Last in a daily changing tongue?

He went on to express what became the battle plan of the new republic of letters:

> Poets that lasting marble seek
> Must carve in Latin or in Greek:
> We write in sand, our language grows
> And like the tide, our work o'erflows.

Early in the next, the eighteenth century, Jonathan Swift echoes and confirms the lament of Edmund Waller. He writes: 'How then shall any Man who hath a Genius for History equal to the best of the Ancients be able to undertake such a Work with Spirit and Chearfulness, when he considers, that he will be read with Pleasure but a very few Years, and in an Age or two shall hardly be understood without an Interpreter?'

Never mind the irony that Jonathan Swift rides into the twenty-first century well able to take care of himself; never mind that most of those who write have very little hope that they will be read at all in the future. Swift's complaint assumed his genius (rightly) and wanted and demanded a language good enough to take it down to a comprehending posterity.

Swift mounted a campaign and one of the first things he did was to rout his enemies, the first of whom were the British aristocracy whose barbaric use of English, he thought, set no example but a bad one. He slated it in his opening salvo, a letter to *The Tatler* in 1710. It was a letter he claimed to have received.

Sir, I *cou'dn't* get the things you sent for *about Town*. I *thot* to *ha'* come down myself, and then *I'd ha' brout'um*; but I *han't don't* and I believe I *can't do't*, that's *pozz*. *Tom* begins to *g'imself* airs because *he's* going with the *plenipo's*. 'Tis said the French King will *bamboozl' us agen* which *causes many speculations*. The *Jacks* and others of that *kidney* are very *uppish* and *alert upon't* as you may see by their *phizz's* . . .

It is fascinating that across the Atlantic Mark Twain would embrace and celebrate even less 'correct' dialect but in London the author of *Gulliver* wanted to eradicate it. Swift is mostly worried about innovations of the past twenty years. He detested words that were clipped: 'rep' (for 'reputation'), 'pos' (for 'positive'), mob, penult, and others (this seems to have been no temporary fad; look at the clipped words of today: phone, bus, taxi, ad). He did not like verbs to be contracted as in 'drudg'd', 'disturb'd', 'rebuk'd', 'fledg'd', 'where by leaving out a Vowel to save a Syllable,' he wrote, 'we form so jarring a Sound, and so difficult to utter that I have often wondred how it could ever obtain.' He hated words he thought merely fashionable – 'sham', 'banter', 'bubble', 'bully', 'cutting', 'shuffling' and 'palming' – the language of the Mohocks.

In the early eighteenth century on the streets of London there were the Mohocks (the posh thugs with their high slang) and the bullies (the common thugs with their coarse slang). One of their 'new inventions' was to roll persons down Snow Hill in a tub; another was to overturn coaches on rubbish heaps. They were said to be armed with razors and knives and 'scared our maids and wives'. As often, it was what they did as much as what they said which caused their language to be disliked and the object of exclusion. The upper classes, the aristocracy, or rather their Mohock sons, were to be of no use in the battle for purification.

It was these aristocratic 'bloods', maybe even a Mohock at the end of the seventeenth century, who had introduced the word 'bloody' as an emphatic, an intensifier. It quickly infected the lower orders. Shakespeare had used the word descriptively: 'What bloody man is that?', but this usage turned it into 'a horrid word'. 'Bloody drunk', i.e. drunk as a blood (cf. drunk as a lord) seems to have diverted it towards obscenity and soon it colonised the mouths of those wishing to be or unable not to be coarse. It alarmed the ears of the polite. Its association with the ancient blasphemy 'Christ's blood' or ' 'sblood' probably helped it along, as did its gory relationship to battle and butchery. Literature, always on the lookout, published it early: in

1684, Dryden writes of bullies who enter 'bloody drunk'; in 1742, Richardson wrote, 'He is bloody passionate. I saw that at the Hill'; in 1743, Fielding, sometimes called the Father of the English Novel after *Tom Jones* and *Joseph Andrews*, wrote, 'This is a bloody positive old Fellow'. Even Swift, in his later years, answered the question 'Are you not sick, my dear?' with 'Bloody sick'.

Swift saw no salvation in the aristocracy and so he turned to his fellow writers, part of that stratum of middle-class talent which was embarking on the remarkable journey of turning the damp little offshore islands of Europe into the centre of trade, science, philosophy, commerce and industry for the entire planet.

To do this, Swift was happy to play politics and appeal, directly, to Queen Anne herself. A stable language, he pointed out, would 'very much contribute to the Glory of Her Majesty's Reign'. If the task of fixing the language were not completed, he argued, then it is possible that future generations would not know of the queen's glory since the texts which record history will be incomprehensible due to changes in the language. If history is not recorded 'in Words more durable than Brass and such as Posterity may read a thousand Years hence' then it cannot be guaranteed that 'Memory shall be preserved above an Hundred Years, further than by imperfect Tradition'.

There is more than one way to interpret this: you could say it was a cynical manoeuvre to get the crown on his side in the fight for his pet project; you could accuse him of overweening ambition in his almost mad attempt to 'fix' something as unfixable as the meaning of words; you could say he was simply besotted by a dubious comparison with classical authors whose reach for posterity depended on circumstances very different from the restless history of English. Or you can, as I do, see it as something of a cry of pain that his words, his life's work, the visible evidence of his racked life and relentless imagination should be at the mercy of a language whose changes would dilute it, obscure it, finally even bury it alive. He looked on his mighty works and despaired.

His friend Addison, of the *Spectator*, the essayist so influential on so many writers of his time on both sides of the Atlantic (Benjamin Franklin used him as a model for his prose), rolled up in support of Swift. In 1711 he wrote:

I have often wished that as in our Constitution there are several Persons whose Business it is to watch over our Laws, our Liberties and Commerce, certain Men might be set apart, as Superintendents of our Language to hinder any Words of a Foreign Coin from passing among us; and in particular to prohibit any French Phrases from becoming Current in this Kingdom when those of our own stamp are altogether as valuable.

Needless to say, we were at war with the French again. Addison used the war as an example of the pestilence he abhorred: 'When we have won Battels which may be described in our own Language, why are our Papers filled with so many unintelligible Exploits, and the French obliged to lend us a Part of their Tongue before we can know how they are Conquered?' (Addison must have known that both the above assertions are laced with words derived from French – for instance: 'liberties', 'commerce', 'language', 'current', 'valuable'.)

What was happening was that the young men, perhaps even the young bloods, over in the wars were having a high old time sending letters home full of new words designed to show off their new knowledge and to baffle, perhaps to provoke, their parents. They wrote of a 'Morass' and a 'reconnoitre', of 'pontoons' and 'fascines', spoke of 'hauteur' of the 'Corps de Reserve' and a 'Charte Blanche' – and many of these, of course, the home tongue quietly digested and served up new as English. Even Addison, even with the fashionable and influential *Spectator* magazine behind him, was unable to dam up the torrent.

Swift wanted an academy – such as French (1635) and Italian (1582) had already – in order to ascertain (in the sense of 'fix') the language. Dryden and Evelyn had suggested it some years earlier but they had not got very far: even forming a committee seemed beyond them. Swift goes on the offensive. He wants the academy to formulate rules for grammar, to discard improprieties, to make corrections and to set up a permanent standard. In 1712, he wrote a *Proposal for Correcting, Improving and Ascertaining the English Tongue.* 'Ascertaining' was the big word. He wanted the language fixed so that (unlike Chaucer) it would be easily and correctly readable for centuries to come. 'I see no absolute Necessity why any Language should be perpetually changing,' he wrote. He wanted it to be as fixed as classical Latin and Greek, even though they themselves had changed hugely in their development and only became fixed when the written form had become a 'dead' language. In *Gulliver*, Swift ridicules and caricatures attempts to change the language.

Like Wilkins' unused 'original' language, Swift's academy did not catch on. As a riposte to Swift's proposal, John Oldmixon spoke for many empirical English speakers when he said that he would rejoice if the language could be fixed but it can't be: 'the Doctor [Swift] may as well set up a Society to find out the Grand Elixir, the perpetual motion, the Longitude and other such discoveries, as to fix our Language beyond our own times . . .' Oldmixon was wrong about Longitude.

And observers noticed that the French, for instance, still changed their language despite their academy. In 1714, Queen Anne died, Swift's Tory supporters were replaced by Whigs in office and the throne was taken by a German with little English and very little interest in it. The idea of the academy crumbled before a stone had been laid.

There is also a telling phrase in John Oldmixon's objection – '*our* Language'. Many of the English were very proud of '*our* Language'. They saw their character stamped on the words and they were right. They believed it embodied, preserved and encouraged the English spirit of individual liberty, of a resistance to central regulation, of not liking being told what to do. If anyone were to make 'the first major attempt to impose order on the language' (David Crystal's phrase), it would have to be an individual and a rare, almost super-humanly knowledgeable, bloody-minded, determined, prodigiously energetic individual. That was what English wanted: a champion, but one who understood the uniqueness as they saw it of the language they relished.

Came the hour, came Dr Samuel Johnson, an intimidating scholar, the monarch of London wits, a beacon of his age, a savage melancholic and, like Newton, an effortless eccentric.

In 1755, Johnson's *Dictionary* was published in two folio volumes. It was the result of seven years' work with little assistance. Forty members of the Académie Française took about fifty-five years in compiling *Le Dictionnaire de l'Académie Française* (1694) and spent another eighteen years revising it. In a conversation with John Adams Johnson calculated his position with regard to the inevitably envied and denigrated French and their forty members and concluded that three Englishmen were worth at least a hundred Frenchmen. This went down very well. (There's an even more flattering figure – 1:500! Forty Frenchmen times forty years divided by one Englishman in three years.) Despite the boast, Johnson's achievement remains awe-inspiring. He rounded up forty-three thousand words and defined them. He pointed out what he had omitted and why and whatever the occasional prejudices, blunders and blemishes it set the mark for English dictionaries. It was the first time there had been a dictionary with illustrative quotations and this was central to its importance. And as he pointed out on the title page, he was careful to use only the 'best writers'.

He began, as his initial plan shows, very much on the side of the Swift–Addison party. His idea was to make 'a dictionary by which the pronunciation of our language may be fixed and its attainment facilitated; by which its purity may be preserved, its use ascertained and its duration lengthened'. Which seems very much like Swift's academy but within two volumes rather than four walls.

But after he had worked on the dictionary and come to write the preface in 1755, his pragmatism and his honesty in face of the force and life of English saw a rueful but radical change of mind:

Those who have been persuaded to think well of my design, will require that it should fix our language, and put a stop to those alterations which time and chance have hitherto been suffered to make in it without opposition. With this consequence I will confess that I flattered myself for a while; but now begin to fear that I have indulged expectation which neither reason nor experience can justify.

With that calm sentence English bade farewell to any serious idea of an academy: just as in its eleventh-century vernacular written form it had been leagues ahead of its 'European' rivals, so now through its non-elected word keeper, Dr Johnson, it declared it would be for ever leagues behind any elected word-fixers. In both cases there is something to celebrate. English would never be lashed down and the power of its freedom gave it, I think, an extra cylinder when it came up against the obstacle or the opposition of other languages. In a sense, Johnson's admission of defeat by the language says as much for English as Alfred's insistence on its powers after his victory. The 1755 preface goes on:

When we see men grow old and die at a certain time one after another, from century to century, we laugh at the elixir that promises to prolong life to a thousand years; and with equal justice may the lexicographer be derided, who being able to produce no example of a nation that has preserved their words and phrases from mutability, shall imagine that his dictionary can embalm his language, and secure it from corruption and decay, that it is in his power to change sublunary nature, or clear the world at once from folly, vanity, and affectation.

Game, set and match to English. The masters had been mastered by it. It would yield to an alphabetical order but to nothing else. To fix pronunciation, as Johnson had said he would do, was equally impossible: 'sounds are too volatile and subtile for legal restraints'.

He made many rules for himself. These included the omission of 'all words which have relation to proper names . . .' such as 'Calvinist', 'Benedictine', 'Mahometan'. Foreign words introduced, in his opinion, through ignorance, 'vanity or wantonness, by compliance with fashion or lust of innovation, I have registered as they occurred though commonly only to censure them'. This first comprehensive dictionary in our language continues on its individual way with such dictates as 'compounded or double words I have seldom noted . . . of thieflike or coachdriver no notice was needed'. He goes on: 'the verbal nouns in "ing", such as the keeping of the castle, the leading of the army, are always neglected'. Participles are usually omitted. Obsolete words are admitted when they are found in authors not obsolete and also included if they deserve revival. He confesses to omitting words he has never found in books and words which 'I cannot explain, because I do not understand them'. On he goes in a manner which enraged, amazed or struck dumb all future lexicographers and pleased so many general readers. 'That many terms of art and manufacture are omitted,' he says, 'must be frankly acknowledged; but for this defect I may boldly allege that it was unavoidable: I could not visit caverns to learn the miner's language, nor take a voyage to perfect my skill in the dialect of navigation, nor visit the warehouses of merchants, and shops of artificers, to gain the names of wares, tools and operations, of which no mention is found in books.'

His dictionary is also lacking in the areas of law, medicine and the physical sciences. Above all, like Swift, he hated what he called 'cant', which he described as words to be found in 'the laborious and mercantile part of the people' where, the doctor decreed, 'the diction is in a great measure casual and mutable; many of their terms are formed for some temporary or local convenience'. It was Dr Johnson, and only he, who was High Priest and sole Tyrant of language and if he decided what you said was cant, cant it was and it was out. Other much lesser but very many dictionaries were to spring up to fill the gaps. Johnson's dislike of bawdy, naughty and slang words, for instance, was surely a major provocation to Francis Grose, whose classical *Dictionary of the Vulgar Tongue*, thirty years later, went where Johnson would not have spent a syllable.

14. Frontiersman Davy Crockett, 'King of the Wild Frontier', became a Congressman and was one of the first exponents of 'Tall Talk' – using new words like skedaddle, hunky-dory and 'splendiferous'.

15. Four generations of a South Carolina slave family photographed in the 1880s. Even today near Charleston can be heard a dialect called Gullah, believed to be close to the English spoken by slaves from Africa.

17. *Brer Rabbit* (*below*) by Joel Chandler Harris, described by Mark Twain as the only master of the 'Negro dialect' the country has produced.

16. Twain's *Huckleberry Finn* (*above*), published in 1885, is powerfully laced with Black English.

18. Robert Burns's first collection, *Poems Chiefly in the Scottish Dialect* 1786 (*below*): his language became a powerful touchstone for national identity.

P O E M S,

CHIEFLY IN THE

SCOTTISH DIALECT,

BY

ROBERT BURNS.

THE Simple Bard, unbroke by rules of Art,
He pours the wild effusions of the heart:
And if inspir'd, 'tis Nature's pow'rs inspire;
Her's all the melting thrill, and her's the kindling fire.

ANONYMOUS.

KILMARNOCK:
PRINTED BY JOHN WILSON.

M,DCC,LXXXVI.

19. Charles Dickens' genius was to use speech as a sign of class – he loved the speed and accuracy with which it placed people.

20. A cockney flower 'girl' – the flower sellers' use of language was the inspiration for Eliza Doolittle in George Bernard Shaw's *Pygmalion*.

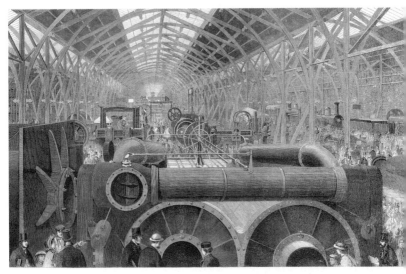

21. By the time of the Great Exhibition of 1851 many new technical and mechanical words had entered the English language.

22. An illustration from *The Bulletin* (*below*), also known as *The Bushman's Bible* which began weekly publication in 1880. One of the poems they printed was *Waltzing Matilda,* which became Australia's unofficial National Anthem.

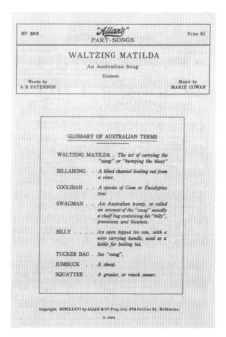

ON A HUNGRY TRACK.
"Mutton, mutton everywhere, yet not a bite to eat."

23. When the sheet music of *Waltzing Matilda* appeared in 1936, the publishers thought it necessary to print a glossary of the dialect used by its composer, 'Banjo' Patterson.

24. In 1965, *Let Stalk Strine* was published to celebrate Australian and its pronunciation, but in the 1970s the McQuarrie Dictionary was the first to officially embrace street and bush language.

25. Anglo-Indian fusion: in the Delhi of the 1820s, Europeans were encouraged to dress in the same way as the Indians they did business with and to embrace local customs – but note the very English portraits on the wall above.

26. The British Raj ended more than fifty years ago but English remains and thrives.

27. Crowds waiting to see *The Jazz Singer* in 1927: the 'Talkies' were fundamental in spreading American English round the globe.

28. Jitterbugging, Harlem, mid 1930s: as Afro-Americans moved north, their language and their music – jazz and blues – influenced English forever.

aw-shucks screenager

fabless

Puffa orgasmatron

heightism

Jedi fashionista

multiculti bizarr

B2C wussy DNR

spinmeister

Viagra ladette

bar-b-q areligious

pear-shaped Gʊ

conjubilant bling-bling

Taliban

29. A selection of the new words included in the latest edition of the
Oxford English Dictionary.

With all his omissions and banishments, it might today seem a wonder that the *Dictionary* carried any weight at all. In fact it carried immense authority at the time and also served a purpose of pride, that English literature could boast such a mighty engine of words, through the genius of one individual. The *Dictionary* and Johnson both seemed to reinforce basic qualities in the English character.

By modern standards it does not stand up. Some of its etymologies are ludicrous. It is prejudiced, capricious and idiosyncratic. That though, I think, only adds to the relish to be had from it. It becomes an autobiography and portrait of an age as well as the first time that a mass of English had been tamed. Here are a few of the entries, selected, perhaps, with less reverence than is due, though we begin on a classical note:

Network: any thing reticulated or decussated, at equal distances, with interstices between the intersections.

Cough: a convulsion of the lungs, vellicated by some sharp serosity.

Dross: the recrement or dispumation of metals.

Little doubt there that a man of serious learning was seriously on the case. The anti-French sentiment is evident.

Ruse: cunning; artifice; little stratagem; trick; wile; fraud; deceit. A French word neither elegant nor necessary.

The Scots are also there to be biffed.

Oats: a grain, which in England is generally given to horses, but in Scotland supports the people.

The inaccuracies are very collectible.

Tarantula: an insect whose bite is only cured by musick.

There is even a rare example of a rude word: perhaps the authority of Middle English 'verteth' helped him here.

Fart: to break wind behind.

> As when we gun discharge
> Although the bore be ne'er so large
> Before the flame the muzzle burst
> Just at the breech it flashes first;
> So from my lord his passion broke,
> He farted first and then he spoke. [Swift]

(There is an anecdote about the absence of rude words from the dictionary: two society ladies commented on this, to which Johnson replied, 'What! My dears! Then you have been looking for them?')

He defined *Excise* as 'A hateful tax levied upon commodities, and adjudged not by the common judges of property but wretches hired by those to whom excise is paid'. The Commissioners of Excise were so offended that they tried (but failed) to take Johnson to court for defamation.

He is good at knocking himself – another trait which could be called endearingly English.

Lexicographer: a writer of dictionaries; a harmless drudge that busies himself in tracing the original, and detailing the significance of words.

Grub Street: originally the name of a street in Moorfields in London, much inhabited by writers of small histories, dictionaries and temporary poems.

Dull: not exhilarating, not delightful: as, *to make dictionaries is dull work*.

The politics of the Tory doctor are set out firmly.

Whig: the name of a faction.

Tory: one who adheres to the ancient constitution of the state, and the apostolical hierarchy of the Church of England.

He felt poorly treated by his so-called patron, Lord Chesterfield, and served his revenge cold.

Patron: one who countenances, supports or protects. Commonly a wretch who supports with insolence, and is repaid with flattery.

His confessions of ignorance are irresistible.

Etch: a country word of which I know not the meaning.
Parsnep: a plant.
Pastern: the knee of a horse.

(When asked by another of the ladies who questioned him how he came to be so wrong in this, he replied, 'Ignorance, Madam, pure ignorance.')

He was fearless in his inclusion of archaic and obscure words such as 'digladation', 'cubiculary', 'incompossibility', 'clancular', 'jobbernowl', 'denominable' and 'opiniatry'.

In this he drew down the criticism of Webster in America, who wrote:

I am inclined to believe that Johnson's authority has multiplied instead of reducing the number of corruptions in the English Language. Let any man of correct taste cast his eye on such words as denominable, opiniatry, ariolation, assation, ataraxy ... deuteroscopy ... discubitory ... indignate, etc. and let him say whether a dictionary which gives thousands of such terms as authorized English words is a safe standard of writing.

American English was not yielding an inch to the high falutin old country. Webster was not the only critic. John Horne Tooke attacked Johnson for violating his (Tooke's) theory that there should only be one meaning per word. William Smellie, editor of the first *Encyclopaedia Britannica*, expressed misgivings. Macaulay called him a 'wretched etymologist'. Even his faithful biographer Boswell questioned his etymologies though he did assert that his hero was 'the man who had conferred stability on the language of his country'. That he did it in such an original, personal, prejudiced and idiosyncratic manner has rather added to his fame as time has rolled over many of his definitions.

There was generous praise from two august keepers of the flame abroad. Marquis Nicolini, President of the Accademia della Crusca (Italy) said it was a 'noble work' which would be a 'perpetual monument of fame to the author, an honour to his own country in particular, and a general benefit to the Republic of Letters throughout all Europe'. And in France itself, a journal declared that Johnson was 'an academy' for this island.

There it still is, in all its dusty but readable glory, the first English academy: in a book.

Johnson's work heralded and triggered a cavalcade of grammars. Everyone wanted to get hold of English and tell it how to behave. They could not wait to lay their hands on this unruly mob of words and smarten it up, sort it out, establish some discipline down there.

The most interesting grammarian was Joseph Priestley who was a noted supporter of civil and religious liberties, wrote about electricity, was a radical dissenting preacher, invented carbonated water (fizzy drinks) and nitrous oxide (laughing gas) and discovered carbon dioxide and oxygen. Science was his chief interest. He also occupied himself with *The Rudiments of English Grammar*, a book in which he expressed a view, novel for that time, that grammar is defined by common usage and should not be dictated by self-styled grammarians.

He had little impact. The battle was won time and again by the men who knew best. Robert Lowth's *Short Introduction to English Grammar* was as conservative and prescriptive as Priestley was liberal and tolerant. Lowth swept the field: twenty-two editions in forty years. Certain grammatical structures were regarded as 'correct', others as not only 'incorrect' but vulgar. The committed corps of codifiers whose admirable descendants exist and in numbers to this day, took to the fight in earnest after Dr Johnson and they have never willingly retreated.

Do we use 'lie' or 'lay'? 'Would' not 'had' is approved as the full form of 'I'd better' (i.e. 'I had better'). Different 'from' is preferred to different 'to'. 'Between you and I' is out. The comparative and not the superlative is to be used when two things are involved. The question of proper case after 'than' or 'as' was a cockpit. Lowth declared, and millions have followed, that it would be determined by the construction that was to be understood or implied, so 'he is older than she [is]'; but 'he likes me better than her [he likes her]'. The double negative, which not unusually had ornamented speech untold times, was sent into exile.

Some of these rules could be seen to make sense. Others were arbitrary. It was a paradise for those terrible twins – Class and Snobbery – and in they came, pat on cue. But in the deep and apparently unstoppable development of language, Priestley's cry that 'custom of speaking is the original and only just standard of any language' is always eventually the case, from Kansas City to Canberra by way of Kingston and Hong Kong. But Lowth's rules will not be denied.

In the nineteenth century at least eight hundred and fifty-six different grammars of English marched into print, ordering the language into shapes. It often obliged them for a while but just as often slid away, went absent without leave, played truant.

It was not only grammar that came in for the often helpful and often infuriating organisation of language. Certain words irritated people, then and now, and there are those who would cut off their heads. Swift tried to execute 'mob' and 'banter' among many others. George Harris attempted to sink 'driving a bargain', 'handling a subject' and 'bolstering up an argument'. 'Subject-matter' drove one writer to a frenzy. 'In the name of everything that's disgusting, nay detestable, what is it? Is it one or two ugly words? What's the meaning of it? Confound me if I ever could guess! Yet one dares hardly ever peep into a Preface for fear of being stared in the face with this ghastly Subject-Matter.' Yet 'subject-matter' has outlived the name of that author.

Hating English words and phrases is not as common as liking them, but the flying squads of opposition are always with us and sometimes they are to be welcomed. There's a sense in which they can't fail and they can't succeed either. English, like water, will find its own level. The language itself through usage and natural selection will see that what is survivable will survive. Those who attack words can hasten the departure of the weak and useless and only hammer into further obstinate strength the words which we all somehow agree have come to stay; for a while longer.

The huge efforts to control English, to rule and order it, had met with some success and no lover of the language would be without one of the many fine dictionaries for whom Dr Johnson's can claim parentage. But what moves language along is mysterious, half hidden and rarely ordered, even by the most erudite and sensible of scholars. Something as ephemeral as fashion, manners or dress can exercise a significant influence. English is open to every influence, however insignificant the source might be.

17

The Proper Way to Talk

The Age of Enlightenment, roughly the latter part of the eighteenth century in Europe and America, saw a loosening of the bonds and ties of religion. It began to create and believe it could control secular cathedrals of the mind. The attempt to control language, whether by Webster and Franklin in America or by Johnson and Swift in England, was part of this attempt to control and it failed. Yet the road to failure can be as influential as the path to success. From the attempts to tame English, to make it jump through hoops, sit up and beg, obey the lash of its superiors, consequences flowed which were to have a widespread, even a worldwide, significance.

Correct spelling was now fully accepted by this unruly language after the pioneering efforts of Caxton and his printing heirs, the necessary legal pedantry of Chancery and the final stamp of Dr Johnson. No more games there. The written word consumed forests, and what was written became available to more people, who had more time and inclination merely to sit and read.

The written word colonised society and a gap grew between what was said on the page and what was said on the tongue. It had always been there but what began to happen now was that the written word dictated to the spoken word. The best spoken English was increasingly supposed to sound like the best written English. But what did written English sound like? Who decided? Out of that argument came 'the best' way to talk and a bewildering number of ingenious distinctions, from scholars, from snobs, from social climbers, from satirists. The attempt to fix the sound of the language became an obsession. But English was too smart to be pinned down, even by the English. It knew that its future lay in freedom. That, though, did not stop those who wanted conformity to their view of the matter.

This chapter is about how, having failed to ascertain or fix the language in Jonathan Swift's 'Words more durable than Brass', the powers that would be attempted to brand it on the tongue. True Pronunciation was now the prize.

The relationship between sound and spelling in English is a nightmare. Our writing system is not phonetic to the point of being anti-phonetic. There are, for instance, at least seven ways of representing what for most people is the same vowel sound – 'ee': free, these, leaf, field, seize, key, machine. What do we do?

As you would expect, given the magnetic attraction of English to everyone who speaks or writes it for whatever purpose (Newton, mathematician and alchemist, took an interest in phonetics and wrote about it), this attempt at fixing pronunciation had been tried earlier.

In 1589, George Puttenham in *The Arte of English Poesie* advised budding poets on which words and which speech to draw on. He is against anything from the north. He is against Langland and Gower because, like Chaucer, though we can revere them we cannot understand them. Puttenham plumps for the speech of London but 'neither shall he follow the speech of a craftes man or carter, or other of the inferiour sort . . . for such persons doe abuse good speeches by strange accents . . .'. The slippery slope has been taken. The ideal sets out to replace all street language, all 'uncouth' usage.

It is in the eighteenth century that the dialects lost most status. This was to do with the codification of writing and the pressure to write 'correctly'. Dialect systems were no longer used for devotional purposes and only rarely used for literary purposes. They continued, with an admirable deep stubbornness, to be the first choice for informal conversation between most equals in the land, but they were as much a casualty of the tidal surge of 'superior' English as any North American Indian tongue.

The pronunciation police came in, led by an Irishman, Thomas Sheridan. His father had been a teacher and friend of Jonathan Swift; his son was to be one of Britain's greatest dramatists. Thomas was a professional actor and theatre manager – and at the centre of London fashion – when, in 1750, he spotted the need for an elocutionist. He seized the opportunity and it warms the heart to know that English as it is most properly spoken by those who set the standard for these things was very much the diktat of an Irish player.

Sheridan's first and crucial book was published in 1756, hard on the heels of Dr Johnson's *Dictionary*. He called it, significantly, *British Education*. Not English. Sheridan was reclaiming the lands and the tongues banished by the Anglo-Saxons twelve hundred years previously: the British were now the subject. And 'Education': no messing about with 'Way of Speaking' or 'Pronunciation'. He went for the key and jugular word: if you wanted to say what you said in the best way, then what you needed was an education and this book, this man could provide it, which, remarkably, he did.

He gave public lectures on elocution in Dublin, Edinburgh, Oxford, Cambridge and London in 1757, which attracted large and influential audiences. He took some members of the ruling elite as his private pupils. He went about the job systematically, which pleased and impressed a culture still happy to live in the shadow of Newton's glory and in the sun of the new Enlightenment. Thomas Sheridan was one of the first to establish the number of distinctive sounds in the English language and the number and types of diphthongs and syllables; he also studied the use of stress in words.

There are two streams of ideas here.

Until about 1750, the metropolitan speech of the court had a higher prestige but there was no social disadvantage for either upper or under class in speaking with a regional accent or a foreign accent – James I, on the throne during part of Shakespeare's reign, spoke and wrote in broad Scots. The Hanoverians were German-speakers just as the Normans had been French speakers. Sheridan found his most responsive audience among the aspiring educated middle classes, those who were taking England and English around the world in thought, word and deed. That middle class, the easily mocked but incalculably influential stratum of British life which wanted to out-Rome Rome, out-Athens Greece, took the mongrel island and turned it into a pack of bulldogs raging across the planet. They wanted their own way. They wanted their own words. Sheridan hit the nerve. In one of his lectures, in 1762, he wrote: 'Pronunciation . . . is a sort of proof that a person has kept good company, and on that account is sought after by all, who wish to be considered as fashionable people or members of the beau monde.' He took no prisoners. 'All other dialects are sure marks, either of a provincial, rustic, pedantic or mechanic education; and therefore have some degree of disgrace annexed to them.'

In case that was not persuasive enough, he supplied a second, a noble reason for laying down your words and following him. 'Would it not greatly contribute to put an end to the odious distinctions kept up between subjects of the same king,' he wrote, 'if a way were opened by which the attainment of the English Tongue in its purity, both in point of phraseology and pronunciation, ought to be rendered easy to all inhabitants of His Majesty's Dominions?' Who could resist such a graceful call?

But of course, in attempting to unite the nation through pronunciation, Sheridan greatly assisted the growth of a deep and continuing social division between 'proper' and 'non-proper' speech. The latter was stigmatised, a bar to social·advancement. The word 'accent' itself which just used to mean how a word was stressed began to mean the manner of pronunciation.

The Sheridan effect was partly as he had intended. Official, High English was hounded and tormented into one and only one 'proper' way of pronunciation. But it fought back every inch of the way.

Who decided? Take the first letter of the alphabet as an example.

Take 'a'. How did you 'properly' pronounce 'a' in 'fast, bath and last'? This became and for years remained the linguistic equivalent of the Wars of the Roses.

Today, the long 'a' in modern southern speech is still thought by many to be the gold standard, the mark of quality. But in 1791, the scholar John Walker, in his *Pronouncing Dictionary*, said that the long 'a' was only used by 'inaccurate speakers, chiefly among the vulgar'. He was emphatic. 'Every correct ear,' he wrote, 'would be disgusted at giving the "a" in these words the full long sound of the "a" in father.' The short 'a', as in 'cat' (or in northern sounds today) is, wrote Walker at the end of the eighteenth century, 'elegant, accurate and precise'. The fight was on.

William Smith, in 1795, called Walker's pronunciation 'a mincing modern affectation ... departing from the genuine [euphonious] pronunciation of our language'.

Over to Walker. Of Smith's long 'a' he writes: 'that this was the sound *formerly* is highly possible from its still being the sound given to it by the vulgar, who are generally the last to alter the common pronunciation'.

It was a split decision: short north – south long: one obstinate but antique, the other polite but a latecomer.

And pronunciation has been an intoxicating, furious, funny and often bitterly serious playground of English ever since. It roared into the nineteenth century with scores of works such as *Hard Words Made Easy*. The letter 'h' alone received as much attention as the ancient scriptures. *Poor Little H – its Use and Abuse* ran to forty editions. *Mind Your Hs, Harry Hawkins' H Book*. The pronunciation of English provided its speakers with a matchless gamut of prejudices and added greatly to the spleen and gaiety of the nation.

Sheridan the Irishman went to Scotland, which has a fair claim to be the motor of the British Enlightenment, to tell them the advantages of 'an Uniformity of pronunciation throughout his Majesty's British Dominions'. The Scots then and now were in at least two minds and various tempers about this but it seems that men of the distinction of James Boswell and Adam Smith did wish to sound like the English upper classes. The Select Society in Edinburgh published a set of regulations which were clear. They were aware of the disadvantages they laboured under in Scotland 'from their imperfect knowledge of the English tongue'. They were able to write it 'with some tolerable purity'. But not enough attention has been paid to the speaking of it which would be an accomplishment 'more important and more universally useful' than the writing of it.

John Walker stepped forward to be of assistance with his *Rules to be Observed by the Natives of Scotland for attaining a just Pronunciation of English*. Sylvester Douglas waded in with a *Treatise on the Lowland Dialect of Scotland* (1779). It was no small matter. The centre of power was increasingly insistent on a centralised accent and powerful Scots were not going to be left out even if it meant publicly demoting their own language. It is a good example of the repressive effect of the official language of authority.

There were two languages in Scotland and oddly the smaller, the Gaelic, is that which has hung on the most tenaciously. As the court and Church were Anglicised, the Gaelic retreated to its brooding fastnesses in the apparently impregnable Highlands and Islands into which even the Romans had not ventured. Lowland Scots had long had close links with the Northumbrian, developing a language separate from though related to the English.

The Act of Union in 1707 meant that Scotland's laws and administrative arrangements were defined in London, in English, and by the time of the Enlightenment, to the anguish of many Scots, Gaelic was peripheral. Scots had become what was called the 'low' language and metropolitan English was now the medium of law, administration, education and religion. From the eighteenth century onwards, the gentry of Scotland increasingly tended to receive an English education. So in Mr Sheridan's 'polite' and Adam Smith's influential circles, English was the standard: no variety of Scots was codified. It even began to be disparaged and by its own people: books proliferated listing Scotticisms to be avoided in polite society. The Scots were assailed and harangued but in one sense of the phrase, they asked for it. And they made English work for them by turning out some of the finest philosophical prose in the language.

But the tutoring must have been hard to bear. To take just one example: 'Mistakes in quantity are not uncommon, and indeed a very principal error in the pronunciation of our northern neighbours is that of lengthening the vowels which we pronunce short, and of shortening those which we make long: thus for "head" they say in Scotland "heed", for "take", "tak" etc.' Mistakes! Errors! Too long here, too short there! And if they worked hard they could get a pat on the head (or heed) from Dr Johnson as he encountered Lowland Scots on his way to the Highlands and Islands. 'The conversation of the Scots grows every day less unpleasing to the English,' he wrote, 'their peculiarities wear fast away; their dialect is likely to become in half a century provincial and rustick, even to themselves. The great, the learned, the ambitious and the vain, all cultivate the English phrase, and the English pronunciation.'

Johnson was right and wrong. The Gaelic language spoken in the far north of Scotland and out on the islands is still spoken today but more pertinently, after the Battle of Culloden of 1746 which marked the end of the attempt of the Stuarts to take the English crown. Gaelic still showed its resilience through the Ossian Poems. These may have been a perverse way of demonstrating energy, and most likely a fraud, but they are evidence of the spell the old ignored tongue could still cast on the new proper world.

In 1760, Macpherson published *Fragments of Ancient Poetry*, a translation, he claimed, of a great Celtic epic created in the third century by the blind bard Ossian. Ossian's admirers included Burns, Scott, Wordsworth, Yeats, Beethoven, Ingres and Napoleon, who is said to have carried the epic into battle. But doubt set in when Dr Johnson denounced the work as a forgery. Despite some recent evidence in its favour, Macpherson is still perceived as a great Scottish cultural con artist. Yet the fact that there was a public, and such a distinguished public, ready to rally to the Gaelic (even in translation, even in a forged translation) demonstrates something of its continuing capacity to command attention.

And Dr Johnson was at most only half right when he predicted of the Lowland tongue that in half a century it would become 'provincial and rustick, even to themselves'. Robert Burns was born in 1759, and his work refuted Dr Johnson. His songs may go on to undermine Johnson's opinion further, given the successful reaching back to its roots to which Scots has recently directed itself in poetry, fiction, drama and song over the past two generations.

Robert Burns, eldest son of seven children to a poor tenant farmer, who somehow managed to find the means to educate the boy, became a Romantic poet whose life was the essence of Romance and Romantic poetry. He was a 'child of Nature', working as a ploughboy until he was fifteen or sixteen. He wrote poetry to find 'some kind of counterpoise' to his circumstances. He loved women to excess and fathered several illegitimate children, including twins to Jean Armour whom he married. He loved Scots. He loved Scotch. His first collection, *Poems – chiefly in the Scottish dialect*, received much critical acclaim and in Edinburgh he was feted, patronised and ruined perhaps, as 'The Ploughman Poet'. He died aged thirty-seven, but his legacy is vast: four hundred songs, some of which are recognised as masterpieces, 'The Lea Rig', 'Tam o' Shanter' and 'A Red, Red Rose'. Ten thousand came to pay their respects at his funeral and that was only the beginning of a reputation which is kept alive wherever Scots with even a smattering of literature meet to talk of Scotland, drink whisky and toast the ladies and the haggis:

> Fair fa' your honest, sonsie face,
> Great chieftain o' the puddin' race!
> Aboon them a' ye tak yer place
> Painch, tripe or thairm:
> Weel are ye wordy o' a grace
> As lang's my arm.

Not only the Scots read him, so did the English, he had readers everywhere. He is not all that difficult to understand. He'll often throw in an English word to help us out, especially in his word clusters 'kiaugh and care' (the same), 'furms an' benches' (the same), 'decent, honest, fawsont' (fawsont means decent). But at a time when Dr Johnson and his heirs appeared to be tramping Scots underfoot, this man from the land itself restored Auld Scotland's grandeur, gave it an inextinguishable heart of genius which resurrected pride and assured it a posterity.

English is there in Burns' work but there is no denying that because it was shot through with Scots, the work did not receive, in the mainstream of English literature, the appreciation its quality deserved. Burns' fidelity to one of the suppressed languages of Britain to some degree cut him off. For generations, Scots suffered the disregard of non-Standard English: only recently has it risen again to claim a place as it were at the high table. For years, Burns' language became such a powerful touchstone for national identity that it was subsumed in politics. In this it was enacting a part often played by language. It can be language alone that holds a nation together, as it did for the English when Norman French threatened to overwhelm it.

A few miles south-west of Burns' country was the Lake District which had nursed and nourished another poet who sought out the common experience and ordinary language for his subject-matter, William Wordsworth.

Wordsworth's contribution to English poetry has been widely recognised. Ted Hughes said that 'looking back he is the first eminence we see'. In ascending order, he said, we 'see' Wordsworth, Milton, Shakespeare. One of Wordsworth's contributions to the adventure of English is that, in the preface to his *Lyrical Ballads* in 1798, he stressed that poetry could be written in 'the language really used by men' and did not need a special poetic diction or an elaborate vocabulary or any other 'fine clothes' to express deep feelings. He also chose to write about the rural life which had surrounded his childhood, a childhood passed, geographically, not very far from that of Burns. But it was in a different world. Unlike Burns, Wordsworth went to an excellent grammar school and boarded; from there he went to Cambridge, took a walking tour in France and Switzerland, enjoyed advantages available to very few. Perhaps even more remarkable, then, that reimmersing himself in the daily life in the Lake District, he should find his main subject-matter in 'low and rustic life'. He explained why: 'because in that condition the essential passions of the heart find a better soil in which they can attain their maturity, are less under restraint, and speak a plainer, more explicit language; because in that condition of life our elementary feelings exist in a state of greater simplicity, and, consequently, may be more accurately contemplated.'

He went even further: 'The language, too, of these men is adopted (purified indeed from what appear to be its real defects, from all lasting and rational causes of dislike or disgust) because such men hourly communicate with the best objects from which the best part of language is originally derived.' There is an entire philosophy there, fuelled by Wordsworth's passion for the first phase of the French Revolution in which he had been caught up.

> Bliss was it in that dawn to be alive
> But to be young was very heaven!

Given that Dr Johnson had criticised Shakespeare for using 'knife' in *Macbeth* – 'a tradesman's word,' he called it, 'an instrument used by butchers and cooks' – Wordsworth's determination to use plain words to convey the weight of powerful feelings was a bold and crucial step. He not only set this out as a manifesto, he followed his own commandment in poems which are now rooted into English literature. He was aware how much he was taking on. 'Readers accustomed to the gaudiness and inane phraseology of many modern writers,' he wrote, 'if they persist in reading this book [the *Lyrical Ballads* of 1798] to its conclusion, will perhaps frequently have to struggle with feelings of strangeness and awkwardness: they will look around for poetry.' He was reviled at first, and for many years, for daring to bring poetry from the voice of the people. In a way he gave it back to its bedrock of Old English.

A few years before, in 1790, Thomas Paine had written *The Rights of Man* in a plain style to demonstrate that 'such a style did not preclude precision of thought and expression'. That a political work of great influence on political thought and a young poet who was to exercise even greater influence on poetic practice, should agree in this way opened up what has become a major thoroughfare for English. A case was now made for the effectiveness, the poetry, the depth of meaning and feeling which could be mined from 'plain English'. It is possible to imagine a world without the influence of Paine, Wordsworth and their followers and one of its aspects would be that a language separate from ordinary English was the only language in which high thinking and profound feeling could be expressed. Wordsworth, I believe, kept English true to its original and tested self. He saved, celebrated and gave lasting literary energy to the ancient language of ordinary speech.

Meanwhile in polite society the way you spoke became one of the subjects of polite society itself. Polite society was organised around a way of talking. If you could not talk that talk you risked ridicule. Richard Brinsley Sheridan, son of Thomas the Elocutionist, led the charge with the invention of Mrs Malaprop.

Her name comes from French 'Mal à propos', meaning inappropriate. Her grave fault was the tendency to substitute a similar-sounding word for the word that she intended to use. 'Make no delusions to the past,' she said, in *The Rivals* (1775), and 'I have interceded another letter from the fellow.' 'She's as headstrong as an allegory on the banks of the Nile,' she said, and, 'If I reprehend anything in this world, it is the use of my oracular tongue, and a nice derangement of epitaphs.' The noun 'malapropism' was first recorded in 1830. Bottom, in *A Midsummer Night's Dream*, often used the wrong word: 'Thisbe, the flowers of odious savours sweet' and he would be laughed at by the Globe audience, but he was a 'rude mechanical' and the laughter came with the territory. Mrs Malaprop was supposed to be a cultivated lady from the aspiring middle classes and even in a world where another character in *The Rivals*, Sir Anthony Absolute, could exclaim, 'Had I a thousand daughters, by Heaven! I'd as soon have them taught the black art as their alphabet,' she ought to have known better. The accent, the use of correct words, correct grammar, everything to do with language was falling into the hands of Those Who Knew Best. Even when done for satire, as in *The Rivals*, or for polite enlightenment, as in Fielding's essay on conversation, in which he gives guidance such as not hogging the conversation or introducing topics not understood by everyone present, with Wordsworth equally with Dr Johnson, the literary men of England were going to tell you how best to use and speak your language and laugh at you, snub you, doubt you or even cut you if you did not follow their own particular and supreme rules.

Out of all this came a literary woman, and a novelist (novels were originally seen as way below the salt, even contemptible, suitable only for women) whose prose was to clarify the England of that Enlightenment/Romantic era to a crystalline standard never achieved before and rarely since. Jane Austen, without a single mission statement, came to rule English. Her gifts for description, for conversation, narrative, the sound of her words on the inner ear, to all these gifts English gave of its best and the Jane Austen style was and is a new highroad opened up in this journey.

Novel reading was taking off in the late eighteenth and nineteenth centuries with the private circulating library which put expensive books into people's hands for a small hire charge. As the nineteenth century rolled on, literacy grew, education spread, books became cheaper, novels increasingly popular and the novel itself, as emphasised severely by Jane Austen herself, came to be seen as a form in which wit, brilliance, depth and variety could find expression every bit as impressive as could be found in the more established forms of poetry and drama. The novel became the benchmark for good English. Dr Johnson would never have believed it. It was 'only a novel!'.

That disparaging phrase comes from *Northanger Abbey*. It is early in the book, when Catherine and Isabella have become close friends, doing everything together, meeting even

in defiance of wet and dirt, and shut themselves up, to read novels together. Yes, novels; – for I will not adopt that ungenerous and impolitic custom, so common with novel writers, of degrading by their contemptuous censure the very performances, to the number of which they are themselves adding – joining with their greatest enemies in bestowing the harshest epithets on such works, and scarcely ever permitting them to be read by their heroine, who, if she accidentally take up a novel, is sure to turn over its insipid pages with disgust. Alas! if the heroine of one novel be not patronized by the heroine of another, from whom can she expect protection and regard? I cannot approve of it . . . And while the abilities of the nine-hundredth abridger of the History of England, or of the man who collects and publishes in a volume some dozen lines of Milton, Pope, and Prior, with a paper from the Spectator, and a chapter from Sterne, are eulogized by a thousand pens, – there seems almost a general wish of decrying the capacity and undervaluing the labour of the novelist, and of slighting the performances which have only genius, wit, and taste to recommend them. 'I am no novel reader – I seldom look into novels – Do not imagine that *I* often read novels – It is really very well for a novel.' – Such is the common cant. – 'And what are you reading, Miss—' 'Oh! it is only a novel!' replies the young lady; while she lays down her book with affected indifference, or momentary shame. 'It is only Cecilia, or Camilla, or Belinda'; or, in short, only some work in which the greatest powers of the mind are displayed, in which the most thorough knowledge of human nature, the happiest delineation of its varieties, the liveliest effusions of wit and humour are conveyed to the world in the best chosen language.

Just as poetry in the Elizabethan Age had been enlisted to fructify the language, novels now took on that purpose. As the written word grew increasingly important, it is not impossible, I think, that the most devoted novel readers, women, who would also be those most likely to teach English to the young, would find in works by Jane Austen, the ideal and the model. An unofficial academy of language was developed through the novel, I believe, which had an effect on styles and speech and writing as great if not greater than that of Swift or Johnson or Sheridan.

But even Jane Austen has her limitations. The language of the streets is kept firmly outside the Austen door; the language of bodily parts was not allowed in the Austen parks; in her own way, Jane Austen was every bit as masterful and controlling as the men whom time has seen her surpass. Her own proper and correct use of English has permeated the minds and sensibilities of hundreds of thousands of her readers, a number of whom carried into their own novels the unspoken but clear and rigid rules of what did and did not do in expression as in behaviour. Swear words would never do. No one is called a son of a bitch; no one is told to bugger off.

In *Tristram Shandy* there is a passage which describes how two nuns, believing that the only way to shift an obstinate mule was to say 'bugger', are hampered by the knowledge that to utter such a word was most sinful. They split it up between them. Neither syllable on its own could possibly be sinful, so one shouts 'bou, bou, bou' and the other 'ger, ger, ger'. In another passage, Sterne goes into great comic detail about the right swear word for the right occasion. 'I have the greatest veneration in the world for that gentleman, who . . . sat down and composed . . . fit forms of swearing suitable to all cases, from the lowest to the highest provocations which could possibly happen to him . . . he kept them ever by him on the chimney piece, within his reach, ready for use.'

Johnson had omitted 'shit' from his dictionary. By the nineteenth century, in polite print in England, this delicacy of feeling or squeamishness had grown stronger and English was being whipped into line. Chaucer, who had used an immense number and range of swear words, would I think have been puzzled at what had happened to that vigorously rude English element in his repertoire. Morality censored language.

The result was that coarse language withdrew from public view. It went underground or into the work of outraged and outrageous writers, from Rochester to D.H. Lawrence. Swift proposed a way for the country to get rich – set up a Swearers' bank which received the one shilling fines which could be exacted by Act of Parliament for swearing.

'Blank' became the 'expletive deleted', as in a sentence quoted in 1854: 'I wouldn't give a blank for such a blank blank.' Mrs Beeton could not bring herself to write the word 'trousers' and so when she writes about how a valet should dress his master she omits the word, and the item, altogether. The dread word was replaced by the 'unmentionables' or 'the indescribables', 'the inexplicables' or the 'inexpressibles'. 'Leg' got away with being 'limb'. But Mrs Beeton's chaps' lower limbs were trouserless.

It was all part of putting English in its place. It was treated by the self-appointed censors as if it were an unruly mob, a subversive faction, a party of revolution. There is something comical in this, but it is also a testament to the power of language. By chopping out words, by executing phrases and assassinating expressions, those who would order society thought they could gain total control. They were a self-appointed word-police. But English was far too dangerous and wild for this new pruned and prudish England. Even Shakespeare was not immune. Indeed, Shakespeare became the prime target of the Bowdlers, named after Thomas Bowdler, whose Family Edition of Shakespeare in 1818 set out to save Shakespeare from himself and make him fit and proper for the nation's Christian families.

Bowdler wrote that the plays were 'stained with words and expressions of so indecent a nature that no parent would chuse to submit them in uncorrected form to the eye or ear of a daughter'. *Othello* was a prime target. So in Bowdler, Iago no longer tells Brabantio, 'Your daughter and the Moor are making the beast with the two backs,' but rather, 'Your daughter and the Moor are now together.' In Shakespeare, Othello worries that Desdemona's 'body and beauty' will distract him from his purpose: Bowdler cuts 'body'. 'Top', as in

'Cassio did top her', was deleted as was 'tup', as in 'an old black Ram is tupping your white Ewe', as was 'naked' – 'naked with her friend in bed'. Shakespeare's 'bawdy wind that kisses all it meets' becomes 'very wind'. 'Cuckold' went, as did 'strumpet' and 'whore'. A generation before Bowdler, an edition brought out by Francis Gentleman had savaged the play, cutting a hundred and seventy-four lines from one scene alone – that in which Othello has an epileptic seizure and falls into a trance. Once censorship began, where and why should it end? Those hundred and seventy-four lines were considered, by Gentleman, to spoil the 'tragic effect'. Dickens' Circumlocution Office in *Little Dorrit* vividly illustrates the trend.

Wherever you land after Swift's failed academy, Johnson's cornerstone *Dictionary* and Sheridan's class-distinguishing elocution, the English are having a high old time tormenting the language into shapes and sounds which reflect strait-laced manners, class prejudice and competing moralities. English was subdued, shorn, trimmed, scrubbed, disciplined and often regarded with distaste. It made no difference in the longer run. It had its own life and, when one door closed, it opened a dozen others. But it was painful for some at the time.

Provincial accents and dialect words became further stigmatised. A gentleman was known as much by his correct pronunciation as by his wealth or breeding. English became a tool for snobs, and a useful ally for hierarchs. These distinctions have entered into the core culture of English and are part of our life today: battles are still fought over the pronunciation of 'controversy'. Grammarians still track public utterances and pounce with glee on 'mistakes'. Correcting English is one of our great indoor sports. And in one way it is all to the good. It shows how much we care about the language; it shows how highly it is regarded; the unnamed army of guardians out there know, rightly, that what we have is of truly incalculable value and they want to keep it in good shape.

Just as English has a remarkable capacity to unite, so it seems to possess infinite powers of division. Countries, regions, cities, towns, even villages had and to an admirable and bewildering extent often still have a hold on ways of speaking you would have thought that the twentieth-century motorways of conformity had bypassed and starved of life. Added to these, though, after the masters and mistresses of the language had their say were accents limited solely to certain groups of families, packs within communities, clubs, even cabals. A single house in one influential public school could have its own recognisable, exclusive way of talking. As could a pit village in Durham. We are, each one of us, all talking advertisements for our history. Accent is the snake and the ladder in the upstairs downstairs of social ambition. Accent is the con man's first resource.

Although the variety is neither as influential, as cruel or as crucial as it was, in my experience, say fifty years ago, it remains and often it matters.

In the nineteenth century, it mattered in ways which seem extreme but which we can still recognise. The example of John Keats is one, as Lynda Mugglestone has pointed out. According to proper rules of communication, it was decreed that the 'r' should be sounded. Many people didn't, then as now, so 'lord' became 'laud'. These were often known as 'cockney rhymes'. Thomas Hood wrote to Keats urging him to be careful of this common habit, to make certain that his rhymes would 'chime to an educated ear . . .' He wrote that 'such atrocities as "morn and dawn" . . . "fought and sort", are fatal to the success of verse.'

Keats was ridiculed for rhymes like 'fauns and thorns', 'thoughts and sorts'. In 1818, John Lockhart in *Blackwood's Edinburgh Magazine* used the notion of 'literate speech' to censure Keats as 'an uneducated and flimsy stripling . . . without logic enough to analyse a single idea, or imagination enough to form one original image' and, most damning of all, without 'learning enough to distinguish between the written language of Englishmen and the spoken jargon of Cockneys'. Gerard Manley Hopkins was still criticising Keats for the same thing in 1880, again as those 'r's which, when not recognised, made his rhymes 'most offensive, not indeed to the ear, but to the mind'.

Finally we have *Pygmalion* just before the outbreak of World War One in which George Bernard Shaw attempts to demonstrate that the character and social position of an illiterate flower seller from Covent Garden can be transformed utterly into that of a society lady simply by cutting the Cockney out of her and implanting 'proper' pronunciation. She can say (in the musical version, *My Fair Lady*) 'hurricanes hardly ever happen' correctly and so pass off to the manner born. What is a comedy is very close to reality. Correct and proper speech became the mark: manners maketh man, they said; well, mouthings made them according to the gospel of Shaw's Professor Henry Higgins. The only word which 'gave her away' was the swear word, unfortunately dropped: 'bloody' as in 'not bloody likely'. The word, used on stage, caused a national sensation which totally eclipsed Shaw's messages about class and language.

In 1914, the *Daily Express* talked to a London flower girl after the opening night of the play. She said that no proper Cockney flower girl would ever say 'bloody'.

18

Steam, Streets and Slang

O f the many revolutions in the eighteenth and nineteenth centuries, the British Industrial Revolution had the greatest influence of all. It changed history utterly. It harnessed and mechanised nature, summoned up an army of inventors whose effect and whose imagination outsoared the makers of the Italian Renaissance and it has both liberated and disciplined millions of men, women and children everywhere. Cities and industries took over from rural dwellings and the countryside: the majority of the population of the world finally began to leave the land after one hundred to one hundred and fifty thousand years of cleaving to it. What would once have been thought of as magic – machines which raced on iron tracks, sound travelling through the air, bulbs which shone brightly all night – and what would have been considered the privilege and preserve of the wealthy – warmth, choice of clothes, travel – became commonplace in fully industrialised countries and available to vast numbers. The Industrial Revolution both exploited and educated the working masses; it changed the possibilities of life. And English met and responded to a challenge which was to make it the global language of economic progress.

In 1756, Professor John Robison went to see James Watt, the inventor of the steam engine, the man whose name marks the language as the unit of power. Robison was anxious to winkle out the latest news from the celebrated engineer and Watt was anxious not to be drawn. In a letter after the meeting, Robison describes the encounter ruefully, but in the course of that letter, the following words are recorded, some new, some revitalised for industry: 'condenser' (new), 'vacuum', 'cylinder', 'apparatus', 'pump', 'condensation', 'air-pump', 'steam-vessel' (new), 'reservoir' (new), 'eduction pipe' (new), 'suck-pipe' (new), and 'siphon'.

Just over half a century later, in 1851, at the Great Exhibition, the English language showed the world what it had made of the machine age. A new vocabulary was on display. The 'trade terms' denigrated by Johnson and outside the ken of his contemporaries, now powered the language as emphatically, I would say, as Tyndale's Bible. The latter had put the Old Faith into English; the former put English at the service of the new and revolutionary Works. The inventors had a wonderful time; they smuggled in familiar terms, they went back when they could to analogies from one of the most formative springs of language for early modern industry – clock making – they looked into the ancient world, the classical world. What they had discovered was a new continent which needed names, directions, signposts, markers, specific locations everywhere, and the language rose to it. The term 'world's fair' entered into the language.

New words had already begun to establish themselves before the cataloguing of 1851. There was 'spinning-jenny', 'donkey engine' (leading to donkey jacket, because donkey engines were usually on board ship and very cold to work) and 'locomotive' (reaching back to Aristotle). Men who had worked as clockmakers were the first to work on Hargreaves' spinning-jennies and they brought their language with them – 'the wheels' they used were referred to as such with 'teeth', 'pinions', 'leaves', 'pivots' – all from horology. The agricultural labourers who came to the mills also brought their own terms, usually based on the shape of things – 'beetles' for hammering, 'rams' for extra heavy hammering. 'Pig-iron' came from the shape made by the casting of molten iron into little blocks which reminded the agricultural men of a sow being suckled by piglets. 'Horsepower' had to be invented as an aid to those who wanted to buy a steam engine and needed to know how many horses it would replace.

These are some of the words from the catalogue of the Great Exhibition, making their first appearance here. Some are plain English, others are coinages from other languages: 'self-acting mills'; 'doubling machines'; 'power looms'; 'electro-plating'; 'centrifugal pump'; 'cylindrical steampress'; 'hair-trigger'; 'high-pressure oscillating steam-engine'; 'lithograph'; 'lorry'; 'anhydrohepseterion' (a machine for stewing potatoes in their own juice).

It is difficult now to realise the excitement and pride in British engineering which the Great Exhibition brought to the country. An extract from the journal of Queen Victoria after her visit gives us a taste of it:

Went to the machinery part, where we remained two hours, and which is excessively interesting and instructive ... What used to be done by hand and used to take months doing is now accomplished in a few instants by the most beautiful machinery. We saw first the cotton machines from Oldham ... Mr Whitworth's planning of iron tools, another for shearing and punching iron of just ½ inch thick, doing it as if it were bread! ... What was particularly interesting was a printing machine on the vertical principle, by which numbers of sheets are printed, dried and everything done in a second ... We saw hydraulic machines, pumps, filtering machines of all kinds, machines for purifying sugar – in fact every conceivable invention ...

Queen Victoria's journal goes on and provides an excellent and enthusiastic review of the exhibition from a surprisingly diligent and, I think, typically amazed visitor.

The scientific and technical vocabularies grew enormously. By the end of the seventeenth century a great number of words had been introduced for basic anatomy and mathematics. From the beginning of the nineteenth century there was a surge in chemistry, physics and biology. 'Biology' itself came in in 1819, 'petrology' (1811), 'morphology' (1828), 'taxonomy' (1828), 'palaeontology' (1838),

'ethnology' (1842), 'gynaecology' (1847), 'histology' (1847), 'carcin-
ology' (1852). In chemistry, 'tellurium' (1800), 'sodium' (1807),
'platinum' (1812), 'silicon' (1817), 'caffeine' (1830), 'chloroform'
(1838), 'cocaine' (1874). In physics, 'sonometer' (1808), 'centigrade'
(1812), 'altimeter' (1847), 'voltmeter' (1882), 'watt' (1882), 'electron'
(1891). In biology, 'chlorophyll' (1810), 'bacterium' (1847), 'sperma-
tozoid' (1857), 'symbiosis' (1877), 'chromosome' (1890), 'photosyn-
thesis' (1898). In geology, 'jurassic' (1831), 'cretaceous' (1832),
'bauxite' (1861). In medicine, 'gastritis' (1806), 'laryngitis' (1822),
'kleptomania' (1830), 'haemophilia' (1854), 'diphtheria' (1857), 'claus-
trophobia' (1879) – a term which might be transferred to the sensation in the mind caused by being so crowded in by lists of words.

English went back to Latin and Greek in many of its descriptions
of the new, often via the French: 'oxygen', 'protein', 'nuclear' and
'vaccine' did not exist in the classical languages but their roots are
there. Some did come straight from Latin, in the nineteenth century,
like 'cognomen', 'opus', 'ego', 'sanatorium', 'aquarium', 'referendum'
and 'myth'; or from Greek, such as 'pylon'. It was considered good
practice to use parts of the classical languages: for example, anthropo-,
or bio-, neo-, poly-, tele- as prefixes; or, as suffixes, -glot, -gram, -logy,
-morphy. A great number of words found a use for the ending -ize.

Part of the fun of invention was to find the name. It is interesting
how very few times a proper name was used – compared with, say,
the British frontiersmen in the American west who freckled the
landscape with names from wives, pals, relations, and names from
the old country. Scientists either through diffidence or wishing to
claim a distinction for their discipline which matched anything in
antiquity, tended to root around in the past. So when John Arnold
made his Chronometer Number Thirty-Six (as blank a title as anything in Bach), it would once have been called a 'timekeeper'. But
together with the Hydrographer of the Navy, Alexander Dalrymple,
he reinvented 'chronometer' (dormant for about a hundred and fifty
years) from 'chronos', meaning time, and 'metron', a measure.

It has been estimated that between 1750 and 1900 half the world's published papers on mechanical, industrial and scientific advances were written and distributed in English. When James Watt needed to pursue his work in mathematics he had to learn and read French and Italian. Now English was the key tongue. Steam technology had revolutionised printing and so information could spread faster and further – telegraphy and telephony – than ever before. Moreover, the language became a magnet for European scientists who came west, to Britain, to pursue their work: the language delivered, among others, Marconi from Italy, Siemens from Prussia and Marc Isambard Brunel, father of Isambard Kingdom Brunel, from France. In the first part of the nineteenth century these small islands had become the world's leading trading and industrial nation, 'the workshop of the world', and the language, built over centuries, supple in all the arts of absorbing, stealing, inventing and restructuring, had matched the economic explosion. The expanded English language, a product of the Industrial Revolution, became an engine which drove it forward.

One aspect of English which has been a recurring feature in its history is the way a word will be adapted from one age to another so that a 'chip' can go from wood to silicon, include golf and a slight and feature as fifty per cent of a British diet. In this boom time for words, the old were often and again recalled to do duty as the new. English had no pride in this. When stuck, it just grabbed what was handiest and let posterity sort out any resulting confusions. 'Coach' is one of the simpler ones. It was part of a horse-drawn carriage in the sixteenth century, became part of a steam-drawn vehicle in the nineteenth century, a bus in the twentieth century, a description of your status on an aeroplane, besides, of course, being the name of a person who tells more talented people what to do, especially at sport. It seems to bear these meanings without showing too much strain.

A word can be a history. 'Industry' has been part of recorded English since 1566. 'Industrious', meaning either skilful or assiduous, was also there in the sixteenth century, as was 'industrial', which meant the distinction between cultivated and natural fruits. It was not until the late seventeenth and eighteenth centuries that 'industry' began to assume a modern meaning. In 1696, there was mention of a 'College of Industry for all Useful Trades and Husbandry'. But the most widespread eighteenth-century use was in 'House of Industry', which meant the workhouse where forced application and useful work came together. Adam Smith wrote of 'funds destined for the maintenance of industry' in 1776 and by the mid nineteenth century this use was common. Disraeli spoke of 'our national industries' (1844); Carlyle talked of 'Leaders of Industry' (1843). There were other developments from the root of the word. In the 1830s, Carlyle introduced 'Industrialism' to indicate a new order of society; John Stuart Mill used 'Industrial Revolution' in 1848. The word 'industry' grew as industry itself flourished.

'Class' is another word whose passage is worth tracking into the Industrial Revolution and from there into the late nineteenth and twentieth centuries where it saturated the pages of so much that was written about society. The different point here is that it did not change its meaning all that much despite great changes around it.

It derives from 'classis', Latin, a division according to property of the people of Rome. Then it became a term used in Church organisation, which was extended to describe other divisions or groups. In the seventeenth century in England 'class' acquired a special link with education, from 'classroom' to 'Second Class Honours'. Defoe, in 1705, seems the harbinger of what was to become something of an English (more than a British) obsession, when he writes: ''tis plain the dearness of wages forces our people into more classes than other nations can show.' Today we nod at Defoe but in fact he was before his time. Until well into the eighteenth century, still in the nineteenth and even in some manner in the twentieth century, the most common words were 'rank' and 'order'; 'estate' and 'degree' were more common than 'class'. All those terms related to birth.

What we see as 'class' relates to a group within society. It is a regression to the Latin to describe the way in which society now chose to describe itself. Placing by birth diminished in importance. Although it has not yet disappeared it is twilight to the noon blaze of Chaucer, Shakespeare and Dr Johnson's day. There is a different sense of society, which the Industrial Revolution midwifed.

Like many words describing the complications of society itself, class as we know or knew it took its time to establish itself. 'The Lower Classes' was used in 1772; 'lowest classes' and 'lowest class' were 'common' from the 1790s. 'Middle class' was recorded in 1756 and by the 1840s it was as widely used a term as 'lower classes'. From the mid nineteenth century it was full industrial steam ahead to 'lower middle class', 'upper middle class', 'lower working class', 'upper working class', 'skilled working class', 'upper class', 'middle middle class', and those who would be unclassifiable, royalty, the aristocracy and the company of artists, vagabonds, thinkers and Celts who often escaped the bondage of these scalpelled classifications. Today 'class' is losing its old certainty and its old sting.

Awareness of class brought accent and pronunciation on to the stage more acutely than ever before. Cockney is a useful example here, partly because by the end of the eighteenth century London was the biggest metropolis in England. Its population was to become four and a half million by the end of the nineteenth century. (In Elizabeth I's reign, the population of the entire country was less than that.) Also rates of literacy were higher in London than anywhere else: seventy per cent of servants could sign their name by 1700; ninety-eight per cent of all books printed in English were printed in London; over half the booksellers were established there. And the Cockney dialect has a fascinating history and in Charles Dickens a genius to give it lasting literary life.

It was, of course, despised by those who wanted to order English into line. In the eighteenth century it was totally discredited, thought of as the language of crime, poverty and ignorance, useful only as comic relief in the less distinguished dramas on the London stage.

In 1791, John Walker, in his *Critical Pronouncing Dictionary of the English Language*, pronounced on it very critically indeed. 'Most [barbarous],' he wrote, 'is the cockney speech of London.' He is very put out that the Cockneys have not learned from their betters in

London; indeed they have made so little of this privileged proximity that their regional tongue is 'a thousand times more offensive and disgusting' than differences in Cornwall, Lancashire and Yorkshire.

In *Piers Plowman* (1362) 'cockeneys' means eggs, small and misshapen as if laid by a cock. In Chaucer, 'cockney' is a mother's darling. By the early sixteenth century it meant people brought up in cities and ignorant of 'real life'. By the early seventeenth century, this low value applied to only one region, 'the Cockney of London' (1611) or the 'Bow Bell Cockney' (1600) – noting that the true Cockney was one born within the sound of the Great Bell of Bow in the City of London. 'Cockneys' soon became Bow Bell Cockneys with, it was said, no interest in anything not on their own patch of ground.

John Walker made them a target. He stated, with contempt, that Cockneys, 'the lowest only', pronounced words like 'fists' and 'posts' in two syllables – 'fistiz' and 'postiz'. The 'v' did the service of the 'w' and vice versa: 'wine' and 'veal' became 'vine' and 'weal'. The 'h' was a culprit once again: no pronounced 'h' in 'while' meant it was indistinguishable from 'wile'; and sinking the 'h' was endemic – ''art' for 'heart', ''arm' for 'harm'. 'F' replaces 'th' as in 'firty' (for 'thirty'), and 'fahsn' (for 'thousand'); and it's 'bovver' not 'bother', 'muvver' not 'mother'. The charges pile up: 'yewmour' for 'humour', 'tewwim' for 'tell him'. The grave crime of the double negative appears ineradicable. 'There ain't nuffink te see.' Question tags litter the sentences: 'That arright then?' 'Ain't it?' which eventually becomes 'Innit?'.

Some writers seized on this with the enthusiasm of Mark Twain across the water. Henry Mayhew, for instance, in his *London Labour and the London Poor* interviewed many of Walker's criminally tongued Cockneys and came out with phrases we now look on with nothing but perplexed pleasure. A tailor, for instance, who issues bills, tells him:

Mr— nabs the chance of putting his customers awake, that he has just made his escape from Russia, not forgetting to clap his mawleys upon some of the right sort of Ducks to make single and double backed slops for gentlemen in black, when on his return home he was stunned to find one of the top manufacturers of Manchester had cut his lucky and stepped off to the Swan Stream, leaving behind him a valuable stock of Moleskins, Cords, Velveteens, Plushes, Swandown &c, and I having some ready in my kick, grabbed the chance, and stepped home with my swag and am now safe landed at my crib.

Mayhew is full of such meat. It is fortunate for us that London as well as claiming one of the greatest social historians in the mid nineteenth century also claimed one of our finest writers – many think our greatest novelist. Charles Dickens was not the first to use speech as a sign of class but he did it so memorably! His genius in this area was to turn John Walker's discredited slum talk into literature. He could and did indicate illiteracy but did not withhold the generosity of his respect for and attention to his characters and their way of talking. An epigraph for Dickens' use of 'lower class' especially London and Cockney speech can be found in *Our Mutual Friend*:

The visitors glanced at the long boy, who seemed to indicate by a broader stare of his mouth and eyes that in him Sloppy stood confessed.

'For I ain't, you must know,' said Betty, 'much of a hand at reading writing-hand, though I can read my Bible and most print. And I do love a newspaper. You mightn't think it, but Sloppy is a beautiful reader of a newspaper. He do the Police in different voices.'.

That last sentence could stand as Dickens' credo. His phenomenal success – the penny edition of *Oliver Twist* sold 150,000 in three weeks – was helped by his experience as a journalist. He observed the London scene and perhaps his shorthand helped him catch its phrases. His mimicking skill honed in amateur dramatics meant that direct speech often carried characterisation and he loved the language of 'the lowest classes'. He loved the speed and accuracy with which it 'placed' people.

In *David Copperfield*, for instance, the linguistic scholar Lynda

Mugglestone, who is a virtuoso on 'h', points out that Clara Peggotty's accent is conveyed by her dropping the letter 'h': this places her immediately as somebody inferior. '"There's the sea; and the boats and ships; and the fishermen; and Am to play with" – Peggotty meant her nephew Ham – but she spoke of him as a morsel of English grammar.'

'H' dropping, according to Alexander Ellis in 1869, was 'social suicide'. Yet Lynda Mugglestone picks out the most famous 'h' dropper in all literature – Uriah Heep – and here Dickens uses the grammatical 'error' as a way to alert us to the uncomfortable, hypocritical nature of the man. '"I am well aware that I am the 'umblest person going," said Uriah Heep modestly, ". . . and my mother is likewise a very 'umble person. We live in a numble abode, Master Copperfield, but have much to be thankful for. My father's former calling was 'umble."'

Interestingly, again spotted by Lynda Mugglestone, when Heep reveals himself in his true arrogance, the 'h', the mark of superior class, the proof of social standing and authority, makes a miraculous recovery: 'You had better not join that gang,' he says. 'I have got some of you under the harrow.'

A lingering myth of English is that the rural poor and the largely rural aristocracy were brothers and sisters under the skin and one piece of evidence is that the aristocrats drop the 'g', as in 'huntin', shootin' and fishin'' as does, say, Mr Peggotty in *David Copperfield*: 'You're a-wonderin' what that's fur, sir . . . when I'm here at the hour as she's a comin' home, I puts the light in the winder.' What is overlooked in this cosy comparison is that the duke would recognise Peggotty's origins instantly and vice versa: accent would outclout the dropped 'g'.

Dickens is excellent on phonetic spelling to give a clear indication of speech and so character. Mrs Gamp says 'minnit' not 'minute', 'pizon' for 'poison': while Mrs Crupp has 'spazzums' not 'spasms'. Sam Weller earned immortality with his 'v's and his 'w's. 'And that was a wery partickler and uncommon circumstance vith me in those days.' But Dickens can be deliberately blind also when a potential genteel hero or heroine becomes involved: Kate Nickleby, a milliner, says 'correctly' 'oblige'; Mr Peggotty used the old and by that time vulgar form 'obleege'. But Kate is a gentleman's daughter and similarly Oliver Twist, though reared in a workhouse, also speaks like the son of a lady, which it transpires he is. Sentiment can outgun genius in Dickens any time he decides the story needs it; and also, he knew that his middle-class or aspiring middle-class readers still loved a lord and lady more dearly as the centre of the book than your common-or-garden creations however lovingly portrayed. And he likes to confuse us: for despite largely holding to the view that speech portrays character, he will still have those of fine speech behaving badly and those of poor speech behaving nobly.

Dickens' mass of characters in their very number and variety express the massing of industry, population, achievement and invention in the nineteenth century. You can use him as a quarry for the speech of the time: equally he can be used to celebrate the fecundity of fictional invention as much as for his vocabulary. The streets and back yards are represented but so are the aspiring parlours and the would-be great houses. And for my generation and possibly others, Dickens was also known to be a writer who had swallowed a dictionary, your own copy of which had to be within reach on first encountering his 'big words'.

It was also the time when slang refused to retreat any more, especially not in London where there were many varieties, such as cant, flash, gibberish, patter pedlars French, slang lingo and St Giles Greek. There was university slang from Oxford and Cambridge: 'wooden spoon' arrived in the nineteenth century – the large spoon was lowered on to the shoulders of those at the bottom of the honours list as they were receiving their degrees; to 'plough' (fail) a paper, to 'floor' a paper (to answer every question), to 'post' (to reject a candidate), to 'spin' (to summon a candidate).

The Cockney rhyming slang was identified by Henry Mayhew in 1851. 'The new style of cadgers' cant is done all on the rhyming principle.' It became the most relished characteristic of Cockney; its wit and innuendo still give it a life. 'Trouble and strife' – wife; 'apples and pears' – stairs; 'a bull and a cow' – row. And more recently: 'Mars Bar' – scar; 'Tommy Steele' – eel; 'Hong Kong' – pong, and a long tail of ruder rhymes for 'D'Oyley Carte', 'Elephant and Castle', 'Raspberry Tart'; 'Becks and Posh' – nosh. There are what might at a stretch be called classics such as those with which the paragraph began and 'Adam and Eve' – believe; 'Dicky Dirt' – shirt; 'frog and toad' – road; 'tea-leaf' – thief; 'whistle and flute' – suit. On it goes still: 'dog and bone' – phone; 'boat race' – face; 'elephant's trunk' – drunk; 'jam jar' – car.

As the Victorian age hit its stride and fired on all cylinders including the censorious, public language, mainly innuendo and slang, became an enjoyably risky way to tweak noses. Marie Lloyd, racy star of the music hall, whose catchphrase was 'a little of what you fancy does you good', outraged the Watch Committee when she sang 'she sits among the cabbages and peas'. Miss Lloyd changed it to 'she sits among the cabbages and leeks' and there was no problem.

Coded gay content came in. 'Earnest' was slang of the period for 'gay'. *The Importance of Being Earnest*, Oscar Wilde's play, takes on another strand of meaning. There are learned theses about this play which deconstruct it as a perfectly disguised description of the place of homosexuals in Victorian society. Sometimes there seems to be hard proof. Jack and Algernon consume muffins: apparently the brighter portion of the audience would know that 'a muffin' was also a gay man, especially a cute one.

It is tempting to see the nineteenth century as the apotheosis of industrialisation with its multitude of interlocking functions and skills being matched by an increase in classes and in the niceties of a language that had taken yet another great leap forward. Accent and language became a game, sometimes cruel, of fine distinctions which seemed intended to put everyone in his or her place. Like an industrial plant, nothing would be left to chance. George Bernard Shaw put it very clearly in his preface to *Pygmalion*. His Irish prejudice and his satirical scorn only lightly tincture a fair view of the truth of that time.

The English have no respect for their language and will not teach their children to speak it. They cannot spell it because they have nothing to spell it with but an old foreign alphabet of which only the consonants – and not all of them – have any great speech value. Consequently no man can teach himself what it should sound like from reading it; and it is impossible for an Englishman to open his mouth without making some other Englishman despise him.

Professor Higgins saw English as still the captive of its original tribes. 'You can spot an Irishman or a Yorkshireman by his brogue. I can place any man within six miles. I can place him within two miles in London. Sometimes within two streets.'

And yet, floating above it all is a language which is not Standard Pronunciation, nor anything like Ideal Pronunciation, but it is nevertheless, as Shaw implies in a letter, the ruling tongue. 'It is perfectly easy,' he wrote, 'to find a speaker whose speech will be accepted in every part of the English-speaking world as valid 18 carat oral currency . . . if a man pronounces in that way, he will be eligible as far as speech is concerned for the post of Lord Chief Justice, Chancellor of Oxford, Archbishop of Canterbury, Emperor, President or Toast Master at the Mansion House.'

It was that eighteen-carat voice, on the back of unparalleled industrial wealth, which took English yet more intensively over the globe.

19

Indian Takeover

In India, English met a unique challenge. It faced a huge empire, initially far greater than its own, a country of intense and elaborate civilisations and one which boasted about two hundred languages, many of them – Sanskrit, Hindi, Bengali, Gujarati, Marathi, Punjabi, Kashmiri and Urdu for example – long and deeply established. They had no need of another language whether for literature or scholarship and certainly not for conversation, trade, religion and gossip. One of the most astonishing feats in this chapter in the adventure of English is not so much that English, the foreign language, was taken on board as a result of imperial rule but that it outlasted imperial rule, that still today in a country of a thousand million people, about three hundred million have some sort of familiarity with it and forty or fifty million speak and write it (often as a second or third language) to the highest level, as the last two or three generations of prize-winning novels from India attest. Yet it was hated, and resented, and India's greatest politician, Gandhi, believed that it 'enslaved' the people of India.

It is thought that the first English speaker to reach India arrived in 882 from the court of Alfred the Great. The *Anglo-Saxon Chronicle* reports that his emissary went there bearing gifts for the tomb of St Thomas, the apostle who is said to have taken Christianity to India and beyond. The story shows the accessibility of India in days when the sea was the key to trade and the reach of Alfred.

Trade contacts grew in the early Middle Ages bringing to English Asian words, from India, often through Latin and Greek, which absorbed them and passed them on. Pepper, for instance, Greek 'peperi', Latin 'piper', Sanskrit 'pippali'; Sanskrit is the deep background for words such as 'beryl', 'ginger', 'sugar', 'musk', 'sandal', 'camphor' and 'opal'. These were just the beginning of a growing procession of words which travelled back west with merchants and sailors; familiar words, many of which we could swear had 'always' been English. Like 'Blighty', 'bungalow', 'cheroot', 'loot', 'thug', 'pundit', 'calico', 'chintz', 'cot', 'dungarees', 'toddy', 'dekko', 'gymkhana', 'jodhpurs', 'polo', 'bangle', 'jungle', 'cushy', 'khaki', 'swastika', 'pyjamas', 'catamaran'. Whole styles and life and fears for it are encapsulated in that modest selection.

What was to become a close and fierce relationship between the English and India started on the last day of the year 1600: it sounds as if it ought to carry a symbolic punch but perhaps it is merely and by chance an easily remembered date. Queen Elizabeth I granted a charter to a few merchants, giving them a monopoly over the rich spice markets of the East. The richest market of all was in Bantam in Java where pepper, spices, silks and aromatic woods could be bought. The English hoped they could increase their profits by taking not just cash but also Indian fabrics to trade in Bantam. It would be too crude to speak of India as a stopover in these early days but it was at first much more of a launch pad than a target.

The fabrics grew in commercial importance. But the English had to work to gain the trade. They wormed their way in. Those merchant adventurers were met by potentates of a complex oriental society and however glorious their Queen in London and fabled their victory over the massively superior Spanish Armada, however dazzling Shakespeare and powerful the philosophies of law and natural science, in India the English had to learn and obey a rigid power system whose stratifications of status made Elizabethan and Jacobean England look like beginners.

They had to learn to be obsequious. It was the only way to trade.

Their problem can be seen in the titles they met – titles, from some of India's many languages, which included Persian: 'maharajah', 'mandarin', 'nabob', 'subahdar', 'sahib', 'sirdar', 'sheikh', 'sultan', 'caliph', 'pasha', 'imam', 'shah', 'mogul', 'khan', 'rajah', 'emir', 'nizam', 'nawab', 'padishah', 'lama', 'seyyid', 'sultana', 'maharani'. This was a country which knew about hierarchy. The English had to kow-tow; and they did. Far from imposing their glittering language, they had to learn Bengali and Hindi; and they did. Instead of gunpowder and the sword, they used soft words and negotiation. They buttered up the Moghuls in their own Persian tongue. They begged. They persisted. Eventually they were allowed to set up trading posts at Madras, Bombay and in the opulence of Surat. John Ovington, the East India Company chaplain, wrote in delight in 1689:

Surat is renowned for traffic through all Asia, both for rich silks, such as atlases, cuttanees, sorfreys, culgars, allajars, velvets, taffetas and satins; and for zarbafts from Persia; and the abundance of pearls that are brought from the Persian Gulph; but likewise for diamonds, rubies, sapphires, topazes, and other stones of splendour and esteem, which are vendable here in great quantities; and for agates, cornelians, nigganees, desks, scrutores (escritoires), and boxes neatly polished and embellished, which may be purchased here at very reasonable rates.

However much they may have despised their own methods, the East India Company merchants had bowed and smiled and held on and finally achieved their aims. As yet, though, the English language did not register in the rich and ancient cultures of the Indian subcontinent.

But they had staked a claim. And if one place could be said to mark the real beginning of what was to be, by whatever standards, a remarkable advance of the English language, it was a tiny village on the banks of the River Houghly, a village called Kolkata, renamed Calcutta by the English merchants and now once again called Kolkata. They established a factory there and from that factory grew one of the world's greatest trading cities. English found a bridgehead in

Calcutta and even today, wherever you walk, you are surrounded by street signs, slogans, advertisements, all manner of vivid print claiming your attention in several languages, one of the most prominent being English.

What the traders found was that the high-quality, brightly coloured, printed and woven fabrics were an instant success in Britain and could and did make fortunes. The relationship between Britain and India was woven through these fabrics. But though trade prospered, English was still peripheral. English-speaking employees at the end of the seventeenth century were still numbered in hundreds, creeping slowly towards a thousand or two. If they wanted to conduct business they had to learn local languages. Here we have an example of English people abandoning their language for that of others and yet bringing back from the relationships words and phrases which would eventually be embedded in their own native tongue. They were encouraged not only to talk like Indians but to take local wives, adopt local habits and wear local dress. And they did. The company's clerks or writers, as they were known, were forced to take on a great number of local business terms, words, rather surprisingly given the takeover nature of the language of commerce, that only very rarely became familiar in Britain.

Words like 'batta' – a travelling allowance; 'bigha' – an area of land; 'cadi' – a civil judge; 'chit' – a note or letter (as in 'chitty'); 'crore' – ten million; 'dawk' – mail; 'firman' – imperial order; 'hashish' – a native drug, which like chitty also made it west; 'jowar' – tall millet; 'jumma' – an assessment for land revenue; 'kotwal' – police officers; 'rahdaree' – toll, duty; 'sunnud' – deed or grant; 'zemindary' – system of land tenure. Most of these came from Urdu and Hindi, sometimes from Persian or Arabic.

English, you might say, was biding its time.

That came in the eighteenth century with an accumulation of events which led to the spectacular and unthinkable collapse of the Mughal Empire. The British navy defeated the French. The East India Company set up its own private army and by 1765 the Mughals formally recognised the company's control of the administration and finances of Bengal, the richest province in India.

The boot was now on the other foot. The British no longer had to beg, worm, flatter, kow-tow. Yet, at first, in what seems a hopeful interregnum, the blinkers of imperial destiny were not put on. They still married local wives, still adapted to local ways and still maintained a true fascination with India. As Governor-General of Bengal, for instance, Warren Hastings actively promoted the study of Indian languages and traditions.

And it was at this time that the deep-rooted connection between Indian languages and English was uncovered by an amateur scholar, a Supreme Court judge, Sir William Jones, mentioned at the outset of this book, but worth putting in context here. Sir William Jones founded the Asiatick Society of Bengal to encourage enquiry into the 'History, Civil and Natural, the Antiquities, Arts, Sciences and Literature of Asia'. He was a one-man representation of the British Enlightenment. When he began to look at the ancient language of Sanskrit – which had been a written language centuries before the Homeric epics – he had a Eureka moment and saw what was effectively a series of root connections between Sanskrit and other languages. The route had been through a distant parent language (which no longer existed) to other language groups. Thus, 'pitar', Sanskrit for 'father', was 'pater' in Latin, 'fadar' in Gothic, 'father' in English; the Sanskrit 'bhrater', Latin 'frater', German 'Bruder', Irish 'braithair', English 'brother'. Even the forms of verbs look similar: English 'am', Old English 'eom', Gothic 'im', Latin 'sum', Greek 'eimi', Sanskrit 'asmi'. English 'is', Gothic 'ist', Latin 'est', Greek 'esti', Sanskrit 'asti'. His insights became one of the chief foundation stones for modern philology. Sir William's work shows, I think, the great respect the small intruding country had at that time for the awesome mass of a subcontinent of which it was edging into control.

The respect of the English can still be seen in 1805 in a letter written by Martha Sherwood, wife of a captain in the 53rd Foot. There is a mixture of showing off and a determination to get on top of her job. There is also an almost scholarly fascination with the complexities of this exotic new culture.

I found when I arrived in Fort William (Calcutta) that our Establishment was already large. Mr Sherwood, as regimental paymaster, a very great man in India because he kept the strongbox, was almost obliged to have a black sirdar or steward. Ran Harry, a Brahmin and a very decent man, was the person recommended to him in Calcutta and through him the rest of our servants had already been provided when I arrived at the Fort. These were:

One kitmutgar, at nine rupees a month: this functionary goes to market, overlooks the cook, and waits at table, but he will not carry home what he purchases in the market.

One mussauldee: his business is to wash dishes, carry a lantern, and in fact, to wait on the kitmutgar.

One Bheesty: his name signifies 'the heavenly' and he carries water in a skin over his shoulders.

We can understand wherefore, in such a climate as India, he might have got his name: Of course the inferior sort of John Bull calls this functionary 'Beasty'.

That last sentence is endearing. Mrs Sherwood then goes on to name and describe five more servants for what must have been a comparatively modest captain's house. The respectful curiosity is still there: so is the respect. But it must have been heady stuff. The British were now allowed to behave like mini-Mughals and they soon eased themselves into the glamour and power of it all. It was their time to shine. A minute number of people now governed a place of such tradition and history and size that it could not but encourage delusions of superiority.

This is not the place to debate the commercial daring and military prowess of the British and set it against the undoubted ruthlessness and miseries inflicted. Keeping to the track of English, though, it needs to be noted that as the nineteenth century opened up, the British increasingly adopted that air of superiority: going native, adopting Indian customs (though not Indian words and phrases), revering its culture largely dropped out of fashion. Perhaps, given the psychological weight of the new situation, this was essential for the security, inner and outer, of such a perilously small number of foreigners on a continent seething with warriors and intelligence. Or power corrupted as ever.

The superior position was justified through religion. In 1813, the Foreign Secretary, William Wilberforce, told Parliament that it must change what he called India's 'dark and bloody superstition for the genial influence of Christian light and truth'. Leaving aside the question which it begs, the result was missionaries, missionary schools and, to our purpose, the first organised drive to take English to substantial numbers of Indians. This was the spirit of the Raj, a word taken from Hindi meaning kingdom or rule. The British would rule and English was called up, the language was enlisted.

There was controversy but a small but influential group of Indians were impressed by western thought – particularly in science and technology. English, they reasoned, would give them access to such knowledge and though not superior to Hindi, Persian and Sanskrit, might be learned alongside them. Rammohan Roy (1772–1833) was the most articulate spokesman for this group. His letter of 1823 reads, in part, when he learned that money would be available for the instruction of Britain's Indian subjects:

We were filled with sanguine hopes that this sum would be laid out in employing European Gentlemen of talents and education to instruct the Nations of India in Mathematics, Natural Philosophy, Chemistry, Anatomy and other useful Sciences, which the natives of Europe have carried to a degree of perfection that has raised them above the inhabitants of other parts of the world.

This judicious mixture of respect, longing and a transparent intention to compete, written in a style of English which would have delighted English purists in London, was followed by disillusion. 'We now find that the Government are establishing a Sangscrit school under

Hindoo Pundits to impart such knowledge as is clearly current in India.'

But there are strands here worth noting. One is that then and since, despite often savage opposition, there has been and remains an influential group of Indians who seized on English as a language which could be very useful to them. They wanted the knowledge and the access it would make them heir to. They were prepared to study and to learn it and they did. It is also implied that while the British wanted English to be imposed, it was more for rule than for liberation; it was to pull the Indians into line and not let them loose on the treasures of the Enlightenment. This became the primary battlefield for English in India: would it be an instrument of empire or the window to a desirable intellectual world? Who would own the language when the smoke cleared?

In 1835, Thomas Babington Macaulay, writer, historian and member of the Supreme Court in Calcutta, wrote his Minute, which became notorious. It laid out why English needed to be taught. It became a landmark document. Edited paragraphs include:

I am quite ready to take the Oriental learning at the value of the Orientals themselves. I have never found one among them who could deny that a single shelf of a good European library was worth the whole native litera-ture of India and Arabia . . . We have to educate a people who cannot at present be educated by means of their mother-tongue. We must teach them some foreign language. The claims of our own language it is hardly necessary to recapitulate. It stands pre-eminent even among the languages of the West.

To Macaulay, the pre-eminence of English made Britain's world imperial role possible. They conscripted Indian clerks or writers, as they were called, to serve the empire's purposes. An English-speaking class of junior officials was needed and in Calcutta a colossal Writers' Building was constructed to house them. English was often eagerly sought by Indians and yet it was also forced on them; it added to the repertoire of Indian languages which then and now multiply seemingly effortlessly on the tongues of educated Indians; and yet it had a special place, it was the language of prestige and preferment and as only a minority of Indians received a formal education in English, it was inevitably elitist and divisive. But without this English-speaking Indian bureaucracy there could have been no Raj, a paradox not lost on Indian intellectuals.

English itself began to frolic on the new continent. What was called 'Butler English' soon sprang up, very similar to the frontier English in America, as in 'long time no see'. It also had similarities with the pidgins in America and the Caribbean. One example is: 'Tea, I making water. Is boiled water. Want anybody want mixed tea, boil the water, then I put tea leaves, then I pour the milk and put sugar.'

There was also a variety called Babu English. Babu was originally a Bengali word for gentleman, but it came to be used of an excessively ornate variety of English which was a product both of social deference (deeply traditional in India and adopted by the English for the first hundred and fifty years) and an education system in which English was often taught by Indians to Indians. So turns of phrase which bore relevance only to a textbook were not weeded out. As in this letter:

Sir,
Being in much need and suffering many privations, I have after long time come to the determination to trouble your bounteous goodness. To my sorrow I have not the good friendships with many people hence my slow rate of progress and destitute state. Here on earth who have I but thee, and there is Our Father in heaven, needless to say that unless your milk of human kindness is showered on my sad state no other hope is left in this world.

'The inferior sort of John Bull' would often mock this and it would be po-faced not to find that irresistible. But in 1903, the viceroy Lord Curzon got as near as it was then possible to comprehend its context and yet have his fun:

It must not be supposed [he wrote] if I, or anyone else, quote amusing specimens of what is commonly known as Babu English that we do it with any idea of deriding the native intelligence or of poking fun at its errors. On the contrary, one of the most remarkable experiences in India is the astonishing command of the English language, to them a foreign tongue, that is acquired by the better educated Indians, enabling them not merely to write but to speak it with an accuracy and a fluency at which I never cease to wonder . . .

Of Babu English he also wrote that 'it often reveals a sense of humour on the part of the writers that is both quaint and refreshing'. If his admiration is rather surprising in such an English nabob for its fulsomeness, his patronising references are also surprising in their gentility.

Babu could be extreme, comparing favourably with any weird or demotic use of English in the English-speaking world. This is part of a speech by a Hindu pleader in a court at Barise:

My learned friend with mere wind from a teapot thinks to browbeat me from my legs. But this is mere gorilla warfare. I stand under the shoes of my client, and only seek to place my bone of contention clearly in your Honour's eye. My learned friend vainly runs amuck upon the sheet anchors of my cause. Your Honour will be pleased enough to observe that my client is a widow, a poor chap with one post mortem son . . .

Slang and word-play became endemic among British officials to such an extent that one newly arrived governor-general complained he couldn't understand the reports written by his staff. The attractions between English and particularly Hindi grew stronger.

The British army relished picking up Indian words. They prided themselves on being able to 'bolo the bat a tora' – meaning to speak the local language a little; if they were 'banged up' – high on bhang – they might be summoned by the 'amen-wallah' – the chaplain, or face 'tori peechy' – delayed repatriation. But a lot of the local lingo did not travel well back to Blighty. Pukka shots in India were blanks in Britain. No one else knew that 'chota hazry' was breakfast, a scoundrel was 'badmash', 'durzee' was a tailor or a 'burra-peg' was a double whisky, that 'gubbrow', 'lugow', 'foozilow', 'dumbcow', 'puckerrow' and 'bunow' meant respectively to bully, to moor a boat, to flatter, to browbeat, to lay hold and to fabricate. Yet they wallowed in it to such an extent that in 1886 a great glossary of Anglo-Indian words was published, almost nine hundred pages, called *Hobson-Jobson*.

Hobson-Jobson is an army term, a corruption of a phrase shouted by Muslims in a procession. The words were 'Ya Hassan, Ya Hassayn'. This became 'Hosseen Gosseen', 'Hossy Gossy', 'Hossen Jossen', 'Jackson Backson' and finally 'Hobson Jobson'. It is now a term in linguistics used for that kind of corruption of words from one language by speakers from another. 'Khakee' was one of the more famous words included. It is taken from the Hindi for 'dust-coloured', meaning a light drab cloth. The first *Hobson-Jobson* dictionary notes that 'it is said it is about to be introduced into the army generally.'

There are thousands of other examples: 'chapati' entered the English language as 'chowpatty', with perhaps a push from 'cowpat'; the Indian plant 'kawanch' became 'cowage'; the fish 'kakap' became 'cock-up'; 'basi khana', stale food or yesterday's dinner warmed up, became 'brass knocker'; 'bringal' – aubergine – became 'brown jolly' and 'cholera morbus' in Anglo-Indian became 'Corporal Forbes'.

Hobson-Jobsonisms take us back to the 'new' words that English captured in India. An alphabetical sampling could read: 'amok', 'ashram', 'avatar', 'bandanna', 'bangle', 'caddy', 'calico', 'candy', 'cashmere', 'cheetah', 'coolie', 'cowrie', 'cushy', 'dinghy', 'doolally', 'guru', 'Himalayan', 'juggernaut', 'jungle', 'karma', 'khaki', 'lilac', 'mantra', 'mongoose', 'panda', 'pariah', 'purdah', 'rattan', 'sacred cow', 'seersucker', 'Sherpa', 'Tantra', 'thug', 'yoga'. Even such a limited and arbitrary selection shows English on its relentless hunt for new words to describe new things, new experiences, new ideas, new shades of meaning, forever swelling the Anglo-Saxon word-hoard, quarrying all the languages it encountered as it moved across oceans and continents. And it was here that the British were introduced to some of what became their favourite foods: curry, it was recently reported, is Britain's most popular dish.

Rudyard Kipling, whose greatness as an author has been shadowed by the strength of his passion for empire and for imperial British supremacy, is the writer above all others who brought the life and plight of the British soldier and the mystery and fabulous difference of India to a wide public. His work is well known. There were innumerable others whose passion for India and for the English in India is also difficult to celebrate naïvely given the darker side of the imperial project.

But this book is to do with the language and here is part of just one of the many tributes which could still, despite the imperial burden, be called warm-hearted and affectionate. The lines are from E.F. Atkinson's verses 'Curry and Rice'.

> What varied opinions we constantly hear
> Of our rich oriental possessions,
> What a jumble of notions, distorted and queer,
> Form an Englishman's 'Indian Impressions'.
>
> First a sun, fierce and glaring, that scorches and bakes;
> Palankeens, perspiration and worry;
> Mosquitoes, thugs, coconuts, Brahmins and snakes;
> With elephants, tigers and curry.
>
> Then Juggernaut, punkahs, tanks, buffaloes, forts,
> With bangles, mosques, nautches and dinglees;
> A mixture of temples, Mahometans, ghats,
> With scorpions, Hindoos and Feringhees.
>
> Then jungles, fakirs, dancing-girls, prickly heat,
> Shawls, idols, durbars, brandy-pawny;
> Rupees, clever jugglers, dust-storms, slippered feet,
> Rainy season and mulligatawny.

With Rajah – but stop, I must really desist,
And let each one enjoy his opinions,
Whilst I show in what style Anglo-Indians exist
In Her Majesty's Eastern Dominions.

It would be romantic and ironic if it could be proved that English alone, or in some great measure, gave many intelligent Indians direct access to the ideas of democracy and independence which were to wrench back India from its latest rulers. But I suspect that a resolution for independence is not confined to one language or one culture.

Yet there are those who do believe that it was the English language and the ideas it carried that created a revolution against the British. Just as English made it possible for Indians to administer the Raj on behalf of the British Empire, so English may have been a factor in enabling Indians to rise up against it.

Macaulay's Minute and the education policy had brought the English language to the Indian people and through the language Rudyard Kipling among others saw a nationalist movement developing. English, he feared, gave it credibility. Kipling observed what he called 'a strong belief among many natives that they were capable of administering the country themselves', and he also observed that many Englishmen shared that belief because, as he wrote, 'the theory is stated in beautiful English with all the latest political colours.'

Kipling of course dismissed Indian independence as no more than a pretty idea. But it was more than that. It was persistent. It met in the houses of wealthy and titled liberals and found voices among the newly enfranchised.

In 1903, Lord Curzon choreographed a spectacular durbar to celebrate the accession of Edward VII. India had never seemed more safely and some self-deludingly thought more happily in British hands. Five years later, a lawyer called Gandhi wrote a pamphlet which was to be the first significant pebble beginning an avalanche. It is fascinating for our story because he concentrates not on the law, not on the military or commercial control, but on the English language. English was the prime and essential target of his attack:

To give millions a knowledge of English is to enslave them. The foundation that Macaulay laid of education has enslaved us. I do not suggest that he has any such intention, but that has been the result. Is it not a sad commentary that we should have to speak of Home Rule in a foreign tongue? . . .

Is it not a painful thing that, if I want to go to a court of justice, I must employ the English language as a medium, that when I become a barrister, I may not speak my mother tongue and that someone else should have to translate to me from my own language? Is not this absolutely absurd? Is it not a sign of slavery?

Gandhi takes this line of thought to what I think is an original and radical conclusion: 'Am I to blame the English for it or myself? It is we the English-knowing Indians that have enslaved India. The curse of the nation will rest not upon the English but upon us.'

And when Gandhi sets out the blueprint for his India of the future, English is banished utterly. Cast off the language, he seems to say, and you cast off the oppressor; his crucial hold over you is to make you speak and so think and so act like him.

It was a view which gathered strength. As India approached independence in 1947, many nationalists regarded the English language as the central fact and symbol of oppression. They wanted rid of it and the end of the Raj was supposed to bring the slow death of English in India. The new constitution assumed that it would continue to be used as an official language only until 1965 and then it would be replaced entirely by Hindi.

It did not happen.

There are many reasons given for this. Non-Hindi speakers objected to the proposed primacy of Hindi. There were riots in the streets – to reject Hindi and to retain English. And, pragmatically, the English language had dug deeply into systems of advancement and status. English gave access to the world; best seen in literature where, since independence, Indian novelists writing in English have made a tremendous contribution and been celebrated not only in India and Britain but in America and throughout the old Commonwealth and been translated all over the world. Yet it is still not straightforward even today. The young novelist Amit Chaudhuri, born in Calcutta and brought up speaking Bengali, writes his fiction in English.

I think that English has played a double role [he says]. Yes, it has been a language of unification. It has also been the language through which people in India became more self-conscious, and therefore conscious of their own differences – from each other, from the English, so it has played this dual role. The English themselves mustn't take too much credit for it because they didn't know this was happening. It's entirely to the credit of Indians that they used this in this way. In modern Indian history English has been very much at the heart of things. It's a lingua franca but it's also more than that, it's part of the growth of the indigenous languages, and the modern forms as well. So it has also increasingly been a part of that self-expression of difference – of different identities – which is also very vital to what India is.

English absorbed much from India. But India absorbed the whole of English as another of its languages. Today it is spoken fluently by four or five per cent of the population, all of whom speak at least one other language just as fluently and often flick from one to the other scarcely noticing the join. Four to five per cent may seem a small proportion, but in a country of India's size this means forty or fifty million people, what Lord Curzon, the viceroy, would have described as the better educated. Beyond that, it has been estimated that upwards of three hundred millions have some contact with it and some knowledge of it.

The Times of India, in English, has treble the sales of *The Times* of London. Calcutta is garlanded with signs in English. India's writers use it with authority on the world stage in many disciplines: scientific, artistic, political, sociological.

The Raj quit India more than fifty years ago. English remains: and thrives.

20

The West Indies

'Indies' was a misnomer from the start. Columbus came on them on his search for a westward route to India, and after such a long open sea voyage, with some justification he thought he had arrived at his destination and christened the inhabitants 'Indians'. This is the first indication of the way in which language has to be examined with more than usual care when it comes from this string of Caribbean islands. 'Caribbean' comes from 'Carib', the local name of one of the tribes.

Professor David Crystal has written that there are six varieties of 'varying distinctiveness' for the area: 'The situation is unique within the English speaking world, because of the way the history of the region has brought together two dimensions of variation: a regional dimension, from which it is possible to establish a speaker's geographical origins, and an ethnic dimension in which the choice of language conveys social and nationalistic identity.'

The Cambridge History of the English Language is no less forbidding:

It is difficult to gain a clear overview of how English and Creole spread in the West Indies – whether as standard or regional British, Caribbean or North American English, or as English-based pidgins and creoles. The general history of English in the region has been fragmented into dozens of histories of English in particular island territories . . . A further difficulty is that the story of the spread of English in the West Indies and surrounding area does not always coincide with the history of the spread of British political power in the region . . .

In some former British colonies, such as St Lucia or Domenica, English is spoken largely as a second language; in some areas that were never British, such as Costa Rica, English is spoken as a first language. Then there are the varieties of pidgin and creole.

This is not altogether surprising. Though we gaily clump the islands together as 'the West Indies', we are talking about dozens of distinctive territories which can be separated by up to a thousand miles of ocean – in itself a certain recipe for variety as Darwin proved in the Galapagos Islands. We are also talking about Spanish, Portuguese, French and Dutch settlement as well as English: and most of all we are talking about the intensive enforced settlement of hundreds of thousands of Africans with scores of different African languages. And finally we are talking about the cross-fertilisation of that mix. What is surprising perhaps is that the prosody – the sound of the spoken language – is broadly homogeneous.

English arrived there late. By the sixteenth century, Spain and Portugal had established themselves in the New World, slavery had been introduced, the Portuguese were running slaves from West Africa and various European diseases had combined with Spanish intolerance to reduce immensely and in some cases to wipe out the indigenous population. The English came much later and at first stood offshore, as pirates, waiting for the treasure ships, especially the Spanish, which were looted by Drake and Hawkins and others with the tacit agreement of Queen Elizabeth. Early words which entered English from the West Indies included 'doubloons' and 'pieces of eight'.

Hakluyt's *Voyages*, a collection of sailors' tales first published in 1589, included this account by John Hawkins of his journey to Guinea and the Indies in 1564, which introduces us to a more domestic vocabulary:

. . . we came to an island of the cannibals, called Domenica, where we arrived the ninth of March, cannibals exceedingly cruel and to be avoided

. . . Near about this place [later, he is now near Santa Fé] inhabited certain Indians who . . . came down to us . . . presenting milk and cakes of bread which they had made from a kind of corn called maize . . . also they brought us down hens, potatoes and pines . . . these potatoes be the most delicate roots that may be eaten, and do far exceed our parsnips and carrots . . .

So we have maize, potatoes and cannibals from 'Indian' languages. 'Cannibals' came from the alternative version of the name for the Carib people; they were also called 'Canibales' and legendary for their ferocity and their ruthless treatment of captives. The Carib language gave English 'cayman', 'curare' and 'peccary' amongst much else. And from the other main local people, the Arawaks, English took 'hurricane' (as well as 'maize'), 'guava', 'hammock', 'iguana' and 'savannah'. 'Canoe' and 'potato' are Haitian.

But once out of the seas to the west, English looted every ship of tongues it encountered. From Nahautl, Aztec and Mexican came 'chocolate', 'chilli', 'avocado', 'cocoa', 'guacamole', 'tamal', 'tomato', 'coyote', 'ocelot', 'mescal' and 'peyote': many of these indirectly through other European languages. It was the Spanish who conquered Peru but English was soon in there, capturing 'condor', 'llama', 'puma', 'cocaine', 'quinine' and 'guano'. The languages of Brazil, like Tupi and Guarani, are the original source of 'cougar', 'jaguar', 'piranha', 'macaw', 'toucan', 'cashew' and 'tapioca'. English was a hunter-gatherer of vocabulary, a scavenger on land and sea. The English sea dog became a popular hero especially when he was annoying the Catholic King of Spain, who had put a price on the head of Elizabeth. Piracy was patriotic. 'Freebooters', they were called, 'filibusters' (sixteenth century) and 'privateers' and the 'old sea-dogs' (seventeenth century). 'Cutlass' was a century earlier, the 'Jolly Roger' a century later, but robbery with violence on the high seas had a good press back in Britain and the words – 'buccaneer' is another – had a chauvinistic swagger about them.

English settlement began in Bermuda in 1609, and reached the

Caribbean in 1624 when Thomas Warner and twelve companions settled in Sandy Bay, St Kitts. In 1626, the first African slaves arrived in St Kitts, which was the first place where the British followed the example of the other European nations and systematically exploited slave labour. To begin with, tobacco was the crop. Sugar proved to be much more profitable – sugar needed more labour; the slave population grew and into the crushed but not wholly eradicated native tongues of the West Indies, soon to be spliced and mated with the European implants, came the invasion of African languages. Even by the end of the sixteenth century, the Africans outnumbered the Europeans and the African population grew massively in the next century.

As always, the language revealed far more than an exchange of information. An eighteenth-century plantation manager called James Grainger wrote an epic poem in praise of Sugar Cane. There were critics in Britain who thought that Grainger was the first real writer to have come out of anywhere in the Americas. One reason must be that they saw their own supremacy of English mirrored in his verse: one will stand for all:

> What soil the Cane affects, what care demands,
> Beneath what signs to plant; what ills await;
> How the hot nectar best to christallize;
> And Afric's sable progeny to treat;
> A muse, that long hath wander'd in the groves
> Of myrtle indolence, attempts to sing.

'Afric's sable progeny' had a different take on this work and different languages in which to express it. It was not made easy.

As I mentioned previously in writing about African slaves going to America, to prevent organised rebellions on board ship, the European slave traders to the West Indies also adopted the policy of splitting up tribes and this resulted in splitting up languages. One notion is that a language bonding began on these boats themselves and took the form of a sort of English picked up from the sailors.

That has been disputed. What is not in question is that these wholly different language speakers once on their plantations soon found ways to communicate, ways which, inevitably given that they were working for British owners, used English.

There were two ways in which this was done (rather as with Gullah in America): one was pidgin; the other creole.

'Pidgin is a reduced language,' according to the *Cambridge History of the English Language*, 'that results from extended contact between people with no language in common ... Simplifications include reduction in numbers of words used and dropping complications such as inflections.' 'Two knives' becomes 'two knife'; accusative forms are used as nominatives, as in 'him' for 'he' – 'him can read'; plurals are formed from a singular noun and 'dem' – 'de dog dem' for 'the dogs'; simplification of verb forms, e.g. the passive form, is avoided – 'de grass cut' for 'the grass has been cut'; auxiliary 'do' omitted from questions – 'why you hit him?'; adjectives used in place of adverbs – 'I do it good'.

Pidgin is a brilliant instant shorthand invented for survival. Creole is a full language developed by the sons and daughters of pidgin speakers. These children would find that their parents' pidgin English was of more general use to them than their native African language. Out of this, the children would organise what was in effect a new language; they would creolise the pidgin. Words would be creolised and grammar would reassert itself. Some linguists believe that this extraordinary and miraculously rapid (a single generation) grammatical development is due to an innate human instinct, that part of the brain 'has' grammar wired in like a whistling whale has a whistle. But there are other scholars in the West Indies who believe that the creole spoken there is directly descended from the Niger-Congo language family to which all the very different West African languages ultimately belonged. The argument here is that forms were borrowed from English but used in a structure which was West African.

Dr Hubert Devenish of the University of the West Indies puts one case. He says 'Me go run school' would be translated into English as 'I ran to school'. The West Indian version would be considered inferior, and ignorant. But he points out that 'go' is the directional marker telling you where you're running to, whereas the English form has a preposition, and the 'go' form which is a straightforward verb, like 'Me go there', would mean 'I went there'. But in 'Me run go school', 'go' would be used as a preposition, i.e. 'me run *go/to* school'. So creole simply switched verbs to prepositions when their grammatical drive needed it: just as, on many previous occasions in the progress of English, nouns had been used as verbs and vice versa. Far from being ignorant this is a wholly valid adaptation. The other case made from this same example is that West African languages like Yoruba and Edo are one of the few groups of languages which do in fact have those sort of constructions and 'run go' is a prize instance.

In the later eighteenth century on St Kitts, at about the same time that James Grainger was being elegant and pastoral about 'the Sugar Cane', a carpenter called Samuel Matthews wrote down some examples of the language he heard used by black creole speakers. He was dealing in sounds which had not been written down before but a close look at four lines can give some insights into the language:

> Vos mottor Buddy Quow?
> [What's matter, Brother Quow?]
> Aw bree Obeshay bong you.
> [I believe overseer bang you.]
> You tan no sauby how
> [You stand not know how]
> Daw boekra mon go wrong you, buddy Quow.
>
> [That white man go wrong you, Brother Quow.]
> i.e. What's the matter, Brother Quow?
> I think the overseer hit you
> You don't seem to know how
> That white man is going to wrong you, Brother Quow.

There is a lot which is characteristic of creole in those few words. Most of them are English – an example, as in Gullah, of the deep flexibility of English, rising to the challenge of as it were binding a new language out of a variety of languages from a different language group entirely. Spoken in a St Kitts accent, and even on the page, the second striking fact is that the sounds have shifted. And some words have been put through the prism of West Africa: 'brother' has become 'buddy' – later a very widely used word but this is the first record we have of it. 'Overseer' has become 'Obeshay' and by repeating these words up against each other a few times we can easily comprehend how that happened. The 'wh' of 'what' becomes a 'v' (Sam Weller would have approved), the 'i' in 'believe' becomes an 'r' in 'bree'; the 'th' of 'that' becomes a 'd' in 'daw' or 'dat'. Many African languages have a rule that a syllable can only have one consonant and one vowel, so when English combines consonants, creoles often reduce it to a single letter: here the 'st' and 'nd' of 'stand' become a 't' and an 'n' – 'tan'. English vocabulary plus African grammar equals a new word: stand – tan.

There are non-English words here too. 'Boekra' comes from the African word for 'white man'; 'sauby' from 'saber', the Portuguese word 'to know'; and as the verses go on there is the word 'morrogou' which is derived from French.

Some other words first recorded in the texts of Samuel Matthews and others on St Kitts include 'How come?'; 'kackar' or 'caca' for 'excrement' (though there is the Old English 'cachus', meaning latrine); 'bong', 'bang' meaning to hit, 'ugly' meaning evil, 'pikni' for 'child', 'grande' for 'big', and 'palaver' for 'trouble' or 'argument'.

There are also French creoles. Derek Walcott, who won the Nobel Prize for his epic poem *Omeros* which is set among the fishermen on the island, was brought up with formal English as his first language and French creole as his 'kitchen and street tongue'. In some of his work they rub together. It is the rubbing together of words as well as the new grammar and the multiple springs they draw on which make creole a rich source for historians and sociologists as well as linguists.

It seems to be agreed that the creole spoken in Jamaica is the deepest in the Caribbean, partly because of the sheer numbers of Africans transported there and partly because a good number of them escaped to the hills and established language groups of their own early on. And although English is very prominent, there are still traces of Spanish. The escaped slaves, for instance, were known as 'maroons', a corruption of the Spanish word 'cimmarón' meaning wild or untamed.

Jamaican English vocabulary followed the by now traditional English pattern and took from everyone and everywhere. From sailors it took 'berth' – later a position of employment, and 'cot' – a portable bed. From Spanish, for instance, it took 'parasol'; 'savvy' from Spanish in St Kitts becomes 'sabi' in Jamaica; 'sabi-so' is 'wisdom'. 'Yard' was used for the Negro yard, the area on the plantation where the slaves lived. By extension it became a house, especially in Kingston. Jamaicans informally refer to the whole island as Yard, hence 'Yardie'.

Sometimes a word seems to be a straight translation of an African tongue. 'Big-eye' for 'greedy' corresponds to words in Ibo and Twi. And also as in Africa you get 'boy-child', 'girl-child'. 'Big-big' for 'huge' is the sort of repetition found in Yoruba. It's catching: 'poto-poto' – very slimy; 'fluky-fluky' – very fussy; 'batta-batta' – to hit repeatedly.

Carnabel Day for Carnival Day (Ash Wednesday); 'catspraddle' in Trinidad is a very undignified fall; 'dumb-bread' is a heavy, flat bread. These are what are called 'loan translations' from West African languages as is 'sweet mouth' – to flatter; from Yoruba, 'eye-water' and 'cry-water' for 'tears'; 'door-mouth' for 'the entrance to a building'.

Rasta is derived from Jamaican creole with elements of the Old Testament and the influence of the black consciousness movement. Rasta uses 'I' to replace the creole 'mi': 'me' is taken as a mark of black subservience. 'I' is respect and solidarity and has extended its domain widely: 'I-lect' is Rasta 'di-alect'; 'I-cient' is 'ancient'; 'I-men' is 'A-men'; 'I-nointed' is 'anointed'; 'I-quality' is 'equality'. The vocabulary has a life of its own, some of which has leaped across the youth culture – 'dreadlocks', 'dub', 'queen' (girlfriend), 'Rasta man', 'sufferer' (ghetto-dweller), 'weed of wisdom' (marijuana). There's also some good word-play: 'Jah-mek-ya' (God made here – Jamaica); 'blindjaret' or 'see-garet' for 'cigarette'; 'higherstand' – understand.

Creole grows. One of the newer words is 'chi-chi man', meaning a male homosexual. The old words still strike deeply, as in the use of 'trouble' meaning disturb – as in 'don't trouble the woman's children'; 'don't trouble my car' – bringing to mind Elizabethan language as in 'the wind troubled the waters' and old dialects such as the Cumbrian: the presence of English dialects in West Indian and black American is strong. I would assume that even more work will be done with creole languages, showing as they do that new lamps can be made from old and borrowed lamps.

Sugar was the most active stimulant in the trade in human beings which led to the pidgins and the creoles and sugar can provide an ending to a chapter which has sidestepped the suffering, looking only for the best that came of it, the sweetest, perhaps.

'Molasses' came from the Portuguese. 'Syrup' was already in use as a word for sugar solutions but also started to be used for the raw liquid in the manufacturing process. 'Treacle' had been a medieval term for a medicinal compound. It too was commandeered.

In the West Indies, sugar yielded alcohol which went through various intoxicating names – 'kill-devil', 'rumbullion', 'rumbustion' – before hitting the buffers of 'rum'. Rum became the naval drink. Admiral Vernon in 1740 ordered that it should be mixed with water before being given to the crew. The admiral used to wear a cloak made of a coarse fabric called 'grogram': his nickname was Old Grog. 'Grog' became rum and water. 'Groggy' began as drunk and moved on to generally shaky.

And still there, but buried deep, are archaic English expressions such as the English seventeenth-century 'from' for 'since', as in 'from I was a child I could do that', and 'aks' for 'ask' ('ax' in Old English), 'cripsy' for 'crispy' – all stewed in with Yoruba, Ibo, Spanish, French, Portuguese and mixed to a language as plaited as any on the planet.

I can think of no better way to end this chapter than to print at some length a poem by Miss Lou called 'Bans a Killin'. Miss Lou, famous as a poet and an inspiration to women and writers in Jamaica, wrote this protest poem to defend Jamaican dialect from the usual charge of that time that it was not proper or correct English and therefore had to be put down. Miss Lou knew her English literature well and used English dialects as her ammunition. Here, she plants her own dialect in the heartland of the English language.

> So yuh a de man me hear bout!
> Ah yuh dem seh dah teck
> Whole heap a English oat seh dat
> yuh gwine kill dialec!
> Meck me get it straight, mas Charlie,
> For me no quite understan
> Yuh gwine kill all English dialec
> Or jus Jamaica one?
> Ef yuh dah equal up wid English
> Language, den wha meck
> Yuh gwine go feel inferior when
> It come to dialec?
> Ef yuh cyaan sing 'Linstead Market'
> An 'Water come a me yeye'
> Yuh wi haffi tap sing 'Auld lang syne'
> An 'Comin through de rye'.
> Dah language weh yuh proud a,
> Weh yuh honour an respec —
> Po Mas Charlie, yuh no know se
> Dat it spring from dialec!
> Dat dem start fi try tun language
> From de fourteen century —
> Five hundred years gawn an dem got
> More dialec dan we!
> Yuh wi haffi kill de Lancashire,

De Yorkshire, de Cockney,
De broad Scotch and de Irish brogue
Before yuh start kill me!
Yuh wi haffi get de Oxford Book
A English Verse, an tear
Out Chaucer, Burns, Lady Grizelle
An plenty a Shakespeare!
When yuh done kill 'wit' an 'humour',
When yuh kill 'variety',
Yuh wi haffi fine a way fi kill
Originality!
An mine how yuh dah read dem English
Book deh pon yuh shelf,
For ef yuh drop a 'h' yuh mighta
Haffi kill yuhself!

Robert Burns, Thomas Hardy, D.H. Lawrence and dialect speakers the length of Britain would surely have approved.

21

Advance Australia

For centuries it was called Terra Australis Incognita. In 1770, James Cook set out on a scientific expedition in search of what might have been a legendary continent. Cook's ship, the *Endeavour*, found its first mooring; Joseph Banks, the botanist, began the collecting of plants and animals. Cook wanted to call his anchor point Stingray Harbour but in honour of Joseph Banks he dubbed it Botany Bay. The naming and claiming of this new land had begun.

It was not until 1788 that English really planted itself on the continent with the arrival of seven hundred and twenty-three convicts who were to found a penal colony: without question the most significant, fertile and successful penal colony the world has ever known. The convict ship made for Botany Bay but a parching summer had turned Cook's primal lush landscape inhospitable. It sailed north and landed at Port Jackson, now Sydney Harbour.

The contact with the local language can be illustrated most directly in two ways. First the naming of the kangaroo. At Port Jackson it appears that the strange creature which beguiled the Brits was called 'patagorong'. Or was it? For, seemingly, there were about two hundred and fifty native languages, many of which were not mutually understandable. It is possible that there were two hundred and fifty words for kangaroo. It is also possible that there never was the word 'kangaroo' at all: that kangaroo was the reply given when one of Cook's crew pointed to this peculiar creature and enquired what it was: 'I don't understand what you're asking,' said his Aboriginal informant and that sentence roughly translates as 'kangaroo'. Wherever it came from, it stuck. These settlers were there under duress and they needed to get their bearings fast. They plundered whatever in the native language helped their furious purpose.

The first cluster of English borrowings came from the Dharuk language spoken around Port Jackson. Words such as 'boomerang', 'dingo', 'koala', 'wallaby', wallaroo' and 'wombat'. One exceptionally happy borrowing was 'cooee', a call word used by the Aborigines to summon one another from a distance. For decades to come 'cooee', the call of the harsh Australian bush, would be the chaste mating call of the English-speaking world, the affectionate signal used in childhood games, the call across the garden fence, the word from the wild that summoned the faithful in domesticated suburbia. There was also an owl known as a 'boobook'; a tree, the 'waratah', which has become the emblem of New South Wales; 'warrigal', another name for 'dingo'; and 'woomera', a throwing stick. From other languages came 'budgerigar'; 'barramundi', a great perch; and 'kylie', another word for boomerang. The experience parallels that of America quite closely. The English held tight to their language – were very resistant to native tongues – but under pressure from the new and the strange they would steal. Not unlike the fifth-century Frisians and the native Celts.

Again, as in America, words from English were grimly applied to local species: 'magpie' and 'apples' are examples here. And the English took their place names with them. North of Sydney, to take just one example, is Newcastle and near Newcastle there are a number of place names from the district around Newcastle-on-Tyne in Northumbria.

It was not until about a century after the first British had settled that the word 'Aboriginal' came into use. At first those found living in the new continent were called Native Australians. 'Australian' derives from the Latin adjective for 'southern'. 'Aboriginal' is a Latin term meaning 'from the beginning': the Romans used it to name the peoples they displaced. As the word 'Aboriginal' came into use for the natives, so the word 'Australian' was appropriated by the settlers.

Language borrowing worked both ways. The Aboriginals had never seen horses: in some of their languages they called them 'yarraman' which most likely comes from teeth.

The Aboriginals also developed pidgins of English, some of which were sucked back into the new tongue. 'Jumbuck', for that curious newcomer the sheep, is widely used in Australia. It could be a corruption of 'jump up' or, less likely, I think, it could come from 'jombok', which means a big white fluffy cloud. 'Walkabout' has gone from the outback to every city street and city square in the English-speaking world.

Dr Kate Burridge of La Trobe University in Melbourne has pointed out the diversity and subtleties in Australian creole. It is, she says, strikingly different from Standard English and again perhaps surprisingly for those who equate creole with simple it can be much more complex than Standard Australian English or English English. She gives a telling example:

Take the pronoun system. Standard English has just one form 'we', so that if I said to you 'We're going now', you don't know whether you're included in that 'we' or who's exactly included in that 'we'. In Australian Creole they have four different 'we's. There's a form for 'you and me' – the two of us; there's a form for 'me and somebody else excluding you'; there's a form for 'you and me and a whole heap of others' and there's a form for 'me and a whole heap of others excluding you'. Much finer distinctions.

About a hundred and fifty thousand prisoners were taken halfway around the world in the eighty years of transportation – interestingly about the same number as is estimated for the Frisian settlers and invaders in fifth-century England. There is evidence that in many cases the offences of these convicts were light – sometimes scarcely enough to warrant even an appearance in court today. Many would now be dealt with by a few days' community work. There are claims that those transported were given adequate medical attention because they would need to be fit at the other end. There were formidable individuals there, as Robert Hughes tells us in *The Fatal Shore*.

But sympathy was very short two hundred years ago. Punishment was the vengeance of the Lord and pity had no place. In his book, Hughes serves up a ballad from 1790 which celebrates the departure of 'thieves, robbers and villains' to Botany Bay. The verses include:

> Some men say they have talents and trade to get bread,
> Yet they sponge on mankind to be clothed and fed,
> They'll spend all they get, and turn night into day –
> Now I'd have all such sots sent to Botany Bay.
>
> There's gay powder'd coxcombs and proud dressing fops,
> Who with very small fortunes set up in great shops.
> They'll run into debt with designs ne'er to pay,
> They should all be transported to Botany Bay.
>
> You lecherous whore-masters who practice vile arts,
> To ruin young virgins and break parents' hearts,
> Or from the fond husband the wife lead astray –
> Let such debauch'd stallions be sent to the Bay.

Little wonder the Australians still love beating the Brits in sporting battles.

As elsewhere, some English dialect words travelled well. Those who came to Australia, just as those who went west, were largely from classes to whom a dialect was standard. Sometimes dialect words which have since withered on the English tongue struck deep abroad. 'Dinkum', for instance, is a word for 'work' from Midlands dialects and 'fair dinkum' meant a fair day's work – hence 'fair play'. 'Cobber', meaning friend or mate, seems to come from the English dialect word 'cob', meaning to take a liking to. The comradely use of 'digger' travelled to Australia's goldfields from England's farmlands.

And the criminals brought their own slang: 'flash', it was known as, or 'kiddy talk'; 'kiddy' coming from 'to kid' – to steal, to fool.

Criminal words slotted in with remarkable ease and time has laundered them impeccably. 'Chum' began life in an Oxford college, someone sharing an apartment, and was taken over as a fellow prisoner; 'swag', the bag of loot, developed into 'swagman', a tramp carrying all his worldly goods in a bundle. There's 'bash', 'cadge' and 'croak' (meaning to die), 'dollop', 'grub' (food), 'job' (robbery), 'judy' (woman), 'mug' (face), 'pigs' (police), 'to queer' (to spoil), 'seedy', 'snooze', 'stink' (trouble), 'swell' (gent), 'whack' (share) and 'yoke'. There's 'beak' (magistrate), 'lark' (prank), 'split' (betray), 'stow it' (keep quiet) – all these are as common in Australian as in *Oliver Twist* and some of them in Shakespeare's Southwark.

There are less familiar words. If you were 'unthimbled' your watch had been stolen, police runners were called 'traps', a thief was a 'prig', to be 'lagged for your wind' meant being transported for life, and if that sentence knocked the wind out of you, you were a 'bellowser'. The voyage itself was being 'marinated' or 'piked across the pond'. To be shackled to another prisoner was to be 'married'. Convict speech such as this was recorded by James Hardy Vaux in 1812. He is said to have written it down in the breaks between his hard labour.

It would have been miraculous had the British not transported their class system to Australia, but the circumstances both streamlined and hardened it. There were the prisoners and their descendants, those born in Australia, known as 'currency', and the British who were 'pure sterling'. The former developed a local dialect, the latter held hard to the standard of London English. If you wanted to climb the ladder of society then it was no different from England at that time, though the gap might have seemed wider – you had to adopt Establishment English. And to say 'caning', meaning a hundred lashes, 'smiggins' for a prison soup thickened with barley, 'scrubby brushes' for bad bread, or 'sandstone' for a man who flaked from a flogging, would be a certain giveaway.

There was also the word 'bloody'. It has a long and interesting history in the literature of war, of words, of violence, of blasphemy and of outright cursing. It was a favourite word among the convicts, unsurprisingly, and it became widely used in Australia. One traveller noted that he heard an Australian use 'the disgusting word' twenty-seven times in a quarter of an hour, and this enterprising observer went on to calculate that it would add up to about eighteen million two hundred thousand uses in fifty years. He added that he thought the said Australian was quite capable of reaching the target. The first verse of John O'Grady's poem 'The Integrated Adjective' illustrates this.

I was down on Riverina, knockin' round the towns a bit,
An' occasionally restin', with a schooner in me mitt;
An' on one o' these occasions, when the bar was pretty full
An' the local blokes were arguin' assorted kinds o' bull,
I heard a conversation, most peculiar in its way,
Because only in Australia would you hear a joker say:
'Where yer bloody been, yer drongo? 'Aven't seen yer fer a week;
An' yer mate was lookin' fer yer when 'e comes in from the Creek;
'E was lookin' up at Ryan's, an' around at bloody Joe's,
An' even at the Royal where 'e bloody never goes.'
An' the other bloke said 'Seen 'im. Owed 'im 'alf a bloody quid,
Forgot to give ut back to 'im; but now I bloody did.
Coulda used the thing me-bloody-self; been orf the bloody booze,
Up at Tumba-bloody-rumba shootin' kanga-bloody-roos.'

As with many dialects, creoles, and non-standard versions of English, what is condemned by the establishment is often held on to with pride and affection in part because it is one in the eye for Proper Speakers. It is a language of Outsiders who are confident enough to set themselves up against the Insiders. It has the comfort of a clan, the edge of being subversive and the freedom of something apparently made up by and for the clannish group that uses it.

The word 'convict' was far more inflammatory than 'bloody'. 'Emancipist', 'government men', 'legitimate', 'exile', 'empire builder' – that is what they wanted to be called.

As the nineteenth century marched on, Australia began a love affair with its new accent and with its ability to invent vivid slang. In 1880, the *Bulletin* or the *Bushman's Bible*, began weekly publication in Sydney and it delighted in 'fair dinkum', 'larrikin', 'bonzer', 'bloody', 'offsider', 'fair cow', 'battler' and 'bludger'. Phrase-making was a speciality: 'better than a poke in the eye with a burnt stick' or 'as miserable as a bandicoot on a burnt ridge'. This was a people finding its identity in the most essential and enjoyable way – through words which started with them and belonged first to them. The *Bushman's Bible* also went in for poetry and one poem became Australia's national anthem, a treasure chest of Australianisms: 'Waltzing Matilda'.

It was written out on a sheep station. (It is said that 'station' was used because the city-bred convicts had little idea of the countryside so they adopted the military words 'station' for 'farm', and 'muster' or 'mob' for 'a flock of sheep'.) Banjo Patterson was the author of this song, in 1895, a song which, I can testify, was sung as lustily in the primary schoolrooms of northern England in the 1940s as ever it was down under – which had by then drawn so many northern British to its shores.

In case you did not enjoy such primary school benefits, it begins:

> Once a jolly swagman camped by a billabong
> Under the shade of a Coolibah tree,
> And he sang as he watched and waited till his billy boiled,
> You'll come a-waltzing Matilda with me.
>
> > Waltzing Matilda, Waltzing Matilda,
> > You'll come a-waltzing Matilda with me,
> > And he sang as he watched and waited till his billy boiled,
> > You'll come a-waltzing Matilda with me.
>
> Down came a jumbuck to dri-ink at that billabong,
> Up jumped the swagman and grabbed him with glee.
> And he sang as he stuffed that jumbuck in his tucker bag,
> You'll come a-waltzing Matilda with me.

Simple as it sings, it is not instantly comprehensible to those unacquainted with late-nineteenth-century outback Australian slang. This, I guess, is partly the point, the clannishness again, the proof of propriety over a new language. The swagman is a drifter. The billabong is a pool and he is shaded by the Coolibah tree, a kind of eucalyptus. The billy can is clear enough. Jumbuck is a sheep; tucker bag is again quite clear but, like the billy can, given an Australian spin. Waltzing Matilda means to hit the road. Matilda was slang for a bedroll, so the swagman is singing about moving on, quickly, presumably. But not quickly enough. He is pursued by a squatter – the farmer who had once squatted on the land to claim it – and the mounted police.

> Up rode the squatter, mounted on his thoroughbred,
> Down came the troopers, one, two, three.
> 'Who's that jolly jumbuck you've got in your tucker bag?
> You'll come a-waltzing Matilda with me.'
>
> Up jumped the swagman and sprang into that billabong.
> 'You'll never take me alive,' said he.
> And his ghost may be heard as you pa-ass by that billabong,
> 'You'll come a-waltzing Matilda with me.'

At school we were always instructed to sing that last line very softly.

It is a rich song for Australia. It is fascinating that the word 'squatter', descriptive of such a degraded condition in England, should have become the name for a wealthy landowner. Sheep stealing was the prime and ancient British capital crime against property, the last resort of the starving, often the talent of the skilled poacher. It rings down English history and to find as it were its last strike in Australia is apposite. And its resounding and defiant ending is equally apposite. It turns the black crime of sheep stealing into something near-heroic, an act of independence against authority, even worth dying for. And the slang gives it a wonderful camouflage as the uninitiated sing along (as we did) imagining a Matilda waltzing away around the billabong.

The pleasure that Australians take in their language is unabated. In 1965, a book was published which celebrated Australian and its pronunciation: *Let Stalk Strine*, by Afferbeck Lauder. It included 'gonnie' (meaning 'do you have?' as in 'Gonnie apples?'), 'harps' (half past two becomes 'harps two'), 'baked' and 'necks', 'emma necks', 'scremblex' – breakfast foods.

'Cossie' is a swimming costume, 'pokies' are slot machines, a 'drongo' is a stupid person, a 'no-hoper' and a 'gutless wonder' are perfectly clear, a 'chine' is a mate. Someone highly esteemed has 'blood worth bottling'. Money, as everywhere, breeds a progeny – 'splosh', 'spondulicks', 'boodle'; drunk is never far behind – 'spifflicated', 'rotten', 'full as a boot'; farting is 'shooting a fairy'. A 'pom' is an Englishman, generally despised but somehow, in my experience and that of many I know, still admitted as a relation; distant.

Yet these typically Australian words were only taken up with tongs by the establishment very recently. It is not until the 1970s that the real street and bush language of Australians, the language that is Australian, finds its way into the dictionary.

The *Macquarie Dictionary* finally put the language between respected hard covers.

Bluey: originally a rolled blue blanket, hence the possessions of a bushman; an ironic nickname for a redhead; 'hump the bluey' – to live the life of a swagman.

Bonzer: adj. + excellent, or as interjection, expression of joy.

Boofhead: a large, stupid fellow, named after a character in a cartoon strip in the *Sydney Daily Mirror*, from 1941, and derived from 'buffalo head'.

Daggy: dirty, slovenly; later uncool.

Dob: to kick accurately, as in football 'he's dobbed another goal'; 'dob in' – to betray; 'dob on' – to inform against.

Druthers: corruption of 'I'd rather' = choice, preference, as in 'if I had my druthers, I'd be in bed'.

Dunny: an outside toilet; used in phrases such as 'all alone like a country dunny' = isolated (from 1960s); 'bangs like a dunny door in a gale';

'couldn't train a choko vine to grow up a dunny wall' = useless (the choko vine being a particularly durable Australian plant); the word is a shortening of 'dunniken', from the British dialect 'danna' (excrement) and 'ken' (house).

All the way to:

Widgie: a woman who embraced the counterculture of the 1950s and 60s, behaviour exemplified by short hair, tight clothes, wild behaviour and free sexuality (male equivalent: bodger, or bodgie).

Woofering: military slang, initiation for a cadet in which a vacuum cleaner hose is applied to the genitals.

Wowser: a killjoy or spoilsport, supposed to be an acronym of 'we only want social evils remedied', a slogan coined by John Norton, journalist and politician (1862–1916).

Dr Kate Burridge has described what she considers 'the most distinctive feature of Australian English'. Hers may seem an undramatic observation but again and again in the history of the English language, the accretion of apparently small matters (the development of prepositions, for instance) has led to big changes. This whole adventure, a word which again earns its keep as a description here, I think, often depends on what seem hairline choices, almost imperceptible forks in the road, but once one path is taken, time and evolutionary circumstance can then channel the language to a completely unexpected and unintended place.

This may be the case flowing from the Australian passion not only for abbreviation but also for adding 'o' or 'ie' at the end of words. Kate Burridge's examples include: 'Robbo, the weirdo journo from Freeo ended up on a dero and metho' or 'I took some speccie piccies of us opening our Chrissie pressies at brekkie' – exaggerations, she admits, but perhaps the actuality will soon catch up because it does seem endemic, one of the ways in which Australian English wants to be its own tongue. It is interesting that this determination is driven not by the Australian establishment, which even as I write keeps its allegiance to Queen Elizabeth II in London and does not wish to sound like 'broad' Australian. But broad Australian is where the action is and perhaps the future too.

These endings can be derided as diminutive, but are also called 'friendly' endings. Dr Kate Burridge finds herself called 'Kato'. A man who works on a wharf becomes a 'wharfie', a musician is a 'muso'; 'mozzie' for 'mosquito', 'maggie' for 'magpie', and most common of all, 'arvo' for 'afternoon'. Dr Burridge is as yet uncertain why some words take 'o', others 'ie' and still others do not lend themselves to friendly endings. But I think she is right to hit on its significance.

The other and for many foreigners the most striking characteristic of Australian English is the Australian accent. For a long time this was a source of annoyance and embarrassment to the authorities in Australia itself. In 1911, in *The Awful Australian*, Valerie Desmond wrote: 'It is not so much the vagaries of pronunciation that hurt the ear of the visitor. It is the extraordinary intonation that the Australian imparts to his phrases. There is no such thing as cultured, reposeful conversation in this land; everybody sings his remarks as if he were reciting blank verse after the manner of an imperfect elocutionist.'

Things had not improved by 1926, when the Director of Education in New South Wales wrote: 'It is said that other people are able to recognise Australians by their speech.'

Would he dare write that now? Through its soaps, its athletes and its writers, Australians now sound the world over like a people unself-consciously proud and totally confident in the way they talk. Australian English sounds young, it has sap in it, there's a kick in the lines. It is not so much that it has found its own voice. It began to do that early on in the unique conditions and the forced mixing of English regional, London, Irish and Scots, to many of whom vivid phrases and semi-secret codes were part of a livelihood. What it has done, in my view, and over the last two generations with a huge surge of energy, is to throw off the shackles of the old country while holding hard to the core of the language it gave them and turning it Australia's way.

22

Warts and All

It is often curious what great men are remembered for. Oliver Cromwell, regicide, first Protector, creator of our only Commonwealth, destroyer of magnificent castles and thought by some 'Our Chief of Men' is also and perhaps equally remembered for saying 'Warts and all' when discussing how his portrait ought to be painted. English no less than the countenance of Cromwell has its 'warts' and in the interest of shade as well as light this chapter touches on what could be called the warts.

There is another reason for this: I was discussing English at a meeting when a student stood up and pointed out that the English language was 'great' (his word), but in the part of the world he came from it had also been very good at racism and racial abuse. He was right. English is astounding in describing and enlarging many areas of our external and internal experiences; these also include swearing and blasphemy, obscenities, vile insults and racism.

The racism was partly a consequence of its fearfully rapid growth. It must have felt dangerous, even perilous and certainly giddy for these small islands within a few generations to have put that essence of national identity, language (by around the turn of the nineteenth century) into America, Canada, the West Indies, then South Africa, Sierra Leone, Ghana, Gambia, Nigeria, Cameroon, Kenya (from 1920), Tanzania, Uganda, Malawi, Zambia, various Pacific Islands, Singapore, Hong Kong, Australia, New Zealand, Tasmania, the

Indian subcontinent . . . not to mention other countries already rather grudgingly taking on English as an essential second language.

But that does not tell the whole story. Racism has to make other groups inferior. Racial denigration is always a demonstration of power, an attempt at total control, the use of language to stave off fears, reinforcing ignorance with prejudice. The best that can be said is that the English language was by no means the first nor the sole nor, sadly, is it likely to be the last language to find racist words.

Perhaps the key to this chapter is to be found in what is often described as the first English novel – *Robinson Crusoe*. Daniel Defoe's shipwrecked Crusoe encounters a black native who has been put on the island as a punishment and expected to die. Crusoe relates:

I understood him in many Things, and let him know, I was very well pleas'd with him; in a little Time I began to speak to him, and teach him to speak to me; and first I made him know his name should be *Friday*, which was the Day I saved his life; I call'd him so for the Memory of the Time; I likewise taught him to say *Master*, and then let him know, that was to be my Name; I likewise taught him to say, Yes and No and to know the Meaning of them.

It is a paragraph exceptionally rich in pickings – there is the saving of life and the use not of force but of language, which is seen as the method of control; and that first word 'Master', a word which tormented so many slaves for certain. But Master it was, in 1719, and in some ways that word alone sets the scene for the next two hundred years.

Friday flows easily. 'Nigger' is in many places now thought the most unsayable word on the planet. No matter that it has a neutral history, that it comes from the word for the colour black in Latin and then in French, adopted by English, 'nigger' carries the lash of a plantation whipping. It is as alive to offence as any of the religious oaths of the Middle Ages. Yet nowadays there are Afro-Americans and others who use 'nigger' with pride. This is a recurring feature of English, where again and again, in many contexts, people have taken on insults and turned them into badges of pride – 'hack' is one, the 'Old Contemptibles' another. But for many years and still now in many places, 'nigger' was denigrating, unacceptable and fighting talk.

So was 'wog', supposedly an acronym for 'worthy' (or 'wily') 'oriental gentleman'; 'sambo', from Spanish 'zambo', meaning a person of mixed Indian and African descent; 'coolie' from the Tamil word for 'a hired person'; 'kaffir' from the Arabic word for 'infidel'; 'dago' from the Spanish 'Diego'; 'frog', applied first to the Dutch and then to the French. 'Savage' is indiscriminate. 'Kaffir' was used to insult the British in India before English absorbed it as an insult-word in South Africa. 'Barbarian' – commonly used, like 'savage' – can be traced back to the Greek word for stammering and used by the Greeks to describe and laugh at the sound of languages other than their own. Like dragons' teeth, a few seeds sprang up in battalions. 'Spic', 'yid', 'paddy', 'chink', 'black', 'spade', 'jock', 'taffy', 'pom' and 'yank' could be included as, I guess, and soon, the way the world goes, 'English' and 'American'.

The black insults, and especially in America, were the most inflammatory and their sores and scars remain: 'Negro', 'nigger', 'niggra', 'thicklips', 'Rastus', 'Uncle Tom', 'cottonpicker', 'coon', 'hard-head' and 'boy'.

Boy is a good example of a word which on the surface seems totally harmless yet in certain mouths, in certain circumstances, in certain times, it became an unbearable stigma, an intolerable insult. Boy! One of the characteristics of language is that no word is safe. No word is wholly clean. Look at 'mother'. Said by some today it can be intended to be the first two syllables of a four-syllable insult; to others it is the most affectionate word of all. Or, at the other end, 'bugger'. Once an insult, it's now routinely used by young men expressing goodwill. 'Where've you been, you old bugger?' Words can whip around from north-east to south-west yet still on the page look precisely the same. 'Wicked' in my youth was near-evil: in my children's it is near-hysterically funny. Such rapid changes remind us that for all their extraordinary subtleties, in the end words express current feelings, passions, sensations often out of control of correct vocabulary and such turbulent feelings will reach out for anything, like a madman about to commit a murder, any object at all to do or express what cannot be repressed any longer. So even a wholly inappropriate 'wrong' word like 'boy' can be used as a weapon in extremis.

These insults are not unique to English. They come partly out of fear which informs every encounter between unfamiliar peoples and has done, I guess, for the last hundred thousand years. Until proven as your friends, the next tribe have to be some sort of enemy and to make yourself feel stronger than them and safe from them you diminish them. It still happens, with the same fearfulness and fury and based in the same ignorance, in our sophisticated, intellectually complex and progressive twenty-first century when we know, for instance, that the range of the human gene pool all over the planet is astonishingly, even dangerously narrow; that all of us came from probably no more than several hundred survivors way back in Africa; and that, literally under the skin, we are precisely the same. It does not stop us using superficial differences to claim profound superiority; and this can be seen in the way in which English began to see itself as not only a rich, varied, powerful and triumphant language, which it was, but an innately superior language.

In 1848, a writer in the austere and academic London periodical the *Athenaeum*, wrote of English: 'In its easiness of grammatical construction, in its paucity of inflexion, in its almost total disregard of the distinctions of gender excepting those of nature, in the simplicity and precision of its terminations and auxiliary verbs, not less than the majesty, vigour and copiousness of its expression, our mother-tongue seems well adapted by organization to become the language of the world.' He was right in that last phrase. There are those who would find themselves agreeing with him to a lesser extent in the rest.

Professor David Crystal, in *English as a Global Language*, took on the *Athenaeum* and took it apart. A language becomes global because of the power which supports it, he argued. Latin became an 'international' language though the Romans (like the British) were by no means as numerous as those in their empire: they were, however, more powerful. Their army, our navy. He writes: 'a language becomes an international language for one chief reason: the political power of its people – especially their military power.' Latin then got a second boost for one and a half millennia through the Roman Catholic Church. There is an analogy between British English (Roman) and American English (the Roman Catholic Church).

Professor Crystal sees no power in innate aesthetic or structural qualities. At different times this has also been claimed for Hebrew, Greek, Latin, Arabic, Italian, Spanish, Chinese and French. This argument, he argues, takes us down a blind alley.

Taking on the *Athenaeum* assertion in detail, he points out that 'Latin was once a major international language, despite its many inflectional endings and gender differences. French, too, has been such a language . . . and so have the heavily-inflected Greek, Arabic, Spanish and Russian.'

He does allow English a certain number of unique advantages, however, and these have counted and still count for something in the often narrow contest for supremacy. The English language is very familiar to many other languages, he argues, because over the centuries it has taken and absorbed so many thousands of new words from so many other languages. (Compared, say, with the French, who have tried to keep other languages out.) It was cosmopolitan from very early on. He says that though it came from Germanic roots it became over its first thousand years more of a Romance language, thus splicing together two of the most powerful forces in language. Professor Crystal also allows that there is an 'absence in English grammar of a system of coding social class differences, which can make the language appear more "democratic"'. Nevertheless he concludes that 'these advantages are incidental' and points out the major disadvantage – the irregularities in the spelling system.

The spread of English, he maintains, comes because having achieved power through the sword and sea power, it retained it through trade. Here we also have a language which benefited from the Industrial Revolution of the nineteenth century and the technological revolution of the twentieth century, especially the new communications technologies: telegraph, telephone, radio and the entertainment technologies: film and television. Language follows trade which follows the flag and the seeding of English in America is the key to its current success and may well be a prime determinant in modern history. Bismarck, the great nineteenth-century German Chancellor, said that the most important element in modern history was the fact that the North Americans spoke English.

Not that American English utterly dominates: British English, as we shall see, still contributes a surprising amount, as do Englishes already described in other parts of the world. But Professor Crystal wants to nail any skulking romantic let alone mystical notion that in English itself, in that unique, enduring complex growth from Frisian to Shakespeare, from Shakespeare to Joyce, from Joyce to Chomsky, there is anything 'special'. It is very hard for a non-linguist to disagree with Professor Crystal. But does not the very scale of the English achievement merit a different take on this?

There is an alternative view expressed admittedly a hundred and fifty years ago, but expressed by a genius. Jakob Grimm was not only one of the two brothers whose *Grimm's Fairy Tales* remain as classic works of literature, psychology, folklore, tales from the darkest forests of an oral imagination, he was also a distinguished linguist and philologist. What he wrote was accepted then, in 1851: it still has interest, I think, today.

Of all modern languages, not one has acquired such great strength and vigour as the English. It has accomplished this by simply freeing itself from the ancient phonetic laws and casting off almost all inflections; whilst from its avoidance of intermediate sounds, tones not even to be taught but only learned, it has derived a characteristic power of expression such as perhaps was never yet the property of any other human tongue. Its highly spiritual genius and wonderfully happy development, have proceeded from a surprisingly intimate alliance of the two oldest languages of modern Europe – the Germanic and the Romanesque . . . none of the living languages can be compared with it as to richness, rationality and close construction . . .

In every war there are casualties. However annoying that cliché might be it is, like many others, true. English was involved in several battles and it still is. You could erect a tall memorial to the languages that fell or were wounded, sometimes mortally, in these conflicts. American Indian and Aboriginal languages, from the Caribbean to the Pacific, have surrendered or left the field. It is not only English that has done this: Greek, Latin, Arabic and Spanish before it had the same history though not on as big a scale because there has never been a language expansion on such a scale. And also it is a fact that languages do die out. They died out before English came on the scene, they have died out over the past hundred and fifty years without the help of English and no doubt some languages will die out in the future. Just as new languages, from pidgin to creoles, will emerge. But English has cut its swathe.

The nearest example to its home turf is Welsh. Welsh derived from the Celtic widely spoken in these islands. It was pushed to the edges of the country by the invading Germanic tribes. It left only a few traces in English as was noted at the beginning of this book. In effect it was a defeated language bypassed, neglected and of no importance to the adventure of advance, check, endure, advance, absorb, attack which shaped the story of English in its rich forward march. Celtic was literally, geographically marginalised on the main island – to the Gaelic north of Scotland, to Cornwall, and to Wales. It seemed penned in for ever, entombed almost, and for centuries it could consider itself an unlikely, fortunate, in some way an exceptional example of survival.

If we skip a thousand years of successful hanging on to the language of the Celts, we arrive at the Acts of Union in 1536 and 1542, ostensibly made to ensure equal rights for the Welsh and English under the Tudors. Welsh people, it said, could speak as they liked, *provided that* '. . . all Justices . . . shall proclaim and keep . . . all . . . Courts in the English Tongue; . . . all Oaths shall be given . . . in the English Tongue . . . no Person or Persons that use the Welsh Speech or Language shall have . . . any . . . Office within this Realm of England, Wales or other of the King's Dominions . . . unless he or they use and exercise the English Speech or Language.'

If this tight rein was thought an improvement by the royal Welsh Tudors, it implies that the subjugation of the Welsh pre-Tudor was very severe. English ruled. Yet the Welsh language held on, went into poetry and song, did not surrender.

Neither was the oppression relaxed. In 1847, a Royal Commission declared that:

The Welsh language is a vast drawback to Wales and a manifold barrier to the moral progress and commercial prosperity of the people. Because of their language the mass of the Welsh people are inferior to the English in every branch of practical knowledge and skill . . . Equally in his new or old home his language keeps him under the hatches, being one in which he can neither acquire nor communicate the necessary information. It is the language of old-fashioned agriculture, of theology and of simple rustic life, while all the world about him is English . . . He is left to live in an underworld of his own and the march of society goes completely over his head.

The Commission was published in two volumes bound in blue and the Treachery of the Blue Books, as it became known in Wales, established a nineteenth-century policy to marginalise even further the Welsh language in favour of English.

This was reinforced by the Education Act in the late nineteenth century which demanded that all Welsh children reach a certain level of ability in English. Teachers were responsible for this and many of them are still remembered to this day as having been particularly harsh. There were those who would not allow Welsh to be spoken at school in any circumstances. Children who broke this rule and spoke their native language had a halter put around their necks and a notice suspended which read 'WELSH NOT'. The WELSH NOT became a symbol of resistance.

For resist it did and eventually through politics, terrorism and a liberalising of official attitudes, it clawed its way up the social scale and although it still has a fight on its hands there is now Welsh radio and Welsh television; Welsh literature, of course, has a long history; there are Welsh road signs and street signs; it has survived the Frisian, the Norman and finally the English yoke. Yet it still has the problem of an overmighty neighbour who also provides it with otherwise unavailable opportunities. There is still the fear that it exhausts its resources in the fight for preservation rather than progression and might become more a heritage language than a vital tongue. And more and more Welsh people speak English. In 1921, thirty-seven per cent of Welsh people spoke Welsh; in 1981, it was nineteen per cent. But over so many centuries its tenacity and its revival have been and are remarkable. And today the number of Welsh speakers is slowly increasing.

Welsh, having been the first casualty, is now a good early example of coexistence. English coexists with Welsh as it does in the far northern islands with Gaelic. It coexists with many other languages. Sometimes other nations replace it: the burgeoning call centres in India, for instance, are staffed by Indians speaking perfect English and replacing English people as once the English replaced Indians in the textile trade. Australia now looks forward and has well lost what was called the 'cultural cringe'; indeed, in some areas it is some of the English who are inclining to that position vis-à-vis their antipodean namesakes now ploughing an independent line. And yet, as in India, and as in the West Indies where, for example, in Jamaica, there are strong moves to make Patwa as socially acceptable as English, the formal mother-ship of English remains. In these countries it is increasingly a tale of two Englishes.

There are many different ways in which to describe the arrival of English in foreign lands. A disaster, an oppression, a misfortune, a cultural massacre – these and even stronger terms have been used and will be used again. But it was also, for many who have and still do take advantage, an opportunity.

Britain now is a place in which many of the nations, groups, peoples it once ruled have come to live. On the streets and in plays, poems and films, languages from the West Indies, Africa, India and Pakistan find their space. American English has been a very strong influence for many generations. Other Englishes are now elbowing their way in. The pot is being stirred yet again and languages once thought of as 'inferior' have come to the mother country of English bringing with them vocabulary and ways of speaking undreamed of even fifty years ago.

23

All Over the World

We as a species must have begun speaking one language. There are linguists who believe that one basic breeding language will eventually be discovered behind every language we now speak. There is a yearning for it among some of us. There have been several attempts artificially to create a one-world language. Esperanto is probably the best known. Invented in 1887 by a Polish oculist called L.L. Zamenhof, it was based on Romance language vocabulary and aimed to provide a universal second language. It has about a hundred thousand speakers in fifty countries. For instance, the sentence 'It is often argued that the modern world needs a common language with which to communicate,' appears in Esperanto as 'Oni ofte argumentas ke la moderna mondo bezonas komuna linguon por komunikado.'

Before that there was Volapuk, invented in 1879 by the German Johann Martin Schleyer; in 1928, there was Novial, invented by the Dane Otto Jespersen, and there has also been Interlingua in 1903, invented by the Italian Giuseppe Peano, and Ido in 1907, invented by the Frenchman Louis de Beaufort. What is happening today despite the population power bloc of China and the resurgence of Spanish in the Americas, is that English, invented by tens of thousands of people from about AD 500 onwards, is making its way all over the world. And in the last hundred years or so, while British English has maintained its astonishing fertility and Englishes from every continent have laced the mix, American English has added the extra cylinders. That has been the most telling injection of all. They have invented and reinvented words to describe their own society.

We can see American English downtown in any city in the States. We would look up a block of 'apartments' to a 'penthouse', be deluged by the 'mass media', go into a 'chain store', breakfast on 'cornflakes', avoid the 'hot dog', see the 'commuters' walking under strips of 'neon', not 'jaywalking', which would be 'moronic' but, if they were 'executives' or 'go-getters' (not 'yes-men' or 'fat cats'), they would be after 'big business', though unlikely to have much to do with an 'assembly line' or a 'closed shop'. There's likely to be a 'traffic jam', so no 'speeding', certainly no space for 'joy-riding' and the more 'underpasses' the better. And of course in any downtown city we would be surrounded by a high forest of 'skyscrapers'. 'Skyscraper' started life as an English naval term – a high light sail to catch the breeze in calm conditions. It was the name of the Derby winner in 1788, after which tall houses became generally called skyscrapers. Later it was a kind of hat, then slang for a very tall person. The word arrived in America as a baseball term, meaning a ball hit high in the air. Now its world meaning is very tall building, as typified by those in American cities.

Then you could go into a 'hotel' (originally French for a large private house) and find a 'lobby' (adopted from English), find the 'desk clerk' and the 'bell boy', nod to the 'hat-check girl' as you go to the 'elevator'. Turn on the television, flick it all about and you're bound to find some 'gangsters' with their 'floozies' in their 'glad rags'.

In your bedroom where the English would have 'bedclothes', the Americans have 'covers'; instead of a 'dressing gown' you'll find a 'bath-robe', 'drapes' rather than 'curtains', a 'closet' not a 'wardrobe', and in the bathroom a 'tub' with a 'faucet' and not a 'bath' with a 'tap'.

All along the way the Americans and the English have hurled mostly genial abuse at each other about their respective tongues. It has its moments. Coleridge raged about the terrible Americanism 'talented' which was in fact an English word. Walt Whitman said that American was a glorious new language reinvented away from the tradition and authority of British English. There is fear that the Americans are mangling 'our' language: who needs 'the inner child', 'have a nice day', or 'authoring' a book; a lot of us do. Just as we use 'cave in', 'flare up', 'fork over', 'hold on', 'let on', 'stave off', 'take on', 'fall for' and 'get the hang of' – all fine upstanding English phrases which very likely originated in America.

Sometimes it seems that America has collared modern life. 'Photogenic', 'beauty queen', 'beauty parlour', 'beautician', 'nutritionist', 'sex appeal', 'sugar daddy', 'pop songs', 'smash hits', 'a record store'. Financial, computer and slang words show more of a balance. Here are a few terms from the last decade or so: 'anorak' (UK), 'Big Bang' (UK), 'Black Monday' (US), 'car boot sale' (UK), 'cashback' (UK), 'cyberpunk' (UK), 'cyberspace' (US), 'derivative' [finance] (UK), 'desktop publishing' (UK), 'enterprise culture' (UK), 'golden parachute' (US), 'hacker' (US), 'Internet' (US), 'World Wide Web' (UK), 'laptop' (US), 'loadsamoney' (UK), 'mattress money' (US), 'PEP' (UK), 'scratchcard' (UK), 'short-termism' [finance] (UK), 'slacker' (US), 'subsidiarity' (UK), 'trailer trash' (US), 'trustafarian' (UK), 'yuppie' (US).

Some even feared – wrongly – that English's 'innings' on its home ground was about to come to an end. In 1995, the Prince of Wales expressed the anxieties of many of his contemporaries when he told the British Council that 'we must act now to ensure that English . . . and that, to my way of thinking means English English . . . maintains its position as the world language well into the next century.' Clearly he feared that the home team would be 'caught on the back foot', even 'hit for six'; however you cut it, he saw us on 'a sticky wicket'. But we 'kept a straight bat' although some of us became so fanatical about using the right word that we banned the flamboyance that had once been a mark of the language. When Rupert Brooke's mother saw it reported that her dashing young son, poet-hero of the First World War, had left Cambridge 'in a blaze of glory', she put her pen through the phrase and substituted 'in July'.

Nothing is alien to the appetite of English. In the First World War,

English English brought us 'shell-shocked', 'a barrage', 'no man's land' (re-charged from the fourteenth century), 'blimp' (an observation balloon). Aerial combat gave us 'air ace', 'dogfight', 'nose dive' and 'shot down in flames'. 'The balloon goes up' is a signal for the artillery to begin firing. 'Over the top' is from the moment you clambered out of the trenches to attack. You muffled a gramophone trumpet by 'putting a sock in it' and the phrase 'at the eleventh hour' stems, via the Bible, from the precise time the Great War ended.

In America the language of the southern blacks moved north as they were sucked up-country to man the booming factories. (In the last thirty years of the nineteenth century, for instance, US steel production rose by over eleven thousand per cent.) In the 1890s over ninety per cent of African Americans lived in the rural south; sixty years later, ninety-five per cent had moved to the urban north. They discovered that they had not left behind the 'colour bar'. Where they settled was invariably on 'the wrong side of the tracks'. But their language took over those for whom they worked. It was often language associated with pleasure. People began to dance the 'cake walk' and then the 'hootchy-kootchy' and 'the shimmy', they started to 'jive' and 'boogie-woogie'. 'Jazz' and 'blues' arrived at the beginning of the twentieth century and changed music for ever. 'Hip' probably came from the African word 'hipikat', meaning someone finely attuned to his/her environment. 'Jazz' later came to mean having sex, as did 'rock'n'roll'. 'Jelly roll', 'cherry pie', and 'custard pie' were all words for female genitalia. 'Boogie-woogie' was a euphemism for syphilis – 'boogie' was a southern word for prostitute. 'Shack up' meaning living together in common-law fashion also came from black speech at this time.

As the twentieth century rolled on, the English-speaking youth of the world adopted 'black' American English as a mark of their generation. You wanted to be 'cool', 'groovy', 'mellow' and certainly not 'square'. Then there's 'to blow your top', 'uptight', 'right on', 'hassle', 'far out', 'bread' (for money), 'make it', 'put down', 'ripped off', 'cop out', 'no way'. 'Man' is very early, first recorded in 1823 as black English. 'Out of sight' and 'kicks' are also from the nineteenth century.

Language has its own force and works, I think, to demands and impulses which cannot always be slotted into the received idea that economic and military superiority alone produce linguistic dominance. Pressure groups and revolutionaries can play a part. African American English came from a minority, mostly poor, often oppressed, all of whom were descended from a different language pool than English, and yet their expressions colonised the English language and not only of youth. Even President Nixon said 'right on' and gave the 'thumbs up'.

A characteristic of English throughout is the ease with which it can borrow or steal words from other languages. By the end of the sixteenth century, there were words from fifty different languages being used as 'English'. The flow of immigrants to America had the same result. On to the bone of Puritan English so tenaciously nurtured by the *Mayflower* families and others who followed from England, came Irish and Scots, especially on the frontier, together with words from Native American, and words from other European languages. 'Ouch!' came in less than a hundred years ago from the German word 'autsch'. German also gave us 'hamburger' and 'frankfurter', 'wanderlust', 'seminar' and the game 'poker'. 'Bum' in its meaning as 'tramp' comes from the German 'Bummler', a good-for-nothing, 'hold on!' from 'halt an!' and 'so long' from 'so lange'.

Yiddish of course. Its words include 'nosh', 'bagels', 'pastrami', 'dreck', 'glitch', 'schmuck', 'schmaltz', 'schmooze', 'schlock' and 'glitzy'. There are phrases too: 'Am I hungry!', 'I'm telling you', 'Now he tells me', 'Could I use a drink', 'I should worry'.

It was not only people who fed the resource; culture did the same. From the gangster culture, for instance, we get 'racketeers', 'hoodlums', 'goons' and 'finks': you could 'take the rap' and end up in 'the hot seat', especially if you'd been involved in a 'hijack' with a 'submachine gun', much to the dismay of your 'bimbo' who was always on the 'blower'. Would she 'spill the beans' or be 'taken for a ride'? The smart thing would have been to have avoided all 'junkies' and 'pushers', cut out the 'hooch' and lead a straight life with no 'gimmicks'.

And there was the culture of 'the Talkies'. You went to the 'movies' at a 'movie theater', to see 'the stars' in 'close up' in 'Technicolor'. The movie could be a 'weepie', a 'tear-jerker', a 'spine-chiller', a 'cliff-hanger' or just plain old 'slapstick' with some 'ham' actors. The 'usherette' would be in uniform. You'd be obliged to sit through 'trailers' and you might well dream of going for a 'screen-test' on some distant day.

When the movies went east to Britain they were gobbled up by millions who absorbed the vocabulary and the phrases as eagerly as they copied the hairstyles and had a go with the American accents. The democratic cultural vote was overwhelmingly pro American English. We flattered it by imitation. This did not deter the objectors. 'Twenty years ago, no one in England "started in", "started out" or "cracked up". We did not "stand for" or "fall for" as we do today' (*New Statesman & Nation*, 1935). 'Those truly loathsome transatlantic importations "to help make", "worthwhile", "nearby" and "colourful" are spreading like the plague' (*Daily Telegraph*, 1935). 'The words and accent were perfectly disgusting and there can be no doubt that such films are an evil influence on our society' (press interview given by Sir Alfred Knox, Conservative MP).

The Americans are more polite about our English than we are about theirs. There was a fear that 'our' English had been taken from us; that its new owners were not looking after it as it deserved; and a deeper fear that they were at the cutting edge now: it was not us who propelled the adventure. But the mother-tongue country was not really daunted, as its leading minds prove to this day. British scriptwriters, songwriters, playwrights, novelists and poets were and are generally delighted with America's words, pillaged them, turned them into English-English and added their own new images ceaselessly. Sometimes it is very difficult to see the joke. That most English of writers, P.G. Wodehouse, lived in America for about half a century.

His plays, musicals, songs and novels enjoy many American characters and who can tell whether some of his more idiosyncratic usages came from this or that side of the Atlantic. 'Vac' for vacation, 'caf' for cafeteria could be UK or USA, 'gruntled' as the opposite of 'disgruntled' is pure Wodehouse, but was the influence English or American? It can be very clear as 'In the matter of *shimmering* into rooms the *chappie* [Jeeves] is *rummy* to a degree.'

Wodehouse went to Dulwich College in south London as did the American-born Raymond Chandler. Chandler named his leading character, Marlowe, after his house at Dulwich College. For many readers and writers his lean prose epitomises an enviably modern style. In 1949, he wrote: 'I'm an intellectual snob who happens to have a fondness for the American vernacular, largely because I grew up on Latin and Greek. I had to learn American just like a foreign language.' There is a thesis waiting for anyone who wants to unravel what could be called the four imperial languages in Chandler – Greek, Latin, English English and American English.

Given the mass of America and the inrush from elsewhere, it is perhaps surprising to find that plain, more or less monosyllabic Old English could still resonate so powerfully and movingly. But it could, as we saw in Winston Churchill's speech: 'We shall go on to the end . . . we shall fight on the seas and oceans . . . we shall fight with growing confidence and growing strength in the air . . . we shall fight on the beaches, we shall fight on the landing grounds, we shall fight in the fields and in the streets, we shall fight in the hills; we shall never surrender.'

That war brought the first mass invasions of Americans into Britain. The GIs arrived and a little handbook was given them to ease their conversation with the natives. They were informed that a kipper was a smoked herring. There were skittle alleys with ninepins rather than bowling alleys with tenpins. They were told that a five and ten store should be called a bazaar and instead of OK, which was already on its way to becoming the most famous word in the world, they should say 'righto'. They were also told: 'the British are tough . . . The English language didn't spread across the oceans and over the mountains and jungles and swamps of the world because these people were panty-waists.' 'Panty-waist' is American for 'sissy'.

By 1944, more than one and a half million Americans were billeted around Britain. And this war, like all wars, brought the recording of new words – from 'jitterbug' to 'doodle-bug', 'smooch' to 'stakeout', 'passion-wagon', 'teenager', 'ballsy', 'gung-ho' (from Chinese 'work together'), 'genocide', 'anti-gravity', 'jet plane', 'chicken' for 'coward', 'laundromat' and 'squillions'.

From the mid twentieth century the English language flooded all over the world until by the year 2000 no one was in any way surprised that a Polish-speaking Pope, the head of a Latin-speaking Vatican, on his arrival in a Hebrew-speaking state, should say in English: 'May this be God's gift to the land that He chose as His own – Shalom.' Nor, as I write this, does it surprise anyone that so many of the diplomats and leaders of states at the United Nations are speaking to the world's press in English.

Countries such as Japan made learning the English language compulsory. The Japanese turned it into a form of Japanese-English: 'biiru' for 'beer', 'isukrimu' for 'ice-cream'. And American soldiers took Japanese words back to the USA: 'honcho' from 'hancho' – leader; 'kamikaze', 'hari-kiri' and 'tsunami'.

In 1945, George Orwell gave the language a new term, 'cold war', and this was yet another war which delivered new words. 'Big Brother', 'Gulag', 'Newthink', 'double speak', 'fallout', 'overkill', 'megadeath'. And from the world of spies, there came 'moles', 'sleepers', 'brainwashing', 'bug' and 'safe house'.

What happened in the second half of the twentieth century has been described rather dismissively as the coca-colonisation of the world. American brand names, American popular music, its movies and television, stormed the world and for a time the jukebox became the shrine of youth. To buy and sell, to enjoy and participate, to sing and be heard, increasingly and everywhere, you needed American English.

Yet English does not have the biggest core-speaking population. There are over a billion speakers who have Mandarin Chinese as their first language. By comparison English's three hundred and eighty million core speakers look quite puny. All the more remarkable then that it has taken such a worldwide hold. For outside the core speakers, it is estimated that upwards of three hundred million have English as a second or third language essential, as in India and Singapore, to enter into many of the central processes of society. There is yet another batch who use English as the preferred adoptive means of communication. Many from different languages now speak to each other in English rather than in either one of their own languages — say Malay or Russian. This figure has been estimated to be over a billion and rising rapidly.

A lateral-thinking way to look at this is to measure the economic strength of different languages. Measured in billions of pounds, Chinese is 'worth' four hundred and forty-eight billion, Russian eight hundred and one, German one thousand and ninety, Japanese one thousand, two hundred and seventy-seven billion, English four thousand, two hundred and seventy-one. English is the buyers' and sellers' language, the stock language of the market.

And English is the first language among equals at the United Nations, at NATO, the World Bank, the International Monetary Fund. It is the *only* official language of OPEC, the Organisation of Petroleum Exporting Countries, the *only* working language of the European Free Trade Association, the Association of Baltic Marine Biologists, the Asian Amateur Athletics Association, the African Hockey Federation . . . while it is the second language of bodies as diverse as the Andean Commission of Jurists and the Arab Air Carriers Association.

And that is not the end of it.

24

And Now . . . ?

For centuries English was outstandingly successful at feeding off other languages and turning them into English, often endowing them with a quality which made them seem agelessly English. Now it is feeding other languages.

So in Russian, for example, they now use 'futbol', 'chempion', 'kemping' (camping), 'khobbi' (hobby), 'klub', 'striptiz', 'ralli', 'boykot', 'lider' (leader), 'pamflet', 'bifshteks', 'grog', 'keks', 'puding', 'myuzikl', 'kompyuter', 'mobilny telefon', 'faks', 'konsultant', 'broker', 'sponsor', 'kornfleks', 'parlament', 'prezident', 'spiker' (speaker), 'elektorat', 'konsensus', 'ofis', 'supermarket', 'loozer' (failure). In Japan we have mentioned one or two; others include: 'raiba intenshibu' (labour intensive), 'rajio' (radio), 'konpyu-ta' (computer), 'kare raisu' (curry rice), 'supootsu' (sports), 'autodoasupo-tsu (outdoor sports), 'sutoresu' (stress), 'insentibu' (incentive), 'akauntabiriti' (accountability), 'ranchi' (lunch), 'kissu' (kiss). Brazil is to ban the increasing number of English words and expressions, such as: 'sale', '50 per cent off', 'spring', 'summer', 'shopsoiled', 'exuberant', 'overtime' (watch shop), 'New Garden'. In São Paolo's Shopping Centre, ninety-three out of two hundred and fifty-two stores featured English words in their names. When President Cardoso recently used 'fast track' in a speech, he was criticised for it. There is no doubt that certain governments think, as Gandhi did to an extreme degree, that the use of the English language is enslaving and a danger to the native tongue.

No one objects more than the French who have contributed many thousands of words to English. The traffic was almost all one way until halfway through the twentieth century, when the flow was reversed. The French dislike this intensely. Yet, inexorably it seems, they say 'le weekend', 'le twin set', 'le look', 'un holiday', 'le midwife', 'le parking', 'le gros rush' (rush hour), 'le garden party', 'les drinks', 'le score', 'le front desk', 'le building', 'le mixed grill', 'un pullover', 'aftershave', 'le babysitter', 'le barmaid', 'le camping', 'le cowboy', 'le cocktail', 'le hold up', 'le jogging', 'le jukebox', 'le jumpjet', 'le know-how', 'le manager', 'le name-dropping', 'le rip off', 'le sandwich', 'le self-made-man', 'le showbiz', 'le stress', 'le supermodel', 'le zapping'. And many more.

In 1994, the French government passed a law prohibiting the use of English words where good French equivalents existed. This can be enforced by a hefty fine. The most recent edition of the Académie Française dictionary admitted about six thousand new words to the French language, including 'le cover girl', 'le bestseller' and 'le blue jeans', but none of those I listed above, from 'le weekend' to 'le zapping'. We'll see who wins: the street talk or the state censors. France's concern for its own language is exacerbated by the drift towards English in the European Union. People who can speak English in Europe outnumber those who can speak French by three to one and the margin grows.

One of many predictions about the future of English is that as time goes on, the mother tongue as we know it, tested and embellished in England, then in Britain, then America, Australia, India, Canada, New Zealand, South Africa, will be spoken only by a minority of English speakers. Other Englishes are being formed all the time.

Singlish in Singapore is a good example. English was used in Singapore for a hundred and fifty years and when it went independent in 1958, Singapore made it the official language of business and government, partly because English united the diverse population of Chinese, Malays and Indians and partly because of its commercial and financial importance. But alongside official English you also hear Singlish which grows and develops despite the efforts of the government to root it out. Some scholars believe that Singlish indicates the way in which future Englishes will develop. In so many ways it fits the tongues and the traditions and the vocal rhythms of the people of Singapore much better than official English and could threaten to replace it. And is it not yet another dialect of English?

Some words come recognisably from English: 'go stun' – to reverse (maritime 'go to stern'), and 'blur' (confused). But others come from Malay and Hokkun. Words such as 'habis' (finished), 'makan' (to eat, meal), 'cheem' (difficult), 'ang mo' (redhead in Hokkun and hence white person), 'kiasu' (very keen, especially of a student). Some of these words are now being used as part of Singapore Standard English and they will change it greatly. Marking plurals and past tenses is a matter of choice and so you get phrases such as 'What happen yesterday?', 'You go where?', 'Got so many car!', 'The house sell already'. The verb 'to be' can be optional. 'She so pretty', 'That one like us', 'Why you so stupid?' These phrases are easily comprehensible to more traditional English users, often full of bite and wit and energy.

A similar thing is happening in South Africa where local words now sit alongside Standard English, indicating total acceptance and signalling the birth of another new English. As in this from a South African newspaper: 'First they told us they would lend us the maphepha to buy the old four-roomed matchbox which masipala put us in . . . So by the time you are eighty years old – if you have survived the marakalas we live under – they can tell you to voetsek out of the house because somebody with the cash in hand wants it now.'

Increasingly even in Europe there is an acceptance of different Englishes. Everything does not have to be put in 'correct' English. The English linguist David Graddol points out that English-looking words in Europe often carry meanings which come from the French – 'federal', 'subsidiarity' and 'community' are three examples he gives. The Germans use 'handy' for a mobile phone and on a Lufthansa flight you will be told to 'turn your handies off'.

The more English spreads, the more it diversifies, the more it could tend towards fragmentation. Just as Latin, which once held sway over a great linguistic empire, split into French, Italian, Spanish, Portuguese and Romanian (all with common roots but – apart from Spanish and Portuguese – not immediately mutually intelligible), so may the future of English be not as a single language but as the parent of a family of languages.

Noah Webster predicted this two hundred years ago. Although he thought it would happen within his native America, the reasons he gave apply precisely to the condition of English around the world today. In his *Dissertations in the English Language* (1789), he wrote:

Numerous local causes, such as new country, new associations of people, new combinations of ideas in arts and science, and some intercourse with tribes wholly unknown in Europe, will introduce new words into the American tongue. These causes will produce, in the course of time, a language in North America, as different from the future language of England as the Modern Dutch, Danish and Swedish are from the German, or from one another.

For Webster's North America two hundred years ago, read 'the world' today. Just as the Old Germanic dialect which fathered English also split into the tribes of Dutch, Danish, Swedish and German, so may English itself diversify. Webster's prediction that the language of North America would become as different from the language of Britain as Swedish is from German has not yet been fulfilled. I suspect it will take a longer time a-coming than Webster anticipated. If ever. But the theory has supporters and it is certainly true that diversity seems to be accelerating.

There are scholars who believe that the future of English will no longer even be shaped by its founding family but by L2 speakers – those who vastly outnumber the 'core' speakers – for whom English is a second language, Language Two. Dr Jennifer Jenkins sees the green shoots of plausibility in this theory. She has pointed out that whereas the traditional English 'talk about' something or 'discuss' something, almost all L2 speakers 'discuss about' something. She believes that phrase is here to stay and will spread into Standard English as, she believes, will the tag 'How can I say?' and many others. Perhaps even words we consider wholly mispronounced will take their place in the *Oxford Dictionary*. In Korea and Taiwan and elsewhere, for instance, a 'product' is a 'produk'. What odds 'produk' displacing 'product' as Asian wealth grows? And the complicated English tag system – 'have you?', 'haven't you?', 'could you?', 'couldn't you?', 'won't you?', 'didn't you?' – will most certainly be simplified, Professor David Crystal thinks. His bet is that 'nesspa?' could replace the lot of them. Innit?

The Internet took off in English and although there are now fifteen hundred languages on the Internet, seventy per cent of it is still in English. And a new form of English has just appeared back at base – Text English.

This appeared in an issue of the *Guardian* early in 2003, under 'English as a Foreign Language'. It was written as a parody by John Mullan of University College London but like all good parodies it captures the essence of a way in which language is used:

Dnt u sumX rekn eng lang v lngwindd? 2 mny wds & ltrs? ?nt we b usng lss time & papr? ? we b 4wd tnking + txt? 13 yr grl frim w scot 2ndry schl sd ok. Sh rote GCSE eng as (abt hr smmr hols in NY) in txt spk. (NO!) Sh sd sh 4t txt spk was 'easr thn standard eng'. Sh 4t hr tcher wd b :) Hr tcher 4t it was nt so gr8! Sh was :(& talkd 2 newspprs (but askd 2 b anon). 'I cdnt bleve wot I was cing! :o' –! –! –! OW2TE. Sh hd NI@A wot grl was on abut. Sh 4t her pupl was ritng in 'hieroglyphics'.

This is yet another English and totally comprehensible to its users who are mostly young and therefore influential on the future of the language.

'I love you' is now more commonly the text 'i luv u'. A texting dictionary is already on the streets. On Valentine's Day in 2003, in the UK, about seventy million text messages were sent, five times the number of Valentine cards. 'i luv u' rules.

At first glance this text looks not wholly unlike one of the Old

Germanic dialects and that is no wonder: for the latest specialist, most technologically driven of written languages is still founded on the word-hoard brought across to England from Friesland more than fifteen hundred years ago.

There are now hundreds of dictionaries of English words – slang dictionaries, science, art, business dictionaries, creole, dialect, sporting, dictionaries blasphemous, humorous, ponderous, omnivorous.

These are some of the latest words recently accepted by the *Oxford English Dictionary*: 'ass-backwards', 'bigorexia', 'blog', 'clientelism', 'clocker', 'dischuffed', 'dragon lady', 'emotional intelligence', 'lookism', 'rent-a-quote', 'rumpy-pumpy', 'sizeist', 'sussed', 'unplugged', 'weblogger'. Still it flows on. English it seems has to name and so claim everything in the world that comes on its radar.

These words are queuing up and knocking on the door to be admitted next to the *OED*:

Whitelist: to place a name, e-mail address, Website address, or program on a list of items that are deemed spam- or virus-free.

Conscientious neglect: gardening in a conscientious manner by using hardy, native plants that don't require chemicals or other environmentally destructive care.

Anglosphere: the collection of English-speaking nations that support the principles of common law and civil rights.

Earworm: a song or tune that repeats over and over inside a person's head.

Google: to search for information on the Web, particularly by using the Google search engine; to search the Web for information related to a new or potential girlfriend or boyfriend.

Zorse: an animal that's a hybrid of a zebra and a horse.

Gaydar: an intuitive sense that enables someone to identify whether another person is gay.

Chambers Dictionary has its own rather racy list of words in waiting:

Bricks and clicks: relating to a company that combines traditional methods of selling with Internet selling – also called 'clicks and mortar'.

Cyberskiver: a person who surfs the Internet while supposedly being at work.

E-lancer: a freelance worker who communicates with clients through a personal computer.

Gayby: a baby born to a surrogate mother on behalf of a gay couple.

Netspionage: the theft of confidential information by abuse of the Internet.

New economy: the sector of the economy involving companies that use the Internet.

Uber-nerd: a person with exceptionally poor social skills.

Again, as with so many of the hundreds of thousands of words which have come into the language since the fifth century, it is all but impossible to discover a single prime creator for these words, words which extend the description and possibilities of our lives. They seem to be conjured out of the air we breathe; just as they are spoken back into that air and carried like pollen on the wind.

An adventure should have an ending but there is no conclusion to the astounding and moving journey of the English language, from its small spring to rivers of thought and poetry and science, into oceans of religions and politics, industry, finance and technology, those oceans swept by storms that poured English on to the willing and the unwilling alike. It is a language that other languages take on, bend, adapt and grow from, just as English itself from its slow fierce forging in these islands has taken on and been tested by and absorbed many other languages. Still it grows. New words line up in their thousands every year to be inspected and selected by compilers of dictionaries: if the guardians of these books of life give them the nod, in they go, into a hoard and a history of words whose ingenuity, democratic sourcing, variety, richness, even genius is all but beyond imagination.

ACKNOWLEDGEMENTS

When I wrote this book I started from scratch, but some of it is based on work I had done in radio and television. It is different from both in very many ways, not least in its greater volume of information and in its ambition. Because it is much longer, I was able to include substantially more material and go into more areas and express more opinions.

All of us who work in broadcasting know that, unlike writing a book, programme making can only be done as part of a team. *The Adventure of English* which I first suggested several years ago was eventually made by a team drawn mostly from London Weekend Television's Arts Department. It was a pleasure to work with them.

First, I want to thank Simon Cherry. He was the Script Editor and his contributions were numerous, thoughtful and good-humoured. He threaded himself elegantly through minefields of the spelling and dating of thousands of words. At various stages I was lucky that the following researchers were employed, sometimes for one programme, sometimes for more: Jonathan Levi, Claire Holland, Andy Marino and Lucy Leveugle. The directors were long-established colleagues and friends: Robert Bee, David Thomas and Nigel Wattis. They brought high skills, many suggestions and great application to what grew into a complicated series, which became tightly stretched as we tried to do justice to this huge subject on adequate but not lavish resources. David Liddiment waved the project on at the ITV

Centre and Steve Anderson, the Head of Factual Programmes, was the sort of constructive ally who matters.

The Adventure of English was the most gruelling work I have done in television. It was difficult because I was the author as well as the series producer and sometimes the two roles rubbed each other up the wrong way. Some of the scripts were drafted ten or more times. The directors developed the habit of convincing themselves that the best time of day to shoot was always dawn.

Before the television series I had made twenty-five radio programmes called *The Routes of English* for BBC Radio 4. These were produced by Simon Elmes, whose deep knowledge of the English language was put into the service of those documentaries which, like the television series, had the rare good fortune of being liked both by audiences and critics. In the course of these radio programmes I met several linguists, including Kate Burridge, Lynda Mugglestone and David Graddol, whose thinking and whose work excited me enormously and eventually led me to chance my arm on the eight hours of television into which we tried to squeeze and shape fifteen hundred years of the English language. We made rules for ourselves, we sought out apposite locations whenever possible, we infested the screen with words, we spoke Old English, Middle English and all other Englishes in the tongue we hope was most authentic, and we had co-operation wherever we went.

I am grateful to all those who agreed to take part in the television programmes including Seamus Heaney, Kathryn Duncan Jones, Lynda Mugglestone, John Barton, Hubert Devenish and Professor Salikoko Mufuene: there were also many scholars and experts who answered our calls with courtesy. Dr Kathryn A. Lowe of Glasgow University was not only a key contributor to the television series but it was to her I turned when I had finished the book to check it through. I am indebted to her for doing this so supportively and scrupulously. She made numerous suggestions, the majority of which I took up. Any errors are my sole responsibility.

A bibliography is attached. It includes those books we found most often most useful. There are some fascinating studies led by Professor David Crystal's fine *Encyclopaedia of English*.

I want to thank Rupert Lancaster at Hodder & Stoughton for editing the book so carefully, and my very good friend Julia Matheson with whom I have greatly enjoyed working for most of my working life.

My final acknowledgement is to the many writers whose work I have read, the many people I have spoken to, all of whom believe, as I do, that the creation and continued life of the English language is fascinating.

I've been lucky three times over. To have had the chance to make programmes on the English language, to do it in the company of many people I admire and to be given the opportunity to start again and write this book on a subject which has fascinated me all my life.

In Wigton, my hometown, in the forties and fifties of the last century I got to know Willie Carrick, who wrote stories in the local dialect. He was Town Clerk, local historian and a great figure in that small landscape. He made me understand that the dialect we spoke was not a debased tongue but something rich, with a history, something to be proud of.

Later, at school, Mr Blacker, the English teacher, taught by making us read aloud from English poetry, stopping every so often to question us on the meaning of key words and phrases, emphasising how rich they were, how much they covered.

Both long dead, but I hope that somewhere behind this book are their voices and their devotion to the English language.

PICTURE ACKNOWLEDGEMENTS

Ashmolean Museum Oxford: 4 photo The Art Archive/Eileen Tweedy. Bodleian Library Oxford: 13. British Library London: 1 (Ms Y.T. 26.f2), 2 (Ms Cott.Vit A. XV. f132), 3 (Ms Harl.2278 f98v), 7 (Ms Roy.18.EI f 175), 8 (Ms Harl.4380 f186v), 10 (Ms Cott.Vesp.f III f8), 11 (G.11586 p. AIIIv), 25 (Ms Add. Or. 2 p17). The Brotherton Library, Leeds University Library: 18 below. Corbis: 15. Corbis/Bettmann: 14, 17, 27, 28. Corbis/Hulton-Deutsch Collection: 24. Corbis/Jane Wishnetsky: 26. Mary Evans Picture Library: 16. Hulton Archive/Getty Images: 20. Illustrated London News 1862: 21. Musée de la Tapisserie Bayeux: 5 photo The Art Archive/Dagli Orti. The National Library of Australia, Canberra: 22, 23 (c) 1936 by Allan & Co. Prop. Ltd., Melbourne. National Portrait Gallery, London: 9 (Unknown artist), 12 (Unknown artist), 18 above (Alexander Nasmyth, 19 (Harry Furniss). Public Record Office, Image Library, Kew: 6 (E36/284 f3).

BIBLIOGRAPHY

I have not listed classic English texts which are available in many editions (e.g. Dickens, Austen, Shakespeare).

General Books on the English Language

Bailey, Richard W.: *Images of English* (Cambridge, Cambridge University Press, 1992)

Baugh, Albert C. and Cable, Thomas: *A History of the English Language* (London, Routledge, 1951, 5th edn 2002)

Blake, N.F.: *A History of the English Language* (London, Palgrave, 1996)

Bryson, Bill: *Mother Tongue* (London, Hamish Hamilton, 1990)

Burchfield, Robert: *The English Language* (Oxford, Oxford University Press, 1985, reissued with corrections 2002)

Crystal, David: *The Cambridge Encyclopaedia of the English Language*, (Cambridge, Cambridge University Press, 1995, reprinted with corrections 2001)

Crystal, David: *English as a Global Language* (Cambridge, Cambridge University Press, 1997)

Crystal, David: *The English Language* (London, Penguin, 1998, 2nd edn 2002)

Elmes, Simon: *The Routes of English*, vols. 1–4 (London, BBC Adult Learning, 1999–2001)

Flavell, Linda and Roger: *The Chronology of Words and Phrases* (London, Kyle Cathie, 1999)

Freeborn, Dennis: *From Old English to Standard English* (London, Macmillan, 1992, 2nd edn 1998)

Graddol, David, Leith, Dick and Swann, Joan (eds.): *English – History, Diversity and Change* (London, Routledge, 1996)

Hughes, Geoffrey: *Swearing* (Oxford, Blackwell, 1991)

Hughes, Geoffrey: *Words in Time* (Oxford, Blackwell, 1988)

Kacirk, Jeffrey: *Altered English* (San Francisco, Pomegranate, 2002)

Katzner, Kenneth: *The Languages of the World* (revised edn) (London, Routledge, 1986)

Leith, Dick: *A Social History of English* (London, Routledge, 1983, 2nd edn 1997)

McArthur, Tom: *The English Languages* (Cambridge, Cambridge University Press, 1998)

McArthur, Tom: *The Oxford Guide to World English* (Oxford, Oxford University Press, 2002)

McCrum, Robert, MacNeil, Robert and Cran, William: *The Story of English* (London, Faber, 1986, 2nd edn 1992)

Montagu, Ashley: *The Anatomy of Swearing* (Philadelphia, University of Pennsylvania Press, 1967)

Partridge, Eric: *A Dictionary of Slang and Unconventional English* (London, Routledge, 1949) (There are later editions, but we looked at this one particularly for Second World War slang.)

Pennycook, Alastair: *The Cultural Politics of English as an International Language* (London, Longman, 1994)

Rees, Nigel: *Dictionary of Word & Phrase Origins* (London, Cassell, 1996)

Ricks, Christopher and Michaels, Leonard (eds.): *The State of the Language, 1990s Edition* (London, Faber, 1990)

Singh, Ishtla: *Pidgins and Creoles, An Introduction* (London, Arnold, 2000)

Watts, Richard and Trudgill, Peter (eds.): *Alternative Histories of English* (London, Routledge, 2002)

Williams, Raymond: *Keywords* (London, Fontana, 1976)

The *Oxford English Dictionary* has been a constant resource, and the search facilities of the online version were particularly helpful.

General History

Morgan, Kenneth O. (ed.): *The Oxford History of Britain* (Oxford, Oxford University Press, 1988)

Canny, Nicholas (ed.): *The Origins of Empire – The Oxford History of the British Empire*, vol. 1 (Oxford, Oxford University Press, 1998)

Marshall, P.J. (ed.): *The Eighteenth Century – The Oxford History of the British Empire*, vol. 2 (Oxford, Oxford University Press, 1998)

Porete, Andrew (ed.): *The Nineteenth Century – The Oxford History of the British Empire*, vol. 3 (Oxford, Oxford University Press, 1999)

Chapters 1–3 (Programme 1)

PRIMARY

Alfred: *On the State of Learning in England* (Hatton Ms. 20, Bodleian Library, Oxford); reprinted in Whitelock, Dorothy (ed.), *Sweet's Anglo-Saxon Reader* (Oxford, Oxford University Press, 15th edn 1975)

Anon.: *Beowulf*, ed. Klaeber, Fr. (Lexington, D.C. Heath, 3rd edn 1950)

Baker, Derek (ed.): *England in the Early Middle Ages: Portraits and Documents* (London, Hutchinson, 1968)

Garmonsway, G.N. (trans.): *The Anglo-Saxon Chronicle* (London, Dent, 1953)

Gordon, R.K. (trans.): *Anglo-Saxon Poetry* (London, Dent, 1926)

Heaney, Seamus: *Beowulf, A New Translation* (London, Faber, 1999)

Henry of Huntingdon: *The History of the English People, 1000–1154*, trans. Greenaway, Diana (Oxford, Oxford University Press, 1996)

Keynes, Simon and Lapidge, Michael (eds.): *Alfred the Great – Asser's*

   Life of King Alfred and Other Contemporary Sources (London, Penguin
   Books, 1983)

Swanton, Michael (trans.): *Anglo-Saxon Prose* (London, Dent, 1975)

SECONDARY

Chapman, John and Hamerow, Helena (eds.): *Migrations and Invasions
   in Archaeological Explanation* (Oxford, British Archaeological
   Report, International Series 664, 1997)

Ekwall, Eilert: *The Concise Oxford Dictionary of Place Names* (4th edn)
   (Oxford, Oxford University Press, 1960)

Golding, Brian: *Conquest and Colonisation* (London, Palgrave, 1994)

Page, R.I.: *Runes* (London, British Museum Press, 1987)

Ward-Perkins, Bryan: 'Why Did the Anglo-Saxons Not Become
   More British?', *English Historical Review*, vol. CXV, no. 462, June
   2000

Wrenn, C.L.: *A Study of Old English Literature* (London, Harrap, 1967)

Chapters 4–6 (Programme 2)

PRIMARY

Baker, Derek (ed.): *England in the Later Middle Ages – Portraits and
   Documents* (London, Hutchinson, 1968)

Bennett, J.A.W. and Smithers, G.V.: *Early Middle English Verse and
   Prose* (Oxford, Oxford University Press, 1968)

Chaucer, Geoffrey: *Works*, ed. Robinson, F.N. (Oxford, Oxford University Press, 1957, 2nd edn 1974)

Davies, R.T. (ed.): *Medieval English Lyrics* (London, Faber and Faber,
   1963)

SECONDARY

Barber, Richard: *The Knight and Chivalry* (revised edn) (Woodbridge,
   The Boydell Press, 1995)

Boitani, Piero and Mann, Jill (eds.): *The Cambridge Chaucer Companion*
   (Cambridge, Cambridge University Press, 1986)

Cannon, Christopher: *The Making of Chaucer's English* (Cambridge, Cambridge University Press, 1998)

Clanchy, M.T.: *England and Its Rulers* (Oxford, Blackwell, 2nd edn 1998)

Paterson, Linda M.: *The World of the Troubadours* (Cambridge, Cambridge University Press, 1993)

Postan, M.M.: *The Medieval Economy and Society* (London, Weidenfeld & Nicolson, 1972)

De Rougemont, Denis: *Love in the Western World* (trans. Montgomery Belgion) (Princeton, Princeton University Press, 1983)

Weir, Alison: *Eleanor of Aquitaine* (London, Jonathan Cape, 1999)

West, Richard: *Chaucer* (London, Robinson, 2000)

Ziegler, Philip: *The Black Death* (London, Collins, 1969)

Chapters 7–9 (Programme 3)

PRIMARY

Davis, Norman (ed.): *The Paston Letters* (Oxford, Oxford University Press, 1963)

Kempe, Margery: *The Book of Margery Kempe* (ed. Staley, Lynn) (New York, W.W. Norton, 2001)

Langland, William: *Piers Plowman*, translated by Economou, George (Philadelphia, University of Pennsylvania Press, 1996)

SECONDARY

Bobrick, Benson: *The Making of the English Bible* (London, Weidenfeld & Nicolson, 2001)

Duffy, Eamon: *The Stripping of the Altars: Traditional Religion in England 1400–1580* (New Haven, Yale University Press, 1992)

Duffy, Eamon: *The Voices of Morebath – Reformation and Rebellion in an English Village* (New Haven, Yale University Press, 2001)

Febvre, Lucien and Martin, Henri-Jean (trans. Gerard, David): *The Coming of the Book* (London, New Left Books, 1976)

Keen, Maurice: *English Society in the Later Middle Ages* (London, Penguin, 1990)

Shiels, W.J.: *The English Reformation* (London, Longman, 1989)

Chapters 10–12 (Programme 4)

SECONDARY

Gurr, Andrew: *Playgoing in Shakespeare's London* (Cambridge, Cambridge University Press, 1987)

Gurr, Andrew: *The Shakespearian Stage 1574–1642* (3rd edn) (Cambridge, Cambridge University Press, 1992)

Kermode, Frank: *Shakespeare's Language* (London, Penguin Books, 2000)

Chapters 13–15 (Programme 5)

PRIMARY

Bergon, Frank (ed.): *The Journals of Lewis and Clark* (New York, Penguin Books, 1989)

Jones, Charles Colcock, Jr: *Gullah Folktales From the Georgia Coast* (Athens, GA, University of Georgia Press, 2000)

Webster, Noah: *Blue-Backed Spelling Book*; Anon.: *New England Primer* (Oklahoma City, Hearthstone Publishing, 1998)

Wood, William: *New England's Prospect* (Amherst, University of Massachusetts Press, 1977)

SECONDARY

Boorstin, Daniel J.: *The Americans: The Colonial Experience* (new edn) (London, Phoenix Press, 2000)

Boorstin, Daniel J.: *The Americans: The National Experience* (new edn) (London, Phoenix Press, 2000)

Brogan, Hugh: *The Penguin History of the USA* (London, Penguin, 1990)

Bryson, Bill: *Made in America* (London, Secker & Warburg, 1994)

Cutler, Charles L.: *O Brave New Words! – Native American Loanwords in Current English* (Norman, University of Oklahoma Press, 1994)

Dillard, J.L.: *Black English – Its History and Usage in the United States* (New York, Random House, 1972)

Dillard, J.L.: *A History of American English* (Harlow, Longman, 1992)

Ellis, Joseph J.: *After the Revolution: Profiles of Early American Culture* (New York, W.W. Norton, 1979)

Kamensky, Jane: *Governing the Tongue – The Politics of Speech in Early New England* (New York, Oxford University Press, 1997)

Mencken, H.L.: *The American Language* (4th edn) (New York, Knopf, 1936)

Mufwene, Salikoko S., Rickford, John R., Bailey, Guy and Baugh, John: *African-American English* (London, Routledge, 1998)

Rickford, John Russell and Rickford, Russell John: *Spoken Soul – The Story of Black English* (New York, John Wiley & Sons, 2000)

Simmons, James C.: *Star-Spangled Eden* (New York, Carroll & Graf, 2000)

Sloan, William David and Startt, James D.: *The Media in America* (Northport, Vision Press, 1999)

Wright, Ronald: *Stolen Continents – The 'New World' Through Indian Eyes* (Toronto, Penguin Books, 1992)

Chapters *14–18 (Programme 6)*

PRIMARY

Jennings, Humphrey: *Pandaemonium – The Coming of the Machine as Seen by Contemporary Observers* (London, André Deutsch, 1985)

Johnson, Samuel: *Samuel Johnson on Shakespeare* (ed. Woudhuysen, H.R.) (London, Penguin Books, 1989)

Mackie, Erin (ed.): *The Commerce of Everyday Life – Selections from The Tatler and The Spectator* (Boston, Bedford/St Martins, 1998)

Mayhew, Henry: *London Labour and the London Poor* (London, Penguin Books, 1985)

Ross, Angus (ed.): *Selections from The Tatler and The Spectator* (London, Penguin Books, 1982)

SECONDARY

Ayto, John: *The Oxford Dictionary of Rhyming Slang* (Oxford, Oxford University Press, 2002)

Colley, Linda: *Britons: Forging the Nation 1707–1837* (New Haven, Yale University Press, 1992)

Crowley, Tony: *Proper English? Readings in Language, History and Cultural Identity* (London, Routledge, 1991)

Fryer, Peter: *Mrs Grundy – Studies in English Prudery* (London, Dobson Books, 1963)

Görlach, Manfred: *English in Nineteenth-Century England* (Cambridge, Cambridge University Press, 1999)

Holroyd, Michael: *The Pursuit of Power* (vol. 2 of biography of Bernard Shaw) (London, Chatto & Windus, 1989)

De Maré, Eric: *London 1851 – The Year of the Great Exhibition* (London, The Folio Society, 1972)

Montagu, Ashley: *The Anatomy of Swearing* (Philadelphia, University of Pennsylvania Press, 2001)

Mugglestone, Lynda: *Talking Proper – The Rise of Accent as a Social Symbol* (2nd edn) (Oxford, Oxford University Press, 2003)

O'Toole, Fintan: *A Traitor's Kiss: The Life of Richard Brinsley Sheridan* (London, Granta, 1997)

Porter, Roy: *Enlightenment* (London, Penguin Books, 2000)

Rogers, Pat: *Hacks and Dunces* (London, Methuen, 1980)

Romaine, Suzanne (ed.): *The Cambridge History of the English Language, Vol. IV – 1776–1997* (Cambridge, Cambridge University Press, 1998)

Chapters *19–21* *(Programme 7)*

PRIMARY

Baker, Philip and Bruyn, Adrienne: *St Kitts and the Atlantic Creoles – The Texts of Samuel Augustus Mathews in Perspective* (London, University of Westminster Press, 1998)

Hakluyt, Richard: *Voyages and Discoveries* (London, Penguin Books, 1972) (includes John Hawkins' voyage to the Indies, 1564)

Krise, Thomas W. (ed.): *Caribbeana – An Anthology of English Literature of the West Indies 1657–1777* (Chicago, University of Chicago Press, 1999) (includes James Grainger's *The Sugar Cane*)

Parkes, Fanny: *Begums, Thugs and White Mughals* (ed. Dalrymple, William) (London, Sickle Moon, 2002)

Yule, Col. Henry and Burnell, Arthur Coke: *Hobson-Jobson* (London, John Murray, 1886)

SECONDARY

Black, Clinton V.: *Pirates of the West Indies* (Cambridge, Cambridge University Press, 1989)

Burchfield, Robert (ed.): *The Cambridge History of the English Language, Vol. V – English in Britain and Overseas: Origins and Development* (Cambridge, Cambridge University Press, 1994)

Crystal, David: *Language Death* (Cambridge, Cambridge University Press, 2000)

Dalby, Andrew: *Language in Danger* (London, Penguin Books, 2002)

Delbridge, A. et al. (eds.): *The Macquarie Dictionary – Australia's National Dictionary* (revised third edn) (Macquarie, 2001)

Farrington, Anthony: *Trading Places – The East India Company and Asia 1600–1834* (London, British Library, 2002)

Hughes, Robert: *The Fatal Shore* (London, Collins Harvill, 1987)

James, Lawrence: *Raj – The Making of British India* (London, Abacus, 1998)

Lewis, Ivor: *Sahibs, Nabobs and Boxwallahs – A Dictionary of the Words of Anglo-India* (Delhi, Oxford University Press, 1991)

Mitchell, David: *Pirates* (London, Thames & Hudson, 1976)

Nettle, Daniel and Romaine, Suzanne: *Vanishing Voices* (Oxford, Oxford University Press, 2000)

Tully, Mark: *No Full Stops in India* (London, Penguin Books, 1991)

Chapters 22–24 (Programme 8)

SECONDARY

Ayto, John: *Twentieth Century Words* (Oxford, Oxford University Press, 1999)

Fussell, Paul: *The Great War and Modern Memory* (Oxford, Oxford University Press, 1975)

Gardiner, Juliet: *Over Here – The GIs in Wartime Britain* (London, Collins & Brown, 1992)

Graddol, David: *The Future of English?* (London, British Council, 1997)

Graddol, David and Meinhof, Ulrike H. (eds.): *English in a Changing World* (AILA Review 13) (Oxford, Association Internationale de Linguistique Appliqué/International Association of Applied Linguistics, 1999)

Partridge, Eric: *A Dictionary of Slang and Unconventional English* (3rd edn) (London, Routledge, 1949) (There are later editions, but this was useful for finding wartime slang.)

Partridge, Eric and Clark, John W.: *British and American English Since 1900* (London, Andrew Dakers, 1951)

INDEX

Abbeville 177

Aboriginal languages 293

Aboriginals 277–8

Académie Française: *Le Dictionnaire de l'Académie Française* 210, 307

Accademia della Crusca 216

Act of Union (1536) 294

Act of Union (1542) 294

Act of Union (1707) 224

Adam and Eve 200

Adams, John 167–8, 169, 173, 210

Addison, Thomas 170, 203, 208, 210

Adeline, St 107

adjective duplication 191

Ælfric 31

Aeschylus 152

thelred, King 31, 32

Aetius, Consul 1

African Hockey Federation 305

African languages 187, 189, 190, 192, 199, 266, 268, 296

Age of Chivalry 46

Agincourt, Battle of (1415) 94, 96

agriculture xi, 26

Aidan, St 8, 11

Alfred, King xii, 6, 32, 50, 56, 98, 211, 250

    saves the English language 18, 19, 30, 33

    translates *Pastoral Care* 18, 29

    English as a rallying force 18, 94

    education programme 18, 45–6

    battle of Ethandune 19

    his Wessex dialect becomes the first Standard English 30

    publications 30–1

    legacy of 32

alphabet 10, 11, 201

Althorp 22

America

    movement of the language which became English 4

    Vikings and 22

    Plymouth Pilgrims travel to 153, 154–8, 301

    the prime inheritor of the English tongue 154

    Indian words enter the English language 159, 160

    first book published in English in America 162

America – *cont.*
appearance of a standard accent 162
spread of colonies 163–4
development of the political system
164
French traders 165, 172
see also United States
American Civil War 183, 196, 197
American English
Native American words 159, 160,
174
first book published in English in
America 162
word flow from French 164, 177
Spanish as the biggest feeder into
American English 164
and development of the political
system 164
accents 165–6
John Adams on 167–8
pronunciation of polysyllables 169
America becomes confident in its
own English language 169–70
keeping the language pure 170
in the west 172–86
Scottish and Irish additions 176
does not totally dominate 292
strong influence in Britain 296
American v British English 298–9,
302–3
American Indian languages 293
American Revolution 166–7, 178,
181, 186
American War of Independence 183
anatomy 239
Andean Commission of Jurists 305
Angles 2, 5, 6, 9, 10, 12, 24, 154
Anglo-Saxon 28, 76, 118, 122, 126,
260

Anglo-Saxon Chronicle 17, 31, 33–5,
39, 42, 250
Anglo-Saxons 35, 42, 96, 221
Angola 189
Anne, Queen 207, 209
Anon: *On The Dialect of the Craven*
204
Antwerp 111
Arab Air Carriers Association 305
Arabic xii, 15–16, 58, 118, 119, 122,
129, 289, 291, 293
Arawak Indians 267
Arden, Mary 142
Ariosto, Ludovico 130
Aristotle 238
Armour, Jean 226
Arnold, John 240
Arthur, King 2, 46
Asante 189
Ascham, Roger 117, 120, 131
Ashmolean Museum, Oxford 30
Ashton 7
Asia 4
Asian Amateur Athletic Association
305
Asiatick Society of Bengal 254
Aspatria 26
Association of Baltic Marine Biologists
305
Athenaeum periodical 290, 291
Atkinson, E. F.: 'Curry and Rice'
261–2
Attwood, Scott 161
Augustine, St 8
Austen, Jane 230–32
Northanger Abbey 230–31
Australia 276–86, 307
Cook's expedition 276
penal colony founded 276

the convicts 278–9
English dialect words imported 279
criminal words 280
Australian pleasure in their
    language 281–4
'Waltzing Matilda' 282–3
word endings 285–6
Australian accent 286
the nature of modern Australian
    English 286
end of "cultural cringe" 295
Australian creole 278
Avon River 5, 93
Awdely, John: *The Fraternyte of
    Vacabondes* 138
Aztec 267

Babu English 258, 259
Bacon, Francis 12, 123, 125, 126,
    142
Ball, John 64–5, 83, 194
Bamoun 189
Banks, Sir Joseph 276
Bantam 251
Barton, John 149, 150
Basque 4
Bassenthwaite 22
Baton Rouge 177
Battle of Britain (1940) 40
Battle of Maldon 31
Bay Psalm Book 162
Bayeux Tapestry 34
BBC English x, 25, 27
BBC Radio 4 x
Beatitudes (from Gospel According to
    St Matthew) 109, 110, 114
Beaufort, Louis de 297
Becket, Thomas à 72
Beckett, Samuel 151

Bede 1, 5, 29, 160
    *Ecclesiastical History of the English
        Nation* 12, 18
Beethoven, Ludwig van 225
Beeton, Mrs Isabella 233
Bellay, Joachim du 130
Belleville 177
Bellow, Saul 292
Bengal 254
Bengali 252
Beowulf 13, 14–15, 16, 48, 50, 90
Berlin Wall 40
Bermuda 267
Bertrand de Born 50
'Rassa tan cries e monte e poia' 47
Bestiary 61–2
Bible, the 80, 81, 83, 84, 142, 153,
    238
    King James (Authorised) version
        26, 109, 113–14, 144–5, 187
    Latin Vulgate version 85
    Wycliffe English Bible 85–9, 91,
        92, 105
    English-language Bibles banned 89
    Latin held to be the language of 92
    Tyndale's Bible smuggled into
        England 110–11
    Matthew Bible 112, 147
    Great Bible 112–13, 147
    Geneva Bible 112, 147
    Bishops' Bible 112, 147
    Douai-Rheims Bible 112
    Catholic Church keeps it from the
        people 113
    Church of England aims to make it
        widely available 113
    Cranmer's Bible 147
    and the Pilgrim Fathers 155, 156,
        160, 162, 198

biology 239–40
Birmingham 7
Bismarck, Prince Otto von 292
Black Death 63–4, 92
black English
    Gullah xii, 189, 190–91
    creation of 187
    emerges in triumph 188, 196
    Sabir 189–90
    pidgin 190
    creole 190
    grammar 191, 192
    prejudice against 191
    influences white speech 192,
        300–301
    literature 192–4
    spirituals 195
    Mark Twain 197–8
Blackfriars, London 89
Blackwood's Edinburgh Magazine 235
Blennerhasset 22–3
'bloody'
    as an intensifier 206–7
    use in Australia 280–81
Bloom, Harold 141, 146
Boccaccio, Giovanni 71
Bodleian Library, Oxford 129
body language x
Boethius, Anicius: *The Consolation of
        Philosophy* 71
Boleyn, Anne 112
Bombay 252
Book of Common Prayer 147
Borrowdale 22
Boston, Massachusetts 182
Boston Morning Post 182
Boswell, James 215–16, 224
Botany Bay, Australia 276, 279
'Bow Bell Cockney' 244

Bowlder, Thomas 233–4
Boyse, Samuel 203
Bradford, William 156–7
Bragg, Melvyn: childhood dialect x,
        25–8
Brazil 117, 267, 306
Breukelen (Brooklyn) 164
Bridlington 7
Britain
    later medieval 80
    multiculturalism 296
    see also England
British Council 299
British Empire xii, 262
Britons 1, 2
    Celtic 6
Brittany 5
Brooke, Rupert 299
Bruges 102
Brunel, Isambard Kingdom 241
Brunel, Marc Isambard 241
Bryson, Bill
    Made in America 158
    Mother Tongue 158
Buffalo Bill (William F. Cody) xii,
        186
Bulletin (*Bushman's Bible*) 282
Bulu 189
Bunyan, John: *Pilgrim's Progress* 91
Burgundy, Duke of 95
Burns, Robert 225, 226–7, 228, 275
    'The Lea Rig' 226
    Poems – chiefly in the Scottish dialect
        226
    A Red, Red Rose' 226
    'Tam o' Shanter' 226
Burnside, Ambrose Everett 196
Burridge, Dr Kate 278, 285, 286
Burton 7

Butler English 258
Byron, George Gordon, 6th Baron 194
Byzantine motifs 12

Cædmon 9
Caesar, Julius 123
Calcutta *see* Kolkata
*Cambridge History of the English
    Language* 265–6, 269
Cambridge University 70, 120, 247
Campion, Thomas 135
Canada 164, 307
cant 247
Cape Girardeau 177
Capote, Truman 177
Cardoso, President 306
Carib language 267
Caribbean 258, 265
Carlisle 26
Carlyle, Thomas 242
castles 36, 51, 54, 96
cathedrals 36, 106
Catherine of Aragon 112
Cawdrey, Robert: *The Table
    Alphabeticall* 129–30
Caxton, William 78, 94, 96, 101–3,
    219
    The Recuyell of the Historyes of Troye
    (trans.) 102
Celtic languages 2, 4, 5, 17, 21, 23,
    27, 28, 35, 42, 122, 293–4
Celts 1, 2, 5, 6, 40, 277
censorship 233–4
Central Africa 42
Central French dialect 45
Central Midlands 78, 99, 103
Centreville 177
Cerne Abbas 31
Chambers Dictionary 311–12

Chancery 98, 103, 219
Chancery Standard 99
Chandler, Raymond 177, 303
Chapman, George 140
Charles, HRH The Prince of Wales
    299
Charleston, South Carolina 189, 196
charters 12
Chaucer, Geoffrey 74, 99, 130, 131,
    170, 203–4, 205, 220, 243, 244
    decides to write in English 69
    his life 70–1
    influence of Italian poetry 71
    vocabulary 72, 75–7
    and dialects 76–7
    the father and founding genius of
        English literature 79
    structure and rhyme schemes 90
    and Caxton 94
    and Mark Twain 197
    swear words in 232–3
    Canterbury Tales 69, 71–7, 78, 79,
        89, 102, 197
    The Parliament of Fowls 71
    A Treatise on the Astrolabe 70
    Troilus and Criseyde 71, 78
Chaucer, John 70
Chaucer, Lewis 70
Chaudhuri, Amit 264
Cheke, Sir John 126–7
chemistry 239, 240
Chesterfield, Lord 215
Chicago 192
China 297
Chinese xii, 15–16, 291, 305
Chippenham 7, 18
chivalry 46, 57
Choctaw Indians 182
Chomsky, Noam 12

Chrétien de Troyes 46–7
Christian Brethren *see* Lollards
Christianity
  reintroduction of 6
  festivals 9
  its words enter the English
    language 9–10
  and writing 10–11
  the unchallengeable belief system
    120–21
  taken to India 250
Church of England 113, 127
churches, and the wool trade 54
Churchill, Sir Winston 8, 303
Cicero 147
cinema 302
Clarence, Duke of 70
Clark, William 173, 174, 175
class 136, 242–3
Clement VII, Pope 112
Cockney 236, 243, 245
  rhyming slang 247–8
'cockney rhymes' 235
Cockneys 244
coffee houses 202
Coleridge, Samuel Taylor 298
Cologne 102, 107
colonialism 117–18
Commonwealth 264
Concord, Massachusetts 166
Connecticut 163, 174
Cook, Captain James 276
Cooper, James Fenimore 166, 180
Corby 22
Cornish 190, 244, 293
Cornwall 2, 5
Cornwell, John 66
Coronation Street (television soap) 136
Costa Rica 266

Council of Constance (1414) 92
court, the
  Latin and French as the chosen
    languages 45
  and chivalry 46
  Henry III strengthens French
    representation 55
  the language of the courtier 136
  and dialect 221–2
courtly love 47
courts
  cases heard in/documents written in
    French since the Conquest 66,
    95
  English replaces French 66
Coverdale, Miles 112
Cranmer, Thomas 113, 147
Crediton 7
creole 266, 269–72, 273
  defined 190
  French 271
  Maican 271–2
Crick, Francis 12
Crockett, Davy 180–81
Cromwell, Oliver 120, 287
Crusades 190
Crystal, Professor David 210, 265,
    310
  Encyclopaedia of the English Language
    69
  English As a Global Language
    290–91
Cuba 118
Cumbria 17, 77
Cumbrian accent 22, 25–8, 137
Cumbrian dialect 273
Curll, Edmund 203
Curzon, Lord 258–9, 262, 264
Custer, General 186

Daily Express 236, 236
Daily Telegraph 302
Dakota 174
Dalrymple, Alexander 240
Danegeld 31
Danelaw 21–4, 43, 191
Danes 17–22, 29, 31, 32, 35, 40, 191
Daniel, Samuel 154
Danish language 24, 35, 309
Dante Alighieri 71, 130
'Dark Ages' 13
Darwin, Charles 266
Darwin, Erasmus 201
Darwinian properties 36
Declaration of Independence 164
Defoe, Daniel xi, 137, 242
  The Journal of the Plague Year 137
  Robinson Crusoe 137, 194, 288
Derby 22
Desmond, Valerie: *The Awful*
  Australian 286
Devenish, Dr Hubert 269–70
Devonshire accent 137
Dharuk language 277
dialect societies 29
dialects
  and the Enlightenment 48
  Chaucer and 77
  obstinacy of 96, 221
  and Chancery English 99
  attitudes harden towards 136
  dialect writing 138
  increased interest in 204
  loss of status 220–21
  Sheridan and 222
  further stigmatisation 234
Dickens, Charles 70, 150, 243, 245–7
  David Copperfield 245–6
  Little Dorrit 234

Oliver Twist 245, 280
Our Mutual Friend 245
Dictes or Sayengis of the Philosophres
  102
dictionaries 311
  the first English dictionary 129–30
  Webster's 171, 174
  black vocabulary 196
  Dictionnaire de l'Académie Française,
    Le 210, 307
  Critical Pronouncing Dictionary of the
    English Language (Walker) 223,
    243
  Dictionary (Johnson) 210–18, 221,
    232, 234
  Dictionary of the Vulgar Tongue
    (Grose) 213
  Hobson-Jobson 260
  Macquarie Dictionary 284–5
  texting 310
  Oxford English Dictionary 122, 134,
    153, 310, 311
  Chambers Dictionary 311–12
diphthongs 221
Disraeli, Benjamin 242
Domenica 266
Domesday Book 38–9
Don River 5
Donne, John 135
Dorking 6
Douglas, Sylvester: *Treatise on the*
  Lowland Dialect of Scotland 224
Dovenby 22
Dover 5
Drake, Sir Francis 124, 266
Drayton, Michael 135
'Dream of the Rood, The' 10
Dryden, John 79, 204, 207, 209
Dublin 22

Dulwich College, London 303
Duncan-Jones, Professor Katherine
    134–5
Dunkirk 35
Durham 235
Durham Cathedral 36
Dutch, the 156, 266
Dutch language 4, 118, 119, 122,
    164, 309

Ealing 6
East, the 43, 58
East Anglia 5, 18, 39, 154
East Germanic 4
East India Company 252, 253–4
East Midlands 97, 99, 103
EastEnders (television soap) 136, 137
Eastoft 22
Edinburgh 226
Education Act 294
Edward the Confessor, St 34
Edward I, King 60
Edward III, King 66–7, 70
Edward VII, King 262
Egbert's Stone 19
Eleanor of Aquitaine 44–7, 50, 73
Eliot, George 150
Elizabeth I, Queen 33, 116–17, 120,
    131, 132, 133, 162, 168, 243,
    251, 266, 267
Elizabeth II, Queen 286
Ellis, Alexander 246
Ellis Island 189
Elyot, Sir Thomas: *The Boke Names The
    Governour* 125, 137
Emerson, Ralph Waldo 146, 166
Encina, Juan del 130
Encyclopaedia Britannica 215
Endeavour 276

England
  Celtic spoken in 42
  Norman French as a percentage of
      the population 42
  merciless conquering of 43
  feudalism 50–1
  the Black Death 62–4
  Renaissance England imports both
      goods and vocabulary 117
  colonialism 117
  population 130
  union with Scotland and Wales 152
  emigration 154
  Act of Union 224
  the world's leading trading and
      industrial nation 241
  trade with India 250–53
  see also Britain
English Channel 45
English language
  originates in German dialects ix, 1,
      291, 309
  a living organism ix
  capacity to absorb others 3, 8–9,
      21, 44, 58–60, 118–20, 121,
      159–60, 267, 277
  movement of Proto Indo-European
      language 4
  the hundred most common words
      in English worldwide 7–8
  early simple directness and
      comparatively limited vocabulary
      8
  begins to compete 12
  Alfred saves the language 18–19
  redefined and made more flexible by
      trade 21
  colonised by Norman French for
      three centuries 37

written English rapidly sidelined
41–2, 44
awaits an opportunity to re-emerge
44
and Henry II's huge kingdom 45
English written word lives on in
the margins 48–50
Arabic words enter English 58
starts to re-emerge 61, 62, 64
the language of protest 65
replaces French in the schoolrooms
65, 66
used by Parliament from 1362
66–7
becomes a royal language again
67–8, 89, 95–6
first book printed in English 102
first dated book printed in England
in English 102
first illustrated book in English 102
flows into religion 112
Elizabeth I's inspirational English
116–17
the sonnet taken into English 131–2
poetry becomes the benchmark for
135
the seeding of continents 154
Pilgrim Fathers' fortunate meeting
with Squanto 158
Swift's proposal 209
capacity to unite or divide 235
industrial words 238–9
scientific and technical vocabulary
239–40
and the Industrial Revolution 241,
292
discredited as the language of
crime, poverty and ignorance
2423

absorbs words from India 251,
259–61
English taught during the Raj
256–8
Butler English and Babu English in
India 258–9
racism 287–9
Crystal's response to the *Athenaeum*
assertion 290–92
maintains its astonishing fertility
297
American v British English 298–9,
302–3
economic strength 305
use by international bodies 305
feeds other languages 306–8
L2 speakers and 309–10
the Internet 310
texting 310
the latest dictionary words 311–12
see also American English; black
English *and under* Australia;
India; West Indies
Enlightenment 48, 219, 223, 230,
254, 257
Eostre 9
Erasmus, Desiderius 107
Esk River 5
Eskdale 22
Esperanto 297
Essex 5
Estonian 4
Ethandune, Battle of (Edington,
Wiltshire) 19, 20
Eurasia 4
Euripides 152
European Free Trade Association 305
European Union 307
Evelyn, John 209

Exeter Cathedral library 13
Exeter Riddles 10, 13

falconry 51–2
Fall, the 200
family names: -son ending 23
Far East 4
Faulkner, William 137–8
Fen lands 49
feudalism 50–1, 74
Fielding, Henry 203, 207, 230
  Joseph Andrews 207
  Tom Jones 207
Finnish 4
First World War 299, 300
Fitzgerald, Scott 177
flash 247, 279
Florida 156
France
  Eleanor of Aquitaine's inheritance
    45
  John loses Norman lands 55
  Chaucer's reputation 75
  Hundred Years' War 94
  a Latin-based language 126
  beaten by the British navy in India
    253
Francien 45, 122
Franklin, Benjamin 170, 171, 173,
  179, 208, 219
Freeman, Thomas 141
French, the 34, 42, 55, 156, 164,
  165, 172, 191–2, 266
French creole 271
French language xii, 7, 27, 122, 132,
  160, 167, 208, 240, 291, 309
  Chaucer and 69, 72, 75
  dispossessed of the language of
    office 96

loan words 118, 119
  dictionaries 129
  Shakespeare learns 147
  enters English in America 164, 177
  in the West Indies 271, 273
  English words imported 307
  legislation on the English language
    307
  Norman *see* Norman French
French literature 130
French Revolution 64, 228
Friar's Crag, Keswick 5
Friesland, Netherlands xii, 3, 16,
  311
Frisian 3–4, 292
Frisian tribes 21, 35, 36, 142, 277,
  278, 295
Fulham 7
futhorc 10

Gaelic 2, 5, 224, 225, 226, 293, 295
Galapagos Islands 266
Gamblesby 22
Gandhi, Mahatma M. K. 250, 262–3,
  306
gangster culture 301–2
Garden of Eden 200
Gay, John 203
gay slang 248
Genesis, Book of 108–9, 200
Genoa 71
Gentlemen, Francis 234
Geoffrey of Monmouth: *Historia Regum
  Brittaniae* 47
geology 240
Geordie 4, 22, 96
George III, King 123
Georgia 163, 192
German 4, 301, 305, 309

Germanic languages ix, 4, 20, 36, 50, 126, 291, 309
Germanic motifs 12
Germanic tribes 1, 2, 5, 17–18, 293
Germans 165, 308
gibberish 247
Globe Theatre, Southwark 73, 139, 140, 229
glossaries 138, 260
Gloucester, Bishop of 84–5
Gloucestershire 107, 108
Goldsmith, Oliver 203
Gordon, Lord 166
Gospel According to Saint Matthew 109, 126
Gospels 12
Gower, John 102, 220
Graddol, David 308
Grainger, James 268, 270
grammar
    adaptability under siege 43–4
    and the Danelaw 21, 24, 191
    black English 191
    retained 58
    Priestley's view 216
    nineteenth-century grammars of English 217
    absence of a system of coding social class differences 291
Grantham 7
Great Exhibition (1851) 238, 239
Great Plains 172
Great Vowel Shift (GVS) 101, 204
Greek xii, 4, 9, 15, 121–7, 240, 291, 293, 303
Greek drama 146
Greeks 289
Greene, Richard 143
Greenwich, London 64

Gregory, Pope 8
    Pastoral Care 18, 29
Grimm, Jakob 292–3
Grimm, Jakob and Grimm, Wilhelm: *Grimm's Fairy Tales* 292
Grose, Francis: *Dictionary of the Vulgar Tongue* 213
Guarani 267
Guardian 310
guilds 81
Gullah tongue xii, 189, 190–91, 269, 270
Gutenberg, Johannes 101
Guthrum 19
gypsies 26
Gyrth, Earl 34

Haarlem 164
Hæsta 35
Haitian 267
Hakluyt, Richard: *Voyages* 266–7
half-uncial majuscule script 11
Hanoverians 222
Hard Words Made Easy 223
Hardy, Thomas 138, 275
Harold, King (Harold Godwineson, Earl of East Anglia) 32, 33, 34, 40, 56, 67
Harris, George 217
Harris, Joel Chandler 192, 193
Hastings 6, 35
Hastings, Battle of (1066) 33–6, 38, 41, 45, 46
Hastings, Warren 254
Hathaway, Anne 142
Hausa 189
Hawkins, Sir John 266–7
Heaney, Seamus 14–15
Hebrew xii, 119, 200, 291

Hellenic 4

Henry II, King 44–5, 46, 50

Henry III, King 55, 56, 67

Henry IV, King 67–8, 89, 95

Henry V, King 94–6, 168

Henry VIII, King 105, 107, 108, 110–13, 131

Herbert, George 135

Hereford 89

Hereford, Nicholas 85

Hereward the Wake 49

Herschel, William 123

Higden, Ranulf: *Polychronicon* 65–6

High English 134, 222

Highland Clearances (1745) 165, 176, 225

Hilda, St 9

Hindi 118, 119, 122, 252, 256, 263

Hobson-Jobson 260

Hokkun 308

Holocaust 188

Holy Island (Lindisfarne) xii, 12, 17, 18

Holy Trinity Church, Stratford-upon-Avon 148

Homer 193

Hood, Thomas, the younger 235

Hooker, Richard 141

Hopkins, Gerard Manley 235

Horace 147

Horton, George Moses 192

Houghly River 252

Houses of Parliament 96

Hughes, Robert: *The Fatal Shore* 279

Hughes, Ted 227

Hume, David 12, 170

Hundred Years War (1337–1453) 70, 94–6

Hungarian 4

Ibo 272

Iceland 28

Ido 297

India 250–64, 289, 305, 307

   movement of the language which became English xii, 4

   the British in 42

   Hindi 118

   Sanskrit dictionary 129

   English persists in 250

   English language hated during the Raj 250

   first English speaker to reach India 250

   trade with England 250–53

   Indian titles 252

   English bides its time 253

   British superior position justified through religion 256

   Indians taught English as part of education policy 256–7, 262

   Macaulay's notorious Minute 257, 262

   English as an elitist language of preferment 258

   Butler English and Babu English 258–9

   independence 262, 263

   Gandhi's attack on English 262–3

   English continues to thrive in India after 1947 263–4

   call centres in 295

Indian languages 27, 199, 250, 252, 253, 254, 258, 296

Indo-European 4, 187

Industrial Revolution 238, 241, 242, 243, 292

industrialism 242

industry 238, 241–2

inflection 4, 24, 25, 291
Ingres, Jean Auguste Dominique 225
Inkhorn Controversy 124, 127, 148,
    181
Interlingua 297
intermarriage 56, 65–6
International Monetary Fund 305
Internet 310
Ireby 22
Ireland 118
Irish Celtic Church 8
Irish Gaelic 119
Irish motifs 12
Irish people 165, 176, 188, 199, 301
Islam 42–3
Isle of Wight 5
Italian language xii, 27, 119–20, 160,
    291, 309
    a Latin-based language 126
    dictionaries 129
    literature 130
    poetry 131
    Shakespeare learns 147
Italy: dominating culture of the
    Renaissance 119
ITV xi

Jackson, Andrew 182
Jacksonville 177
Jamaica
    Jamaican creole 271–2
    Jamaican dialect 274–5
    Patwa 295
James I, King 113, 161, 222
Jamestown, Virginia 155
Japan 304
Japanese 305, 306
Jarrow 12, 18
Jefferson, Thomas 172, 175

Jenkins, Dr Jennifer 309–10
Jespersen, Otto 297
'Jim Crow' laws 196
John, King 55, 56
John of Gaunt 70
Johnson, Dr Samuel 141–2, 203, 219,
    225–8, 230, 231, 232, 238, 243
    Dictionary 210–18, 221, 232, 234
Jones, Charles C., Jr 193–4
Jones, Sir William 4, 254
Jonson, Ben 135, 140, 141, 147,
    151–2
Joyce, James 12, 150, 292
Jutes 2, 5, 6, 9, 10, 12

Keats, John 235–6
Kent 5, 8, 40, 96, 101, 138
Kentucky 174
Kermode, Sir Frank 141
Keswick 23
kiddy talk 279
Kilbracken, Lord 183
King James Bible 26, 109, 113,
    114–15, 144–5, 187
King's College, Cambridge 126–7
Kingston, Jamaica 272
Kipling, Rudyard 138, 261, 262
Knox, Sir Alfred 302
Kolkata (Calcutta) 252–3, 264
    Writer's Building 257
Korea 310
Ku-Klux Klan 196

L2 speakers 309–10
La Trobe University, Melbourne 278
Lafayette 177
Lake District 5, 22, 23, 227, 228
Lancashire dialect 244
Langdale 22

Langland, William 220
  Piers Plowman 70, 90–1, 244
language
  as the finest achievement of culture
    x
  a shared language 20
  clarity for commerce 24
  used to reinforce invaders 37–8
  writing brings uniformity to 101
  supports the professional writer 153
  Lavoisier's 'non-natural' language
    201
  clarification of (Locke) 201, 202
  censored by morality 233
  power of 233
  and trade 292
  has its own force 301
Latin xii, 4, 15, 27, 164, 167, 174,
    194, 293, 303
  and Celts 2, 6
  Church 8, 9, 36, 81, 82, 83, 160,
    291
  Bede and 12
  inflection 24
  Alfred and Latin translation 29, 30
  Ælfric and 31
  and Norman French 39
  and Magna Carta 56
  the Bestiary 61
  loses its grip as clergy die in the
    Black Death 63
  Chaucer and 69, 72
  and Wycliffe's Bible 85, 87
  Bible 85, 92, 103
  as the language of classical thought,
    science and philosophy 120
  the universal language 120
  the language of international debate
    and controversy 120

  no longer associated with
    suppression 120
  thousands of words co-opted to
    English 121
  and medicine 122
  exclusivity 123
  and Old English 124
  Shakespeare learns 147
  and science 199, 240
  splits into other languages 309
Lauder, Afferbeck: *Let Stalk Strine*
    284
Lavoisier, Antoine 201
Lawrence, D. H. 137, 233, 275
laws 12, 15, 123
Lazenby 22
Leeds, Yorkshire 77
Leo X, Pope 112
Leofwine, Earl 34
Lewis, Captain Meriwether 173, 174,
    175
Lindisfarne *see* Holy Island
Lindisfarne Gospels 11, 12, 18
Linguistic Atlas of Late Mediaeval
    English 97
Linthorpe 22
literacy
  growth of 230
  in London 243
Little Bighorn 186
Little Domesday 39
Little Sudbury, Gloucestershire 103–4
Lloyd, Marie 248
Lloyds Coffee House 202
loan words 8–9, 23, 37–8, 100, 118
Locke, John 201–2
  Essay on Human Understanding 201
Lockhart, John 236
Lollards 88, 89, 90, 93, 105, 107

London
  Celtic name 5
  population 54, 99, 243
  power in 69–70
  development of printing in 78
  Chaucer's base 90
  speech of 103
  and the Spanish Armada (1588) 116
  street slang 138, 139
  Shakespeare arrives in 142–3
  cosmopolitan nature of 147
  Puttenham chooses the speech of
    220
  slang 247
London, Bishop of 108
Lord's Prayer 12–13, 15, 85
Los Angeles 177
Lou, Miss: 'Bans a Killin' 274–5
Louisiana 172, 173, 183
Louisiana Purchase 172, 173
Low Dutch 118
Lowe, Dr Katie 43
lower classes 243, 245
Lowestoft 22
Lowland Scots 224, 225
Lowth, Robert 217
  Short Introduction to English Grammar
    216
Lucan 120
Luther, Martin 83, 105, 106, 107,
    112
Luton 7
Lydgate, John 102
Lyell, Sir Charles 192

Macaulay, Thomas Babington, 1st
    Baron 215, 257, 262, 263
McCoy, Joseph 184–5
McCrum, Robert 190

Machiavelli, Niccolò 130
Macmillan, Harold, 1st Earl of
    Stockton 301
Macpherson, James 225
  Fragments of Ancient Poetry 225
Macquarie Dictionary 284–5
Madras 252
Magna Carta 56
Maican creole 271–2
Mainz 101
malapropism 229
Malay 119, 305, 308
Maldon, Battle of (991) 31
Malory, Sir Thomas: *Le Morte d'Arthur*
    102, 131
Malvern Hills 90
Mandarin Chinese 305
Manning, Harold 28
Marconi, Guglielmo 241
Marie de France 46–7, 49
market towns 24
Marlowe, Christopher 140
maroons 272
Marshall, William, Earl of Pembroke
    48
Marston, John 140
Maryland 163
Massachusetts 163, 174
Masters of Chancery 98, 99, 103
mathematics 239, 241
Matthews, Samuel 270, 271
Mayflower 154, 155, 172, 188, 301
Mayflower Compact 155
Mayhew, Henry 247
  London Labour and the London Poor
    244–5
medicine 122, 240
Mediterranean Sea 22, 43
Memoirs of John Ker of Kersland, The 203

Mennonites 165
Merchant Adventurers 102
Merchant Taylors' School 128
Mercia 5
Mexican 267
Mexico 118
Micklethwaite 22
Middle Ages 38, 46, 50, 52, 59, 94,
    251, 288
middle class 222, 243, 247
Middle East 118
Middle English 52, 69, 81
Middle Passage 188, 190
Middlesex 136
Middleton, Thomas 140
Midlands 17, 97, 99, 279
Milan 71
Mill, John Stuart 242
Milton, John 120, 227
Mind Your Hs, Harry Hawkins' H Book
    223
Miramichi River 159
Mississippi 174
Mississippi River 164, 172, 177, 178,
    186
Missouri Negro 197
Missouri River 172
Modern English 127
Mohocks 206
Monboddo, Lord 201
Monmouthshire 89
Montfort, Simon de, Earl of Leicester
    55
Moorfields, London 214
More, Sir Thomas 110, 112–13
    Utopia 120
Morrison, Toni 138
movie culture 302
Mugglestone, Lynda 235, 245–6

Mughal Empire 253
Mughuls 252, 253–4
Mulcaster, Richard 128
My Fair Lady (musical) 236
Myrrour of the Worlde, The 102
Mystery Plays 81–2

Nahautl 267
names
    Old English names begin to die out
        55
    increasing use of the surname 77–8
    place *see* place names
Napoleon Bonaparte 35, 40, 225
Naseby 22
National Trust 5
Native American languages 159, 160,
    301
Native Americans 156–8, 159, 180
NATO 305
New Amsterdam (later New York)
    156, 164
New England 158, 161, 188
New England Primer 162–3
New Hampshire 163
New Jersey 163
New Orleans 164, 172, 177, 178
New South Wales 277, 286
New Statesman and Nation 302
New Sweden (later New Delaware)
    164
New Testament: Tyndale translates
    from Greek and Hebrew 107–8
New World 118, 164, 176, 188, 266
New York (previously New
    Amsterdam) 164
New Zealand 307
Newcastle, Australia 277
Newcastle-on-Tyne 26, 77, 166, 277

Newton, Sir Isaac 201, 202, 220, 221
   Opticks 120, 200
   Principia 199
Nicholas of Guildford, Master: 'The
   Owl and the Nightingale'
   (attrib.) 49
Nicolini, Marquis 216
Niger-Congo language family 269
Nixon, Richard 301
Norman barons 55, 56
Norman Conquest 24, 33, 37, 41, 42,
   52, 64, 66
Norman French 41, 122, 227
   swamps the English language 36–9,
     43, 52–3, 57
   English emerges after three hundred
     years 40
   anglicised and plundered by English
     59
Norman French army 38
Normandy 31, 34, 35, 41, 45, 55, 61
Normans 3, 21, 33, 36, 37, 39, 49,
   55, 222, 295
Norse 122, 132, 159–60
   see also Old Norse
Norsemen 36
North Africa 118
North Carolina 163
North Germanic 4
North Lincolnshire 48
north-south divide 22, 28
Northumberland 96
Northumbria 5, 9, 11, 12, 17, 27, 28
Northumbrian accent 22
Northumbrian language 224
Norwegians 17, 21, 22
Norwich 54
Nottingham 7, 54
Nottinghamshire accent 137

novel, the 230–32
Novial 297

Odo, Bishop 35, 39
O'Grady, John: 'The Integrated
   Adjective' 281
Ohio River 172
OK, derivation of 182–3
Old English 27, 32, 103, 118, 229,
   271, 273
   and the hundred most common
     English words 7
   existing terms given new powers 9
   alphabet 11–12
   the greatest poem (*Beowulf*) 14
   fights its way to pre-eminence 16
   Bede's book translated 18
   sense carried by inflection 24
   word order 24
   poem describing the Battle of
     Maldon 31
   nearly all lost due to the Battle of
     Hastings 33
   determined to take on no other
     tongue 35
   takes what it needs from the Danish
     language 35
   in 'Sumer is icumen in' 50
   religious homilies 61
   and the Bible 80–1
   historical sound changes in 100
   and Latin 124
   in Stratford 147
Old Norse x, 4, 7, 21–4, 28, 36, 58,
   72, 102
Old Testament 80–1, 111, 272
Oldham 239
Oldmixon, John 209
Onslow, Lord 183

OPEC (Organisation of Petroleum
    Exporting Countries) 305
Oregon trail 180
Orm: *Ormulum* 48–9
Ormskirk, Lancashire 157
Orwell, George 304
Ossian 225
Ossian Poems 225
Ovid 120, 147
Metamorphoses 147
Ovington, John 252
Oxford 86
Oxford English Dictionary 122, 134,
    153, 310, 311
Oxford University 70, 83, 85, 120,
    247, 280

Pacific Ocean 4
Paine, Thomas: *The Rights of Man* 229
Pakistan 296
Palace of Westminster, London 66,
    67, 96
papacy 83, 91, 105, 304
parchment 11
Parisian French 122
Parliament: English rather than French
    used from 1362 66–7
Paston Letters 99
patter pedlars French 247
Patterdale 22
Patterson, Banjo 282
Patwa 295
Peano, Giuseppe 297
Peasants' Revolt (1381) 64, 90
Penkridge, Richard 66
Penn, William 159, 165
Pennsylvania 163, 165
Pennsylvania Dutch (Deutsch) 165
Penrith 5

Penshurst Place 132
Persia 252
Persian 119, 252, 256
Peru 267
Peterborough 39
Peterborough Abbey 42
Peterborough Chronicle 42, 44
Petherton, Somerset 71
Petrarch 71, 130, 131
Pettie, George 125
Petty France, London 54
Pevensey Castle 5, 34, 36
Philadelphia 165
Philip II, King of France 55
Philip II, King of Spain 35, 116
Philip IV, King of France 60
philology 254
phonetics 220
physics 239, 240
Picardy 45
pidgin
    Australian 278
    defined 190
    in the West Indies 258, 266, 269,
        273
Pike County dialect 197
Pilgrim Fathers (Plymouth Pilgrims)
    153, 155–8, 160, 163, 172, 176,
    194–5, 198
Pineville 177
Pinker, Stephen x
place names 22–3
    -by ending 22
    -dale ending 22
    -ham ending 7
    -ing ending 6
    -thorpe ending 22
    -thwaite ending 22
    -toft ending 22

-ton ending 7
in New England 161
Plantagenets 44
Plimouth Plantation, Massachusetts
157, 161
plurals 44, 100
Plymouth Pilgrims *see* Pilgrim Fathers
Plymouth Rock, New England 155
poetry
runes and 10
the greatest poem in Old English
(*Beowulf*) 14–15
Arabic and Chinese 15–16
describing the Battle of Maldon 31
Eleanor of Aquitaine patronises
poets 46, 47
and courtly love 47
Romantic 47, 226
the heartland of written English 49
Italian 71
alliterative verse 90
Elizabeth I writes 132
the sonnet 131–2, 133
becomes the benchmark for English
135
enlisted to fructify the language
(Elizabethan Age) 231
polysyllables 168, 169
Poor Little H – its Use and Abuse 223
Pope, Alexander 203
Essay on Criticism 204
Port Jackson (Sydney Harbour) 276,
277
Porter, Professor Roy 123
Portuguese language 117–18, 119,
271, 273, 309
Portuguese, the 156, 266
Potomac River 159
prefixes 128

prepositions 24–5, 44
Priestley, Joseph 216, 217
The Rudiments of English Grammar
216
printing 78, 101–3, 108, 202, 203,
219, 241, 243
pronunciation 222–3, 234
Protestantism 90, 107, 111, 112,
156
Protocollum books 127
psalms 81
Public Record Office 98
Puritanism 6, 173, 301
Puttenham, George 137, 138
The Arte of English Poesie 136

Quakers 165
Queen's College, Oxford 85
Queen's Men, The 139

racism 287–9
Raj 256, 258, 262, 263, 264
Raleigh, Sir Walter 137, 142
Rasta 272–3
Reading 6
Reading Abbey 49
'rednecks' 177–8
Reformation 91
Renaissance 116, 120, 121–2, 130,
138, 146, 160, 237
Rhode Island 163
Richard II, King 64, 66, 67, 71
Richard III, King (Richard of
Gloucester) 78
Richardson, Samuel 207
Richmond, Yorkshire 83
riddles 10, 13–14
Roanoke Island 155
Robison, Professor 237, 238

Rochester 36

Rochester, John Wilmot, 2nd Earl of
    233

Rocky Mountain News 184

Roet, Sir Payne 70

Roget, Peter Mark: *Thesaurus of
    English Words and Phrases* 201

Rojas, Fernando de 130

Roman alphabet 11

Roman Catholic Church 80
    arrival of Augustine and Aidan 8
    loan words 8–9
    becomes more pervasive in the
        country 9
    Norman French take up positions of
        power 41
    and elevated morality 57
    Latin and French as the controlling
        languages 60, 68
    English claims its proper place 62
    power of 76, 80, 83, 106
    wealth of 83–4, 106
    schism 83
    and Wycliffe 83–4, 87, 91, 92
    Council of Constance (1414) 92
    and assaults on the Latin Bible 103
    as the gatekeeper to God 106
    growing protest against 106
    the Bible kept away from the
        people (up to 1530s) 113
    and British/American English 291

Roman Empire 1

Romance languages 291, 297

Romanian 309

Romans 6, 42, 224, 277–8, 291

Romantic love poetry 47

Romanticism 47, 226, 230

Romany xi, 26

Rome 8, 10, 106, 242

Ronsard, Pierre de 130

Rosthwaite 22

Routes of English, The (BBC Radio 4
    programmes) x

Roy, Rammohan 256

Royal Navy 188, 253

Royal Shakespeare Company 149

Royal Society 200, 201

Rugby 22

runes 10

runic alphabet 10

Russian 291, 305, 306

Ruthwaite 22

Ruthwell Cross, near Dumfries,
    Scotland 10

Sabir 189–90

St Austen's Green, Little Sudbury
    104, 105

St Giles Greek 247

St Kitts 268, 270, 271, 272

St Lawrence River 156

St Louis 176, 177

St Lucia 266

St Paul's Cathedral, London 105

Salisbury Plain 19

samizdat press 85

Sandtoft 22

Sandy Bay, St Kitts 268

Sanskrit xii, 129, 192, 254, 256

Santa Fé 267

Santa Fe trail 180

Sao Paolo 306

Savage, Richard 203

Saxons 2, 5, 6, 9, 10, 12, 49, 191,
    192

Scandinavian languages 4, 28

Schleyer, Johann Martin 297

science 239–40, 256

Scotland
  Gaelic 2, 225, 293
  Norwegians invade 17
  English spreads to 118
  dialect 138
  union with England and Wales 152
  Highland Clearances (1745) 165,
    176, 225
  and the Enlightenment 223
  Act of Union 224
Scots language 222, 224–5, 227
Scots people 165, 176, 183, 188, 199,
    223–4, 226, 227, 301
Scott, Sir Walter 225
Scottish Highlands 224
Scunthorpe 22
Seafarer, The 13
Second World War 40, 303–4
Select Society 224
Seneca 120
Senegal 191
Shakespeare, John 142
Shakespeare, William 12, 73, 76, 126,
    139, 140, 141–53, 160, 165,
    181, 187, 206, 227, 243, 251,
    292
  new words x, 144, 148
  sonnets 47, 143, 144
  the greatest writer 141
  the most written about writer 141
  background and early life 142–3,
    146–8
  his vocabulary 144–5
  quotability 145–6
  Midlands dialect 148–9
  monosyllables 150
  inventiveness 151
  editions of his works 152–3
  film adaptations 153

  Bowlderised 233–4
  Antony and Cleopatra 145
  First Folio 152–3
  Hamlet 116, 144, 145–6
  Henry V 144, 149
  Macbeth 144, 228
  The Merry Wives of Windsor 145
  A Midsummer Night's Dream 153,
    229–30
  Othello 144, 233–4
  Summer's Day Sonnet 204
  The Tempest 152
  Timon of Athens 150
  Titus Andronicus 140
  Troilus and Cressida 150
Shaw, George Bernard: *Pygmalion* 236,
    248–9
Sheridan, Richard Brinsley 232, 234
  The Rivals 229, 230
Sheridan, Thomas 221–4
  British Education 221
shire fyrds 19
Sidney, Sir Philip 132–5, 139, 142
  Astrophel and Stella 143
  A Defence of Poesy 133, 134
Siemens, Ernst Werner von 241
Sigismund, Emperor, King of
    Hungary 92
Singapore xii, 305, 307–8
Singlish 307–8
Sir Gawain and the Green Knight 70
slang 247–8, 259, 281, 282, 283
slang lingo 247
slavery 187–96, 266, 268, 272
Smellie, William 215
Smith, Adam 224, 242
Smith, William 223
Smith, Captain William: *A New
    Voyage to Guinea* 189

Smithfield, London 64
Somerset 19, 30
sonnet, the 47, 131–2, 133, 143, 204
Sophocles 152
South Africa 289, 307, 308
South America 156
South Carolina 163
South Cumbria 28
Southwark, London 73, 139, 280
Spain/Spanish 118, 156, 165, 185, 266
Spanish Armada (1588) 35, 116, 117,
    124, 251
Spanish language 27, 117, 118, 119,
    289, 291, 293, 309
  dictionaries 129
  literature 130, 135
  the biggest feeder into American
    English 164
  in the West Indies 272, 273
  resurgence in the Americas 297
Spectator 170, 208
spelling 219
  variety in 97–101
  American English 169
  and sound 220
  phonetic 246
  irregularities 291
Spenser, Edmund 126, 127, 131, 142
spirituals 195
Squanto (Tisquantum; a Native
    American) 157, 158, 160
Stalin, Joseph 85
Stamford Bridge, Battle of 34
Standard English x, 70, 78, 94, 190,
    191, 278, 308, 310
Standish, Brabary 157
state, the
  Latin and French as the controlling
    languages 60, 68

Norman French take up positions of
    power 41
Sterne, Laurence: *Tristram Shandy* 232
Stevenson, May 170
Stratford School 147
Stratford-upon-Avon, Warwickshire
    142, 146–9, 152
Strauss, Levi 183–4
stress, use in words 221
Stuart, Prince Charles Edward (Bonnie
    Prince Charlie) 225
Suffolk 166
Sullivan's Island 189
'Sumer is icumen in' 49–50
Surat 252
Surrey 136
Susquehanna River 159
Sussex 5
swearing 76, 232–3, 236
Swedish 309
Sweyn, King 31
Swift, Jonathan 203, 205–10, 212,
    214, 217, 219, 220, 221, 232,
    234
  Gulliver's Travels 209
  *Proposal for Correcting, Improving and
    Ascertaining the English Tongue*
    209
Swift River 92
Sydney 282
Sydney Harbour 276
syllables 221

Tabard Inn, Southwark 73
Taiwan 310
Tamil 119, 289
Tamperers (illogical irregularities of
    spelling) 100–1
Tangier 190

Tangier Island 155
Tatler 205
Taunton 7
technology 122, 256
television drama 136, 137
Temne 189
1066 and All That (Sellars and
    Yeatman) 33
Ten Commandments 85
Tennessee River 172
Terra Australis Incognita 276
Terschelling, Friesland 3
Text English 310
Thames River 5, 21, 41, 73, 116
Thomas, St 250
Thornby 22
Thursby 22
Tilbury 116, 132
Times, The 182, 183, 264
Times of India 264
Todd, Mike 182
Tooke, John Horne 215
Torpenhow 5
Tottenham 7
Toussaint L'Ouverture 194
Tower of Babel 189, 200
trade
    and the Danelaw 21
    language clarity for commerce 24
    French terms 54
    French the international language of
        58
    Renaissance England 117
    the French in America 165, 172
transubstantiation 84
Treachery of the Blue Books 294
Trevisa, John 65, 66, 77
Trinidad 272
troubador style 61

troubadors 46, 47, 64
Troyes, Treaty of (1420) 95
Tudors 294
Tunbridge Wells 96
Tupi 267
Turkish 119
Twain, Mark 138, 192, 197, 206, 244
    Huckleberry Finn 197-8
Twi 189, 272
Tyler, Wat 64
Tyndale, William 147, 156, 165, 194,
    238
    an Oxford scholar 107
    preaches at St Austen's Green
        103-4, 105
    influence of his book 104
    compared with Wycliffe 107
    translates the New Testament
        107-8
    aim of 108
    the quality of his writing 109-10,
        114
    influence on the King James Bible
        109
    Tyndale's Bible smuggled into
        England 110-11
    spends his life on the run 111
    prints his Old Testament
        translation 111
    imprisoned and executed 111-12
    and the King James Bible 113

Ulster/Ulstermen 176
Uncle Remus stories 192, 193-4
United Nations 304, 305
United States
    House of Representatives 169-70
    early years as an independent
        country 173

United States – *cont.*
  Lewis and Clark open up the west
    176–7
  wagon routes 180
  the gold rush 183
  Levi Strauss 183–4
  cowboys 185–6
  slavery 187–96
  Ku Klux Klan 196
  black migration to the industrial
    north 196
  coca-colonisation' of the world
    304–5
  see also America; American Civil
    War; American War of
    Independence
university slang 247
University of the West Indies 269
Utah 174

van Buren, Martin 182
Vaux, James Hardy 280
Vedic hymns 4
vellum 11
verb serialisation 191
Vernon, Admiral 273
Victoria, Queen 186, 239
Vikings 17, 21, 22, 28, 35
Villon, François 130
Vilvorde Castle 111
Virgil 102, 147
Virginia 163
virtue 57–8
Volapuk 297

Wace (Norman-French poet) 47
Walcott, Derek 271
  Omeros 271
Wales 2, 5, 118, 152

Walker, John 244, 245
  Critical Pronouncing Dictionary of the
    English Language 223, 243
  Rules to be Observed by the Natives of
    Scotland for attaining a just
    Pronunciation of English 224
Waller, Edmund: *Of English Verse*
  204–5
'Waltzing Matilda' (Patterson) 282–3
Wanderer, The 13
Warner, Thomas 268
Warwickshire 143
Wasdale 22
Watch Committee 248
Waterloo, Battle of 40
Watling Street 21
Watson, James 12
Watt, James 237–8, 241
Webster, John 140
Webster, Noah 168–9, 171, 173,
  215, 219
  his dictionary 171, 174
  American Spelling Book (*Blue Backed*
    Speller) 168–9
  Dissertations in the English Language
    309
Weever, John 144
Welsh language 119, 293–5
Welsh people 5, 123–4, 165
Wessex xii, 5, 18, 29, 69
Wessex dialect 30
West Africa 189, 266, 271
West African languages 269, 270, 272
West Country 190
West Germanic 4
West Indies 189, 265–75, 295, 296
  dozens of distinctive territories 266
  settlement by other countries 266
  slavery introduced 266, 268

English piracy 266
first English settlement (St Kitts, 1624) 268
pidgin and creole 190, 269–75
West Midlands 78, 97
dialect 90
West Saxon dialect 21
West Saxon rule 21
Western Indo-European family 4
Westminster Abbey 34, 36, 44, 60, 71, 79
White Tower, London 41, 64
Whitman, Walt 299
Whitworth, Sir Joseph 239
Wiggonby 22
Wigton, Cumbria 7, 22, 26, 77
Wigtonians 25–6
Wilberforce, William 194, 256
Wilde, Oscar: *The Importance of Being Earnest* 248
Wilkins, John 202, 209
   An Essay Toward a Real Character and a Philosophical Language 200–201
William I, King, the Conqueror 34–5, 36, 38–9, 41, 44, 45, 50, 55
William X of Aquitaine 44
William de Waterville 42
William of Malmesbury 41
William of Nassington 60
Wilson, Thomas 125
   The Arte of Rhetorique 127
Wilson, Woodrow 182
Wilton 7
Wiltshire 19
Winchester 21, 30–1, 70
Witherspoon, John 166
Wittenberg 105

Wodehouse, P. G. 303
Wolof 189, 191
Wolsey, Cardinal 105, 107, 108, 110
women
   as a fifth column among the Norman French 56
   novel reading 232
Wood, William: *New England's Prospect* 160–61
wool trade 54
word endings 24
word games 13–14
word order 24, 25
Wordsworth, William 27, 137, 194, 225, 227–9, 230
   Lyrical Ballads 125, 227, 228–9
working class 243
World Bank 305
Worthing 6
writing
   Christianity brings 10–11
   importance of 11
   brings uniformity to language 101
   the great writing rift 138
Wulfstan, Archbishop: 'Sermo Lupi' 31–2
Wyatt, Sir Thomas 131
Wycliffe, John 83–93, 103, 106, 107, 156, 194
   an Oxford scholar 83, 107
   and the Church 83–4, 87, 91, 92
   main arguments written in Latin 84
   inspires two biblical translations 85
   completion of the Wycliffe English Bible 86–7
   organises and trains itinerant preachers 87–8

Wycliffe, John – *cont.*
a synod of the Church examines his works 89
his Bibles outlawed 89
illness and death 89
Langland and 90
condemned by the Archbishop of Canterbury 91–2
condemned as a heretic 92
his remains disinterred and burned 92–3
his Bible continues to circulate 105
Tyndale compared with 107

Wye River 5
Wyoming 174

Yeats, W. B. 225
Yiddish 301
York 36, 82
York Minster 36, 82
Yorkshire accent 22, 166
Yorkshire English 77, 244
Yoruba 191, 272, 273

Zamenhof, L. L. 297